D0066109

BEYOND PLURALISM

ETHNIC POLITICS IN AMERICA

EDGAR LITT
University of Connecticut

SCOTT, FORESMAN AMERICAN GOVERNMENT SERIES
Joseph C. Palamountain, Jr., Editor

SCOTT, FORESMAN AND COMPANY

Library of Congress Catalog Card No. 79-81169

Regional offices of Scott, Foresman and Company are located in
Atlanta, Dallas, Glenview, Palo Alto, Oakland, N.J.,
and London, England.

FOREWORD

The American System of government strikes a balance between unity and diversity. There is a unity to our system, but it is a unity which tolerates—indeed, requires for its vigor and viability—a broad diversity of institutions, processes, and participants. By organizing the analysis of the sprawling complexity of the American system into smaller, coherent, but interlocking units, the Scott, Foresman American Government Series attempts to reflect this pluralistic balance.

This approach, we believe, has several important advantages over the usual one-volume presentation of analytical and descriptive material. By giving the reader more manageable units, and by introducing him to the underlying and unifying strands of those units, it puts him in a better position to comprehend both the whole and its components. Moreover, it permits us to tap the expertise and experience of distinguished scholars in the fields of their special competence.

It is hard to conceive of a more timely or more relevant study than the one Edgar Litt offers the reader in the following pages. His subject is one for which the reader can find illustrations from each day's newspapers. His analysis will aid the student concerned for relevance in his academic work in understanding the most acute domestic problems our society confronts.

Professor Litt's subject is an old one in American political science—one which, but a few years ago, we political scientists mistakenly thought we were about to relegate from politics to history. His reinterpretation of American ethnic politics in the light of today's ethnic and social conflicts promotes a better understanding of our past. More important, he demonstrates how and why ethnic politics persist in an era when—a few years ago, at least—we naively thought the melting pot had just about completed its mission.

More important, Professor Litt ably demonstrates that while the social base for ethnic politics displays surprising persistence, it does not result in the same political game that was being played forty years ago. Consequently, and most important, he points the reader to the great unfinished task remaining before us.

Relevant as his work is to the core problems of our society, his analysis derives from a carefully conceived theoretical position and method. It will, I believe, win him the respect and gratitude of both scholar and activist as a happy marriage of the relevant with the academically sound.

Joseph C. Palamountain, Jr., *Editor*

PREFACE

There are three major themes in this book about American ethnic politics. First, I have tried to synthesize a decade's research on the influence of race, nationality, and religion in our Republic's life. The "older" theories of ethnic politics were based on the examination of European immigrant groups adapting to the urban industrial order. The "newer" ethnic politics, however, involves non-Caucasians dealing with a highly complex urban environment. This means that we must pay careful attention to the common and distinct factors that have shaped the politics of our diverse minorities.

Second, I have drawn particular attention to the public policy dimensions of ethnic politics. Until recently, ethnic politics usually meant the study of the urban political machine and the ways in which group leaders were dealt with in the political party, machine, or legislature. The imperatives of our times require that we think more clearly about the large-scale and aggregate nature of ethnic politics, that is to say, about its impact on the life chances and distributed values of the citizenry.

Third, I have been concerned about theories and practices of conflict resolution in the modern history of American ethnic politics. In particular, I have examined the limits of pluralistic, accommodation techniques—techniques that were more relevant to New England Italo-Americans and Midwestern Slavs than they are to the black masses in contemporary New Haven and Chicago. In large measure, each major ethnic group has contributed to the intellectual (as well as to the political) history of American politics. Thus, the questions of Jewish liberalism, Irish Catholic organization, and Negro concern about participatory democracy inform us about the cumulative interplay between ethnic politics and the state of the Republic's public order.

Since I began research on the political attitudes of American Jews a decade ago, I have come to realize the immense variety of ethnic groups and political styles in America. But I have been even more impressed by the commonality of structure, purpose, and theory that underlies the social pagent of these "strangers" in our midst. Many scholars have aided me in this quest, among them, Robert E. Lane, Raymond Wolfinger, James Q. Wilson, Herbert Kaufman, Allan P. Sindler, Fred Greenstein, Matthew Holden, and Nathan Glazer. However, the culmination of this particular book owes most to the scholarship and cogent criticism of my friend, Michael John Parenti. It is not a false sense of modesty that leads me to say that his contributions are reflected in whatever is valuable within these pages.

A new generation of scholars and activists, fired by the scent of "Black Power" and "Participatory Democracy," are making their mark upon the real and analytical worlds of the politician and the scholar. This book is a watershed between their aspirations and the legacy of Handlin, Myrdal, and Lubell, who pointed the way to my generation. And that is how it should be because the saga of ethnic politics has always been the meeting of the Establishment and the Newcomer in the arenas of commerce, culture, and political life.

Edgar Litt

TABLE OF CONTENTS

PART ONE * THE PERSISTENCE OF ETHNICITY IN POLITICAL CHOICE 1

CHAPTER ONE * THE SOCIAL BASE OF ETHNIC POLITICS 4
American Society and the Ethnic
The Melting Pot
Cultural Pluralism
The Core Culture
Acculturation and Assimilation

CHAPTER TWO * THE INDIVIDUAL BASE OF ETHNIC POLITICS 16
The Tribe Endures
Three Important Conditions of Ethnic Political Choice
Functions of Ethnic Political Choice
Social Stability and the Economy of Tradition
Material Goals: Economics and Patronage
Psychic Goals: The Esteem of the Victim
Civic Values as Ethnic Political Goals

PART TWO * PATTERNS OF ETHNIC POLITICS 39

CHAPTER THREE * THE ORGANIZATIONAL BASE OF ETHNIC POLITCS 42
Ethnic-Based Politics: From Association to Party
Religious Institutions and Ethnic Politics

CHAPTER FOUR * THE POLITICS OF ACCOMMODATION 60
Divisible Benefits and Recognition
Accommodation and Collective Welfare Benefits
Preferments and Secondary Benefits

CHAPTER FIVE * THE POLITICS OF SEPARATISM 75
The Search for a Past and a Future
Rehabilitation
Organizational and Institutional Supports
The Function of Symbols
Longevity and Transition: From Revolution to Institution
Organizational Maturity and Efficacy
From Have-Nots to Haves
Signs of Accommodation
Conclusion

CHAPTER SIX * THE POLITICS OF RADICALISM 92
Two Styles of Radicalism
Old-Style Radicalism: The Politics of Forensic Ideology

The Liabilities of Ideological Radicalism
Ideology and Political Congruence
New-Style Radicalism: Passion and Anomic Politics
The Anomic Personal Situation
The Weak Social Base
The Governmental Presence

PART THREE * VARIETIES OF AMERICAN ETHNIC POLITICS 111

CHAPTER SEVEN * LIBERAL POLITICAL CULTURE AND THE JEWS 113
The Sources of Jewish Political Liberalism
The Future of Jewish Liberalism: Absorption, Adaptation, Antagonism

CHAPTER EIGHT * IRISH CATHOLICS: THE POLITICS OF ADJUSTMENT 127
Patterns of Political Learning
The Critical Triad: Family, Church, Community

CHAPTER NINE * THE NEGRO REVOLT AND DEMOCRATIC PARTICIPATION 142
The Concern About Mass Politics
Assumptions About Participation
The Reconstruction of Democratic Participation

CHAPTER TEN * ETHNIC POLITICS IN AMERICA: RETROSPECT AND PROSPECT 155

FOOTNOTES 169

BIBLIOGRAPHICAL ESSAY 187

PART ONE

The Persistence of Ethnicity in Political Choice

Although the American political culture is highly inclusive, ethnic forces play a surprisingly persistent role in our politics. The unexpected tenacity of the ethnic factor in American politics requires explanation for three reasons. First, we have associated ethnic politics with the period of initial immigration and thus have tended to assume that ethnicity was short-lived and that it was eliminated by assimilation and affluence. Such a "deprivation thesis" overlooks long-term ethnic factors in the politics of supposedly well-integrated group members. Second, ethnic politics has had an important impact on the basic structures and processes of public life. It permeates political institutions, just as the position of a group in society alters with the passage of time and the undergoing of new experiences. Third, it has become increasingly obvious that the politics of white immigrant groups differs in many respects from contemporary politics within the black community. In order to compare "old-style" and "new-style" ethnic politics, we must first comprehend the durability of race, religion, and nationality within American politics; then, we must relate ethnic politics to the changing quality of the public system being influenced.

This book focuses first on the social bases of ethnic politics, particularly on the variety of ways in which racial, religious, and nationality groups were Americanized. Three divergent theories, the melting pot, cultural pluralism, and core values, provided great flexibility to political leaders. The persistence of ethnicity in political decisions of leaders and citizens is analyzed. The ethnic factor is found to contribute to political leadership and the choices of mass publics.

Next, the persistence of ethnic politics is traced in relation to the needs of organizations and institutions formed along ethnic lines. The process of accommodating themselves to the American social system perforce involved these agencies in politically relevant situations. In addition, the pursuit of organizational goals involved distinct political decisions that influenced both each organization's impact on the lives of its members and its choice of which formal political channels to use. These ethnic organizations were at once socializing agencies ministering to the needs and aspirations of co-ethnics *and* sources of power through which ethnic groups could exert leverage on the polity. The ability of ethnic institutions to reconcile these two functions has perpetuated the relevance of ethnicity itself to American politics. That relevance was accentuated as political power that had been formed along the lines of ethnic institutions was subsequently challenged by other ethnic groups seeking a larger share of political rewards.

Finally, a salient character of the politics developed by each of three American ethnic groups, namely, the Irish, Jewish, and black communities, is discussed. Ethnic pluralism is criticised from the perspective of contemporary race politics. The conflicts within and limitations upon classic ethnic political accommodation are reviewed, and several reforms are offered.

The relevance of ethnic politics and institutions has currently become a matter of national urgency because persistent "old-style" ethnic politics lacks the resources and the will to cope with demands of the urban Negro. The federal presence in civil fights, the urban discord about racial justice, and the dilemma of integrationist efforts in many communities contribute to the enduring ethnic distinctions that have fashioned a major portion of American politics today.

CHAPTER ONE

The Social Base of Ethnic Politics

As one studies ethnic groups in America, one becomes increasingly aware that the questions encountered, seemingly so peculiar to our "nation of immigrants" and our rapidly changing industrial society, are ancient and primitive ones. The problem facing all human groups is older than the parable of the Good Samaritan, one of the earliest preachments on brotherhood, and older than the book of Deuteronomy, which prescribed one code of ethics to govern internal tribal relations and another less exacting set of rules to guide contacts with outsiders. This problem may be stated as follows: The shared symbols, interests, affections, and real or imagined traits which draw some men together into the group or community are the walls which separate those men from others. Hence, the communion that nurtures intragroup cohesion is often the first condition for intergroup conflict. To state it more tersely, for there to be "brothers" there must also be "others." Boundaries, whether they be geographical or psychological, have a way of being both cohesive and divisive.

We cannot long ponder this phenomenon without realizing that it is one of the age-old problems of political science. Aristotle understood that the bonds of nature and necessity which make man a communal animal also make him a political animal. Without such communal-political ties, "he is like the tribeless, lawless, heartless one" that Aristotle described in the first book of *Politics.* Yet given such ties, we are confronted with a dilemma: Despite this tendency to cluster together in common passion and loyalty, men draw distinctions that set them apart in some way from the whole of mankind. Indeed, Aristotle himself, the Greem supremicist, testified to this by disapproving of the universalist vision and polyglot entourage of his former student Alexander.

That mankind suffered an irresistible propensity to divide itself into conflicting groups was one of James Madison's great concerns also. According to Madison, "the most common and durable source of faction" may well have been "the unequal distribution of property." However, while he was something of an economic determinist, he also knew enough about politics and about men, ancient, English, and colonial, to appreciate that class differences were not the sole generator of divisions. Thus he could write in number ten of the *Federalist Papers:* "Where no substantial occasion presents itself, the most frivolous and fanciful distinctions have been sufficient to kindle . . . unfriendly passions [of the people] and excite their most violent conflicts."

We cannot accept Madison's warning without concluding that we are dealing with some innate human perversity. Suffice it to say that faction breeds faction, or, to use modern parlance, if there is an in-group, there undoubtedly will be an out-group. Furthermore, it is in the nature of social organization that the way men define and desire things will be, in part, determined by the positions they occupy within the existing social system. Moreover, the positions occupied and the identifications structured will differ with the range and diversity of that system. The impoverished Negro farmer in South Carolina and the New York corporation executive, while they may not hate each other or, indeed, even be aware of each other, will operate from quite different perspectives. Wherever distinctions arise, there is the potential for conflict, and wherever conflicts occur, there is politics. To be sure, confronting and mediating the demands, interests, and values of competing groups is the stuff of politics.

The distinctions that men make may be drawn along regional, economic, occupational, and ideological lines, they may involve clearly defined material and psychological interests which we readily identify as "political," or they may be as senselessly competitive as the Eatanswill town politics witnessed by Dickens' Mr. Pickwick. Among the pervasive distinctions that have brought men together are those which we designate as "ethnic," that is, those distinctions based on race, religion, or national origin. In most of the world the bonds of Blood, Believer, and Brother as strongly define political interest and conflict as do the bonds of class or locale. All too often, moreover, ethnic distinctions correspond with regional, class, or caste interests and thereby aggravate the fissures, and fortify the fusions, that obtain in the polity. Sometimes, on the other hand, they cut across such divisions and provide unity where none seemed possible.

In any case, ethnic politics should not be viewed as a parochial phenomenon, something peculiar to the likes of Tammany, for there are few places on earth where ethnicity is not presently of political import. Even if we confine our attention to those distinctions that exist principally within national boundaries and say nothing of the usual rivalries between nations, which themselves are often as ethnic as they are political, we are left with an imposing list: Afrikander v. Bantu, Kikuyu v. Luo, Yoruba v. Ibo, Bahutu v. Watusi, Kurd v. Iraqim, Moslim v. Hindu, Ukrainian v. Great Russian, Great Russian v. most Eurasian groups, Mongolian v. Chinese, the overseas Chinese v. most of Southeast Asia, the overseas Indians v. most of eastern and southern Africa, Turk v. Greek Cypriot, Arab v. Jew, Ladino v. white Spanish, Welsh v. English, Walloon v. Flemish, Czech v. Slovak, Christian v. Jew, Protestant v. Catholic, Catholic v. Buddhist, black v. white, and on we could go; this list merely scratches the surface. One can even discern conflicting subgroups within the opposing groups (thus, orthodox v. reform Jews, Afrikans-speaking v. English-speaking whites, Ulster v. Celtic Irish), particularly in Africa and the Middle and Far East.

What makes all men alike in their common humanity may be truly greater than what makes them different; yet most of mankind does not see it that way. As Madison said, men are never at a loss to find the most fanciful distinctions to stir their passions, and it does seem that among people who most resemble each other, lesser differences become distinctions of great moment. Thus, much of "world politics" is ethnic politics.

What is true of the world seems true of America. With the exception of the American Indians, who have been one of the groups most victimized by the distinctions that divide mankind, America is entirely populated by immigrants and their descendants. In the view of one English student of the subject, Maldwyn Jones, immigration has been "America's historic *raison d'être*." A nation composed of such a cultural, linguistic, racial, and religious conglomeration will experience at least its share of ethnic politics. This book is an investigation of that kind of politics in America. It purports to be neither an exhaustive compendium of every study on the topic nor an historical account of every ethnic group that has ever expressed a political need or desire in this nation. It is motivated by no preordained intent to demonstrate the special desirability or, for that matter, undesirability, of ethnic politics. What we have attempted to do is lend systematic articulation and analysis to the wide-ranging, variegated, and complex phenomena that comprise ethnic political behavior.

The primary questions guiding us are: What have been the impact, styles, and conditions of ethnic political behavior? In other words, how can we best describe and account for ethnic politics and locate the causes and consequences of such politics?

The key factors in the analysis of such questions seem to be: (1) The American socio-cultural system, that is, the social institutional structures of this society that orchestrate and provide a means for the inculcation and achievement of cultural goals, values, beliefs, cues, and symbols. How does the socio-cultural system of the national community affect ethnic political life? (2) The components of ethnic politics themselves. What basic patterns of ethnic politics dominate in the relationship between the cultural and political systems? (3) The American political system. What are the pervasive consequences of ethnic politics for its core values, major public policies, and functioning? Guiding all of these inquiries is another major question: How do the values, predispositions, and social positions of ethnic members and groups influence the varieties of ethnic politics?

The kinds of ethnic political behavior we encounter cannot be treated purely as the simple products of social, political, and ethnic life. As is frequently the case, cause and effect cannot be fully separated, and the consequences of any set of forces themselves become causal factors by changing the very conditions in which the initial forces operate. With ethnic political behavior, therefore, we turn our attention in the latter portion of this book principally to the consequences and the feedback of such political behavior on social, political, and ethnic life in general, and on policy formation and the American creed in particular.

The themes and theories formulated by others interested in this field will be investigated, criticized, and brought together. Wherever possible, we will introduce data from original sources. Sometimes widely different materials will be used to demonstrate the same hypothesis; at other times, the same material may support a variety of related propositions. Much of what we have to say is amply documented, although some of our observations, given the present state of empirical research, necessarily rely on cautious inference. Our final analysis of theory and trend is presented with the hope that the reader may come away with a clearer and deeper understanding of ethnic politics in America and, at the same time, of man's overall social and political life.

AMERICAN SOCIETY AND THE ETHNIC

Before attempting to assess the effects of the American system on the persistence of ethnic politics, we must direct our attention to the relationship between that system and the minority groups that are a part of it. First, it must be noted that the number of minority groups viable in American society is extensive. However, for the purposes of this volume, only a few, such as the Negroes, the Jews, and the Irish Catholics will be discussed in detail. This is not to imply that the other ethnic groups have not been important to American history and society; it is merely to say that the groups examined were chosen because it is felt that they have, over the years, had the most *obvious* effect on the American political process.

Next, we must ask such questions as: Is the American socio-cultural system a unique blend of the multifarious groups that compose it, as the melting pot thesis argues? Or is this society really less a blend than a patchwork of ethnicity, held together by the necessary minimum of common loyalties but retaining more or less distinct subcultural groupings, as the cultural pluralism thesis would have it? Or should one speak of a dominant white Protestant core socio-cultural system, in which ethnic groups enjoy a more or less marginal status? Individual observers have adhered firmly to one or the other of these ostensibly mutually exclusive models. Here we will briefly examine all three.

THE MELTING POT

As early as 1782, the French-born American farmer Crèvecoeur observed, in what was to become something of a classic statement, that the American was "that strange mixture of blood, which you will find in no other country." Crèvecoeur could point to four sons of mixed Dutch, French, and English stock, who had married four wives of different nationalities.[1]

Other observers, from Ralph Waldo Emerson to Frederick Jackson Turner to the Jewish immigrant writer Israel Zangwill, who wrote a play entitled "The Melting Pot" in 1908, saw the congested great cities as caldrons in which old bloods, cultures, and rivalries would be simmered into an invigorated and uniquely American blend.[2] Indeed, even before the eighteenth century was over, it had become evident that Americans were not Englishmen, and that American society was not a replica of that found in the mother country. At the time of the Revolution, the English, while the largest single element, comprised scarcely half the total American population; the rest consisted of large concentrations of

Germans, Dutch, and Scotch-Irish and a substantial number of Negroes, Scots, Frenchmen, and Swedes, plus a scattering of people who were to appear in great numbers in the next two centuries.[3]

A few groups, like the French Huguenots, were swift to change; names were anglicized, French gave way to English, and even the Huguenot churches were absorbed by the Anglicans. For other groups the pot bubbled more slowly. The Hudson Valley Dutch and Swedes, for example, retained distinctions in language, custom, and religion for half a century after the Revolution. Whatever the varying rates of assimilation, however, most of these groups eventually have disappeared into the larger cultural totality.

CULTURAL PLURALISM

History and the passing of generations have reduced ethnic uniqueness, but what is striking, some argue, is not the scope and rapidity of assimilation but rather the persistence of unassimilated ethnic identifications. A recent study of New York City finds that the melting pot has never eradicated ethnic politics there. Some older groups may have been lost sight of in the tide of more recent arrivals, but New York still retains rather clear, long-standing ethnic distinctions which are operative in the city's social, economic, and political life, and which show every evidence of persisting.[4] "This is not to say," Glazer and Moynihan write, "that no individual group will disappear. This, on the contrary, is a recurring phenomenon. The disappearance of the Germans is a particularly revealing case." There are many Germans in New York, but they do not constitute a major political bloc; no special group appeals are made to them by politicians, and there is no German component in the city's ethnic interest structure. Yet what seems to make "the disappearance" of the Germans a "particularly revealing case" is that they are *not* disappearing. German influence can be seen "in virtually every aspect of the city's life." German American societies still flourish; the Germans have begun an annual Steuben Day Parade, "adding for the politicians of the city yet another command performance at an ethnic outing." Thus, what Glazer and Moynihan first described as "the disappearance of the Germans" they later term an account of a "mild German resurgence."[5]

Rather than a melting pot, New York is a patchwork of ethnic enclaves. Besides the major groups, such as the Irish, the Jews, the Negroes, the Puerto Ricans, and the Italians, there exist several dozen smaller communities, from the Ukrainians and Armenians to the Chinese and Vietnamese,[6] some of which, like the Chinese community, are growing substantially. Moreover, although New York may be exceptional in the extent of its cosmopolitanism, there are highly concentrated ethnic enclaves all over America. Thus, ninety per cent of the population in Fredericksburg, Texas, is German American, and Westby, Wisconsin, is ninety-five per cent Norwegian, both in number and in language and custom. In short, one can emphasize the extent to which ethnics have melted into a new American mixture only by overlooking the great plurality of customs, subcommunities, and minority group ties that still exist. So argue such proponents of cultural pluralism as Horace Kallen, who considers America to be "a democracy of nationalities, cooperating voluntarily and autonomously in the enterprise of self-realization through the perfection of men according to their own kind."[7]

THE CORE CULTURE

In attempting to assay the extent of assimilation, one should not overlook the question: assimilation into what? If in colonial times the French Huguenots were already embarking upon this process, into what were they assimilating? In language, family name, and religion, they were absorbed into the dominant English American society of that day. One may speak of a new blend pouring from the American crucible or a pluralistic patchwork of Germantowns, Chinatowns, and Little Italies, but most students of ethnicity have explicitly or implicitly assumed that there is a "core culture" pattern in America, composed of essentially white Anglo-Saxon Protestant values, life styles, and identifications, to which the ethnic cultures are in some way related.

Using language as an index of cultural diffusion (as the medium by which cultural forms are transmitted and social relations conducted, it often serves this purpose well), one can see that the American language, while not identical to that used in the British Isles, is not a melting-pot blend of different tongues. A measure of ethnic influence is found in the wealth of foreign words that have been osmosed into a language that remains English. While the pluralists may point to bilingual communities in America, from French Canadians in Maine to Mexican Americans in Texas, these exceptions prove the rule: in the United States, both officially and in practice, the language is English.

To operate acceptably in the mainstream of American society extending beyond the confines of his group, the ethnic must achieve a certain minimal proficiency in and adaptation to the linguistic skills, behavioral patterns, and attitudinal values of the dominant community, as well as a certain minimal acceptability by that community. If ethnic groups suffer a marginal status in

American life, toward what are they marginal? If minorities experience feelings of inferiority, toward what do they feel inferior? Indeed, it may be argued, how can we even speak of minority groups unless we presuppose a majority identification and standard in a core culture?

That all three theories have enjoyed some currency is partly because each expresses long-standing value preferences; each claims not only to describe what actually is the case, but what ethically and ideally ought to be. The appeal of the melting pot has been a compelling one since this nation's earliest days. It feeds upon and is fed by the larger myth of America as mankind's grand experiment. The rich and spacious environment, the carefully balanced political institutions, and the vigorous energetic mixture of new peoples stood in sharp contrast to a crowded, impoverished Old World with its despotic rule, its encrusted social order and its age-old legacy of hatreds and rivalries.[8] Today, "America, the melting pot," remains one of the most easily grasped and popularly held ideas.

Although not so widely disseminated, the concept of cultural pluralism has been proffered as the most desirable solution to the problem of ethnicity. Kallen, the originator of the term, believed that ethnic heritages should be preserved and a pride in ethnic group membership encouraged. In his view, American society would be enriched not by melting down group identities into an amorphous mass crushed under the standardized imprint of Americanization, but by protecting and fostering distinctive ethnic identities. In this way, the richness and variety of heritage would be retained and an ethnic sense of self-respect rather than one of inferiority and self-hate would be propagated.

It is equally evident that the "core culture" concept has been for many less of an analytical explanation than a battle cry. Shielding "the American heritage" from popery, pauperism, radicalism, and foreign contamination has been the self-appointed task of nativists, civic leaders, and educators since the birth of our nation.[9] For example, the old "national origins" quota system (recently replaced), severely restricting immigration from Asia, Africa, and southern and eastern Europe, gave twentieth-century moral confirmation to the idea of a core culture as the special preserve of the descendants of an Anglo-Teutonic tradition.

Clearly, each social theory has had political implications. The melting pot refrain discouraged the organization of distinctly ethnic political organizations and interest groups. Under this theory, ethnic politics was viewed as the perpetuation of divisive factions and parochialisms inimical to the best interests of a homogeneous society organized around individual talents. The individualism of the melting pot had no room and little tolerance for the urban problems and organization of American group life. On the other hand, the recognition of cultural pluralism enhanced the mosaic of fraternal, party organization, and social groups woven into the fabric of distinct racial, religious, and nationality differences within America. Cultural pluralism provided ample flexibility to the corps of political and ethnic group leaders who bargained from a position of electoral strength with "their own kind." The republic in miniature that exemplifies so much of recent American politics found its intellectual base under the pluralistic rubric.

The implications of the core culture idea are probably more subtle. Originally rooted in Anglo-American institutions, the theory is now equally suited to enhance the dominance of international corporate structures that have significant impact on our lives. In essence, a core culture suggests a unified political elite whose public behavior provides an adequate guide to public policies. Under this theory, those who have learned the proper cultural norms are most qualified to govern the polity. White Protestant civic leaders working for the good of the total community with the tools of "good government," namely, at-large elections, professional staffs, and a belief in managerial and fiscal efficiency, represented models of political leaders preserving the American core culture in an earlier era of urban life. Today, the interactions among corporate, political, and military professionals working for the organized interests of our dominant institutions reinforce the belief in a basic set of "higher values" perpetuated within the polity. Moreover, the core culture thesis has provided broad criteria for detecting and curtailing the influence of "alien" politics that have threatened the stability of the society. Radicals importing foreign ideologies, group efforts to promote racial and nationality pride, and religious solidarity forged into political power have been seen as undermining the core values of American society.

Our interest is not, however, in exploring the respective ethical implications of the three models but in considering whether they explain something about present reality. As might be evident, one reason why all three models may seem plausible is because each enjoys some kind of empirical base. To say, however, that there is some truth in each of a variety of persuasions does not provide much clarification to any question. For instance, of the three themes, the "melting pot" is probably the most popular and the least substantiated. There is evidence that some groups disappear into a larger cultural totality, and insofar as members of these groups contribute to a distinct American life, the melting pot idea has empirical support. But while the contribution of immigrant groups can be measured in demographic and economic terms, viz., manpower, labor, talent, and population, there seems little evidence that they have contributed much of their original cultures.[10]

The scattered linguistic and culturally autonomous ethnic communities lend some support to the idea of cultural pluralism. But, as has been noted previously, such communities represent the exception rather than the rule. If they are truly culturally autonomous, they are, by definition and in fact, isolated from the mainstream of American life. Ethnicity contributes to the pluralistic differences in American society, as do class, locale, occupation, and social and political ideology. Nevertheless, over and above such pluralism, there exist dominant and basic standards, values, and living styles which, while not free of contradictions and variations, still seem to represent established patterns that are far more than merely federations of quasi-autonomous cultures. It is toward these established patterns that the newcomer often feels alien but into which he may eventually assimilate. If such uniformities obtain and predominate, however, how do we explain the persistence of ethnic identifications? The answer to that question is forthcoming when we recognize that ethnic identification and assimilation involve a multiplicity of factors and processes.

ACCULTURATION AND ASSIMILATION

In colonial times, nearly every group that came to America attempted to form a community that replicated the Old World society from which it emanated. This effort was repeated in the eighteenth, nineteenth, and twentieth centuries by each succeeding group of newcomers. With few exceptions, they failed. The story, especially in relation to the more recently arrived groups, has been adequately recounted and will be dwelt upon only briefly here.[11]

If what we call culture means the values, styles, accumulated patterns, solutions, and practices which represent a society's total adjustment to its physical and social environment, it would follow that no specific form of culture can be transplanted from one environment to another without at least some substantial change. The nineteenth- and twentieth-century immigrants, and even many who arrived earlier, were confronted with an established society possessing cultural forms, values, and behavioral patterns which in many respects differed from theirs. The newcomers experienced heavy social pressure to conform to the new culture, and the instruments of conformity became ever more efficient with the growth of large-scale social organization, industrialization, mass communication, and public education.

In addition to the shocks of migration, resettlement, and adjustment to the new society, the immigrant family usually experienced a conflict of serious dimensions during the second and third decades of habitation in America, i.e., that time of familial life when the children began to involve themselves in the wider American world. (If and when the ghetto wall is demolished, it will occur not only by a frontal assault on the part of the dominant community, but also by a process of subversion, as it were, a "boring from within" the family matrix by offspring acting as agents of alien American values and ideas.) Generational disparities increased as the children, exposed to the indoctrination of the American schools, the settlement houses, the city, places of work, military service, the mass media, and American recreations, were drawn into a web of life which implanted in their minds an image of a glorified "American way" and "American type."[12]

The American-born youth knew his life and future were to be made in the new society and not in the far-off villages that survived in the reminiscences of the old folks. Unable to offer or draw upon a complete cultural base of their own, and with no larger constellation of societal forces and institutions to back them, the immigrants eventually lost the battle. Not infrequently, even the immigrant parents became reconciled to, and practitioners of, many of the new American ways.

It has been characteristic of most ethnics in America that, with varying degrees of rapidity—although frequently by the second generation—they have discarded most of the cultural practices, styles, and trappings of their groups. The evidence accumulated by historians and social scientists indicates that the "melting pot" has more often operated as a "smelting furnace . . . burning out the alien culture elements like slag from the pure metal of American culture."[13] By the same evidence, it would seem that cultural pluralism, with the exception of the situation in a few scattered culturally autonomous communities,[14] exists more as a sentiment than a reality. Yet, the idea of an ethnic pluralistic society persists, and discernible ethnic group loyalties and identifications are to be found in all regions of the nation. However, what is often missing in "cultural pluralism" is the "culture." This can be illustrated by the two studies, done twenty years apart, of working-class Italian American communities in Boston. Sociologists W. F. Whyte and Herbert Gans, respectively, demonstrated that the second generation Italian American manifests little concern for, or knowledge of, Italian culture other than its cuisine. Rather, his interest is directed toward American events, sports, recreation, work, dress, and the popular media. But to conclude that Whyte's North-End Italians and Gans' West-End Italians are acculturated is to tell only half the story. In fact, they retain a pronounced Italian American group identification, and they distinguish ethnically between themselves and the representatives of the outside world, whom they tend to distrust and resist. That outside world is personified by social workers, officials, librarians, and teachers who, as agents of a core white, Protestant, middle-class society, are often outspokenly disdainful of the ethnic community.

The important lesson to be drawn is that ethnic identifications usually persist without the benefit of the Old World ethnic cultural systems and long after cultural and linguistic differences have faded. To explain how this is possible, it is necessary to differentiate between "acculturation" and "assimilation." Acculturation refers to the process whereby the minority member absorbs the cultural ways, values, and life styles of the wider community, or that portion of the wider community which operates within the regional and class confines available to him. Assimilation pertains more to a subjectively-felt identification and attitude. With total assimilation, no value or status distinctions on the basis of ethnicity are made by the ethnic or the host community. On the other hand, the ethnic who undergoes "acculturation" is not necessarily freed from feelings of marginality or minority group status. He does not necessarily feel assimilated, i.e., totally identified with and accepted by the host community and free of a sense of distinction or difference.

This explains why some observers speak of an almost ubiquitous Americanization and the absence of ethnic pluralism when, in fact, they are referring to acculturation; while others can speak of persistent pluralistic ethnic identification when, in fact, they are referring to assimilation. The persistence of unassimilated and/or unacculturated ethnic groups provides a dual source of politics tinged with ethnic components. It is this duality that helps to explain why ethnic politics has so long endured in the American political system. Nor does ethnic group identification require isolation from the mainstream of American life. Psychological identification with an ethnic group continues long after group members have learned those values and behaviors necessary for survival in a complex industrial system. Such identification endures beyond physical proximity in the area of original group settlement and acculturation. The American melting pot has never steamed away the layers of group sentiment and symbols that underlie ethnic identification. Herein lies the durable base for the varieties of racial and religious politics within the ongoing system.

CHAPTER TWO

The Individual Base of Ethnic Politics

Q. Are you going to vote for Kennedy because he is a Catholic?
A. . . . No, because I am.[1]

For the Irish, Jewish, Italian bright boys who pursue it, politics is a status-conferring occupation. . . . As successful politicians, they can demand deference from the greatest capitalists, the toughest union leaders, the oldest of the old families.[2]

THE TRIBE ENDURES

"It doesn't matter any longer what you do to me; you can put me in jail, you can kill me," wrote James Baldwin. "By the time I was seventeen you had done everything that you can do to me. The problem now is, how are you going to save yourselves?"[3] It is not difficult to explain the Negro's use of politics to redress grievances. But others—the third generation Jew, the Catholic businessman—how do we account for the durability of their ethnic affiliations in political life? Students of political behavior have repeatedly commented on the surprising persistence of ethnic voting throughout metropolitan America.[4] For instance, Robert

Alford found no evidence of a decline of religious influence in presidential voting between 1944 and 1960,[5] and V. O. Key, Jr., observed that "a special feature of American urban class structure has been its association with differences in national origins."[6]

To be sure there have been profound changes in the political impact of nationality, race, and religion in recent decades. Nevertheless, the persistence of ethnicity as a political variable in the face of urbanization and other "modernizing" social changes is striking and was not anticipated by American social scientists. Alford cautions against assuming the withering away of ethnic politics when he observes:

> Whether there is any tendency for those [modern] societies to become secularized and to create a different kind of political orientation, specifically a greater tendency to vote according to class rather than region or religion, are really open questions. That urbanization and industrialization tend to break down "traditional" loyalties of all kinds, specifically religious ones, has long been a cliché of sociological theorizing about broad trends of social change since the Industrial Revolution. As with all clichés, this may have a germ of basic truth, but it is vastly oversimplified.[7]

Why is this cliché an oversimplification? Ethnicity influences the broad range of choices made by most political actors in the pursuit of diverse goals under varying conditions. This statement points to the multiplicity of ethnic political behavior. It leads us away from thinking of ethnic politics in a stereotyped manner, that is, as only public responses made by poor or unacculturated ethnic group members. Before accounting for the multiple manifestations of ethnic political choice, however, it may be useful to look closely at three political conditions that structure the choices to be discussed.

THREE IMPORTANT CONDITIONS OF ETHNIC POLITICAL CHOICE

In theory, a person's racial or religious identification may guide him in voting for political candidates or in making up his mind about public issues. In practice, ethnicity is most likely to be politically important to *practicing politicians*, for there is a close connection between their ethnicity and the political choices facing them. Let us call the major conditions affecting their choices political activism, political saliency, and political visibility, and let us see how these conditions structure the responses of ethnic groups to events.

Discussing political activism, Robert Dahl observes that, "one of the central facts of political life is that politics—local, state, national, international—lies for most people at the outer periphery of attention, interest, concern, and activity."[8] Most members of ethnic groups fall within the category of inactive citizens most of the time. Politics per se is not very compelling for them, especially if the personal gardens of family, job, and home life are reasonably well tended. By contrast, politists, e.g., those individuals highly active in politics, are more likely to be sensitive to the *political* consequences of ethnicity as well as any other factors likely to have a bearing on *public* outcomes. For example, in the spring of 1960 several prominent Catholics looked skeptically upon the prospects of a young co-religionist who was seeking the Democratic presidential nomination through the primaries of Wisconsin and West Virginia. Mayor Richard Daley of Chicago, Governor David Lawrence of Pennsylvania, and Manhattan leader Carmine DeSapio were not "bad" or insensitive Catholics. In fact, they were behaving like "good" politicians rationally calculating the probable impact of a Catholic presidential candidate, John F. Kennedy, on their state and local party tickets.[9]

Ethnic ramifications of politics are especially important to politists who have invested considerable amounts of their scarce political resources (time, money, interest, influence) in public activities. Thus, political choices and the potential influence of race, religion, and nationality on politics are usually more salient to politicians than to average citizens. Nevertheless, ethnicity has often become highly important in the political behavior of the latter. Witness the Buffalo worker quoted at the beginning of this chapter. While the political party leaders of such places as Chicago, Pennsylvania, and Manhattan may have had more at stake, the industrial worker revealed a close connection between his status as a Catholic and the religious issue that permeated the Kennedy-Nixon presidential election in 1960.

The political salience of ethnicity is usually strongest in crisis situations when an ethnic group is making a concerted and dramatic bid for political power. From the immigrant political machine to the current drives for "Black Power," social divisions in America have frequently been registered in ethnic politics. The saliency and psychic investment in ethnic politics determines its political impact upon the community. Compare an Irish Catholic vote for Al Smith in 1928 or John F. Kennedy in 1960 with a vote cast by the same man for the fifteenth Irish American to represent his state senatorial district. Ethnicity and voting for one's own kind are factors in all three choices, but the qualitative differences are vast. It follows that ethnic politics is most salient when it involves major group goals including the initial election of a co-ethnic to high public office.

Third, ethnic factors are more important in some political processes, particularly those involving a high degree of visibility, than in others. Most of the studies about ethnicity and politics are based on investigations of voting and party behavior. These choices are usually grosser and intrinsically more divisive than administrative and judicial decisions, in which ethnicity is often less overt and the outcomes supposedly integrative and "nonpolitical." The importance of ethnic influence is readily apparent in those choices that consistently involve the general public. Despite public avoidance of the religious issue by Nixon and Kennedy in the 1960 presidential campaign, the myth that religious affiliation was irrelevant to presidential ambitions had little impact on the "off-stage" public discussions of Kennedy's Catholic faith among face-to-face groups in Oklahoma, Tennessee, and other sections of America. Ethnicity, which is probably less visible in decisions made by and for political elites than when the citizenry is directly involved, becomes politically visible when citizens, and politicians representing them, have intense feelings about changes in the distribution of public goods and the personal qualities of elected public officials.[10]

In summary, this chapter contains expressions of doubt about the assumed death of ethnicity in American political life. Moreover, it indicates that one of the reasons for the lack of clarity in discussions about ethnicity in American politics is a failure to specify the choice being made by different political actors operating in different contexts and with diverse saliency of ethnic factors in political life.

FUNCTIONS OF THE ETHNIC POLITICAL CHOICE

Just as ethnicity's political impact varies with the abovenamed conditions, so, too, does the utility of ethnicity determine its political importance. Political leaders play up ethnic group grievances in order to win election to public office. Moreover, in a democratic system there is an important link between the choices and concerns of citizens and those of political leaders or politicians.[11] However, ethnicity has a different significance for politists, who constantly seek to influence choices made by the few, than it has for the average citizen, who exhibits low or moderate political involvement. Nevertheless, the variety of functions ethnic political behavior has fulfilled for average citizens should not be forgotten. The basis of "normal," traditional American ethnic politics is the selective use of ethnicity amidst usually low levels of political involvement. Even in a politically slack system, citizens united from time to time by ethnic bonds have used politics to stabilize their environment, to secure material goals, to satisfy basic psychic needs, and, on occasion, to bring about fundamental changes in civic values.

SOCIAL STABILITY AND THE ECONOMY OF TRADITION

"They dreaded political change," wrote Oscar Handlin of the great migration's immigrants, "because that might loosen the whole social order, disrupt the family, pull God from his throne."[12] With rare exception, the story of religion and nationality in American life is that of adaptation to a changing political and social environment. Immigrants and their descendents who secure reasonably satisfying material and psychic benefits usually are contented civil men who decline the more demanding role of political man. Such sporadic political behavior as they do display results from a desire to harmonize their plural ethnic and political loyalties.

The impact of immigrant politics can be seen in the congruent roles of ethnic and citizen found in their descendents. Sam Hodder, a subject in the Smith, Brunner, and White volume *Opinions and Personality*, could well be a grandson of a Polish peasant whose letters were studied in the classic work of Thomas and Znaniecki.[13] Hodder is no passive object of an omnipotent feudal system. He has citizenship rights and knows how to exercise them. He is concerned about politics only to the degree that he feels that political change might rob him and others like him of concrete benefits. He has no conception of the modes whereby political power secures or protects interests. As long as concrete experience within his perceived world goes on normally, his loyalties will also proceed as usual.[14] Moreover, these loyalties—Polish American, Catholic, union man, Democrat—will persist in harmony during most trips to the polling booth.

A major explanation of the channeling of ethnicity in political choice is its translation through the mediating path of stable party identification.[15] Voting studies show a tenacious relationship between specific ethnic memberships and party affiliation, a tenacity that points to a striving for congruity and clarity between a man's ethnic and party memberships.[16] Ethnicity becomes Americanized, so to speak, when it underlies stable party identification.

Ethnic considerations are also likely to endure when average citizens must search diligently for a meaningful political choice, i.e., when salient ethno-party factors are not present. Ethnicity may "rationally" simplify and stabilize choice among ambiguous stimuli or in the absence of politically compelling cues. In particular, voters are especially likely to fall back on ethnic cues in nonpartisan elections. For instance, in an experimental study of a Canadian mock election, English and French Canadian voters were given fictitious ballots. Both ethnic groups "overchose" hypothetical candidates of their own ethnic character. When in a second survey sample the same fictional candidates were given party affiliations, both the English and the French voters were guided by the candidates' affiliation; the ethnic connotations of their names had no significant effect.[17]

A study of Italo-American political attitudes also reveals the impact of ethnic identification in the absence of party labels. Asked to choose between hypothetical Italian and non-Italian candidates, respondents invariably selected the former—until party labels were introduced, whereupon in most cases ethnic favoritism gave way to party loyalty. Moreover, when affiliations are given, ethnic voting on the basis of name recognition is most likely to occur among those with strong ethnic identification and little political interest or information about the political choice. Thus, a Michigan study found that strong Catholics who could recall only the ethnic affiliations of congressional candidates were most likely to cross party lines in search of a co-religionist.[18] As a further example of the relationship of nonpartisanship to ethnic voting patterns, in Detroit's nonpartisan system, the vote for Negro candidates varies sharply with the racial composition of the district, while the strong party system of Chicago increases ticket voting sharply and reduces variance among the votes received by Negro and white Democratic candidates.[19] In New Hampshire's low-keyed and fragmented Democratic politics, an Irish or French Canadian background is often the most pertinent factor in voting in primary contests.[20] The late V. O. Key, Jr., provided a relevant generalization when he wrote that "elements of . . . national origin [and] religion have far greater bearing on votes in the primary than in the general election when party considerations come into play."[21]

Ethnic voting also promotes social harmony because it reinforces the most stable and satisfying elements in a person's milieu. Thus, voting for an Italo-American representative in a predominantly Italo-American ward requires no special set of political circumstances or grievances; it merely reflects the primary social and psychological experiences of the local resident.[22] Furthermore, the expression of ethnic homogeneity by voters is reinforced when there are few sharp fluctuations in the social and economic composition of the ward or the local community. (It should be noted, however, that ethnic voting based on name recognition, party attachment, and social harmony usually has conservative consequences.) The root proposition of this discussion is advanced by Berelson and his associates:

> Political stability is based on social stability. . . . Ethnic affiliations . . . do not change rapidly or sharply, and since the vote is so importantly a product of them, neither does it. In effect, a large part of the study of voting deals not with why votes change but rather with why they do not.[23]

Ethnicity also tends to preserve existing political choices. The close tie between ethnic and party identification works both ways. If party affiliation, or, in its absence, direct ethnic choice, is of use in making political choices, it is also useful in reducing tensions faced by ethnic groups in dealing with the larger society. In the face of the host society's hostility and in support of its religious goals, the American Catholic Church, for example, constructed separate educational, social, religious, and professional institutions. The norms of the then emerging Catholic subculture often ran counter to the emphasis on secularism, mobility, achievement, and impersonality in society as a whole.[24] Thus, the long-standing association between the Democratic party and the American Catholic community provided an opportunity to accommodate some of these fundamental differences within the normal political process. Moreover, persistent Catholic support of Democratic candidates reveals the durable nature of the ethno-party affiliations.

Those attempting to explain the convergence of Catholic-Protestant voting patterns in recent years miss the point that Catholic-Democratic allegiances after 1937 stood up in the face of two decades of secular, liberal control of foreign affairs and of noneconomic domestic concerns, such as civil liberties and the communists-in-government issue, that severely strained Catholic attachments to the party of Al Smith.[25] Gerhardt Lenski found, for example, that in Detroit involvement in the Catholic subcommunity strongly correlated with Democratic preferences, and Greer discovered that a middle-class, suburbanization process has had surprisingly little effect in eroding continuous Democratic attachments among the Catholic electorate in St. Louis county.[26]

These Catholic-Democratic ties reduced the conflict between society's norms of individual, secular achievement and communal values anchored in religious affiliation, thus preserving ethnic group cohesion. Continued Catholic responsiveness to the equalitarian appeals of the Democratic party reinforced communal values of Catholic family, peer, and friendship in the face of countervailing secular pressures to achieve, compete, and depersonalize social relations.

The conserving function of ethnic political choice is most evident among group members with high ethnic and low political involvement. For instance, Episcopalians, with the most church-related memberships and the fewest political or nonchurch activities, most narrowly define the political activities they think legitimate for their clergymen to engage in, thus increasing group cohesiveness against divisive external political pressures, and incidentally increasing the potential for clerical political influence cloaked in spiritual vestments. By taking an apparently nonpolitical stance and invoking moral pieties agreeable to the ethnic membership, clergymen may acquire a limited influence over political events. For example, in a kind of reverse effect, arguments against clerical involvement in open housing and integrated school politics effectively sustained opposition to Negro political demands among ethnic-based congregations in Boston and Milwaukee. There is ample evidence, too, to support the contention that ethnic politics frequently conserves acquired group sentiments. In 1952, Jewish women with few non-Jewish social contacts clung most strongly to acquired Jewish-Democratic voting norms despite a national swing to Eisenhower among most groups. An Oregon study shows that frequent attenders of both "fundamentalist" and "liberal" Protestant religious services are highly likely to vote in accord with the prevailing sentiments of their respective clerical leaders. In the process, interdenominational links between social class and voting habits are weakened and parishioners move toward intradenominational political agreement.[27]

Indeed, the political homogeneity of ethnic groups is both cause and consequence of the group's cohesion. Ethnicity has often provided the glue for political and group stability. In a society where political ideology is not usually compelling, most citizens are likely to utilize residual group memberships, such as ethnicity, to govern their infrequent expenditures of political attention and effort. In a society where large-scale organizations depersonalize human relations, men fall back on the primary bonds of blood, believer, and nationality. Moreover, reliance upon ethnicity in political activity further sustains group cohesion within a complex society. The persistence of ethnic political choice is due in no small measure to the enduring need to maintain social relations. Although many citizens see voting as a marginal act, it does provide an important means of maintaining social stability as well as perpetuating the existence of American ethnic groups themselves.

MATERIAL GOALS: ECONOMICS AND PATRONAGE

Two key relationships stand out in any investigation of ethnicity and political choice. One is the politically significant association between ethnic group membership and social class. The second is the relation between ethnicity and affiliation with political parties, candidates, and interest groups. Membership in an ethnic group unites an individual to a party and colors his perception of political demands made by other groups. Thus, it is often the case that a "party or candidate is simply endorsed as being 'for' a group with which the subject is identified . . ."[28] and opposed to other, competing groups negatively viewed by members of the subject's ethnic group.

Group conflicts anchored in racial and nationality differences have severely retarded the development of class politics, especially by preventing cohesion among the less well-off strata of society. For example, antagonisms between poor whites and Negroes in the South seriously curtailed efforts to unite "have-not" groups in that part of the nation, thus contributing to the long-term power of the ruling "Bourbons." For decades, southern elites have effectively utilized race to keep poor whites and Negroes in similar economic straits apart. In another illustration of this point, despite their common religion and social class position during the formative years of urban life, lower-middle and working class Catholics persistently fought their political battles along ethnic lines. In the Northeast in particular, there were decades of Irish, Italian, Polish, and French Canadian competition for control of party and electoral posts among politicians of the Catholic faith.[29]

The traditional explanation that ethnic groups have turned to politics in order to provide governmental employment stems from the supposed absence of alternative channels of social and economic advancement. Indeed, political institutions have functioned as major mechanisms of social mobility and economic sustenance for the Irish and other ethnic groups. Today, material incentives for political participation obtain especially among American Negroes, Puerto Ricans, and other groups with generally low socioeconomic status. The federal government is the major employer of Negroes, followed by the city of New York. In 1966, 23 per cent of New York City's employees were Negroes, although Negroes comprised only 14 per cent of the city's total population. Among "professionals," moreover, 14 per cent of the city's employees were Negroes compared with a figure of 6 per cent representing the contribution of Negroes to the total professional labor force employed by all private industry in New York.[30]

The significance for Negroes of government jobs is evident

when proposals that might reduce black access to public posts are offered. Considering how important government positions have been to members of minority groups, one can understand a Negro political leader's response to a certain metropolitan proposal in St. Louis:

> That charter would write the protection out of Civil Service, and you know how important Civil Service is to my people. They have better jobs and if you put those jobs into a county government without Civil Service, the chances are that a lot of people will lose their jobs.[31]

Such tangible rewards also account for the high rates of participation by urban Negroes and the foreign-born constituents in local politics, despite the fact that low social status is usually a barrier to regular voting and other political activities.[32] However, "economic deprivation" does not explain the political pull of ethnicity as the ethnic groups become more economically self-sufficient, less dependent on public employment, and more heterogeneous in regard to class distribution. The durability of ethnic politics beyond the initial period of group economic deprivation, when ethnicity was practically synonymous with low socioeconomic status, can probably be explained in the following manner:

> 1. *Relative* differences in the economic positions of both ethnic groups and individual group members persist long beyond the period of economic deprivation. Indeed, numerous studies of ethnicity and social class indicate that: (a) native born are better off than foreign born; (b) Jews and urban white Protestants are better off than Catholics; and (c) groups of northern European stock are better off than groups of southern and eastern European extraction (Jews excepted).[33]
>
> Variations in social position may also explain persistent differences in political behavior among these people. The fact that "professional class" patterns, e.g., business-professional occupations, high income and education, and high achievement orientations, are prevalent among American Jewry influences those Jews in lower social class positions. For instance, higher incidences of political participation, achievement orientation, and noneconomic liberalism, and lower incidences of psychological impairment and anomie (suicide, alcoholism) among low socioeconomic-status Jews are related to a high degree of Jewish group cohesion and the dominance of professional class life styles in the Jewish commu-

nity.[34] However, Catholics, specifically Irish Catholics, occupy a middling position with respect to occupation, education, and achievement orientation, suggesting that "there may be some kind of lower-middle or lower class orientation . . . to education and occupation which tends to anchor Catholics in the lower socioeconomic groups and which limits those who do achieve higher education to certain fields which appear to offer more security."[35] In the context of the Catholic subcommunity, a lower-middle class orientation is related to low participation in issue-oriented and liberal reformist politics, low support of noneconomic liberalism, and highly conventional appraisal of programs and candidates. More importantly, the evidence suggests that better-off Catholics must usually strain against dominant group patterns when they behave politically like better-off Jews. Thus, the dominant social and economic characteristics of a group produce policies that are displayed even by those group members of different social and economic accomplishment.

2. The memory of past material benefits achieved or opportunities secured through politics is likely to be strong to create party loyalties that are not lightly altered. The normal national Democratic majority, based to some extent on welfare gains under Democrats since 1932, reflects the translation of urban, ethnic gains into partisan affiliation. Thus, a Jewish businessman, prosperous in his suburban ranch house, recalls that:

> The Republicans are for big business. . . . They always have been and always will be. Jews have prospered under the Democrats since the depression when Roosevelt kept this country from falling to pieces.[36]

Party identification is a "bridge" between secondary group memberships, such as race and religion, and political events. The bridge is most stable when many factors converge to sustain party loyalty. For instance, Jews who identify as Democrats solely because of their "Jewishness" are more susceptible to ethnic appeals from Republicans than are Jews whose Democratic allegiance is rooted in social and economic attitudes.[37]

A group's political heritage and political strategy often dictate loyalty to a party. Group leadership, too, is frequently wedded to a party and can switch support to another party only with great difficulty. However, in the absence of party ties and economic autonomy, bloc voting is more frequent, more profitable to group leaders, and sometimes benefits the citizenry. For example, Mexican American politics of South Texas was built on the *jefes*, Latin strawbosses who traded blocs of votes in *quid pro quo* arrangements. At times, whole counties such as Duval, Starr, and Webb swung their votes almost unanimously for favored candidates, especially incumbent governors who controlled the largesse of patronage. More often, the less dramatic one-party politics rooted in the dominant party's primaries found individual *jefes* making their own deals in a free market and canceling out the bloc vote of a rival political merchant.[38]

3. Ethnic politics enjoys a durability beyond the initial phase of economic deprivation for another reason: As the group's lot in life improves, leaders emerging from its ranks capitalize on ethnic consciousness. Indeed, one might go so far as to suggest that ethnicity actually *increases* rather than decreases in saliency when ethnic politicians acquire necessary resources (skills, education, finances, organization, motivation). Electoral successes and political influence come to those groups having skilled professional leadership and a citizenry sophisticated enough to believe the ballot has meaning for their respective destinies. Both of these conditions occur only *after* ethnic politicians seek political offices. In Providence, Rhode Island, about three decades elapsed after the end of mass immigration before the newer minorities obtained ward committee positions.[39] In New Haven, Connecticut, about seventy years intervened between the end of the mass immigration of Italo-Americans to that city and the onset of that group's ability to elect major candidates proportionate to their numbers.[40] Furthermore, Al Smith's presidential bid came nearly ninety years after the first substantial waves of Irish immigrants came to America.

The ability of an ethnic group to produce men of social and economic achievement affected the success and quality of its political leadership. Politicians emerged among ethnic group leaders who had achieved some social stature, men such as the Italian funeral director, the Irish saloonkeeper, and the Jewish evening law school graduate. Group leaders who entered politics helped to translate ethnicity into political power for the less fortunate members of their ethnic groups. Today, the impact of black leaders and civil rights activists produces the same type of political awakening among the masses. For instance, in those counties of the contemporary South where youthful middle-class political leadership has been strongest, political demands and demonstrations initiated by Congress of Racial Equality and Student Non-Violent Coordinating Committee organizers exceed the level of political participation one would normally expect from residents with low socioeconomic status.[41] Here again, members of the ethnic group enjoying some social and economic advantages, such as ministers and college students, serve as political leaders. Raymond Wolfinger's analysis of Italo-American political behavior in New Haven supports the argument that ethnic politics becomes more prevalent as group members obtain economic stakes within American society.

One view of ethnic assimilation into politics would suggest that ethnic politics decreases as group members become more economically sufficient and socially secure. However, this view analyzes too short a time span. "The clearest demonstration of political proximity is a fellow ethnic's candidacy for major office (mayor, governor, senator, president), [but] . . . middle-class status is almost a prerequisite for such a candidacy, [and] it takes a generation before an ethnic group's political solidarity can be mobilized."[42] Moreover, this solidarity is likely to reappear as fellow ethnics seek additional offices on the totem pole of American federalism. Thus, middle-class Catholics who had been attracted to Eisenhower Republicanism supported John F. Kennedy's bid for the presidency in 1960.[43] This delayed impact of ethnic politics at various political levels, that is, ethnic voting for group members seeking higher offices, erodes the idea that groups will cease using ethnicity in politics once they have achieved some wealth and recognition.

Although social mobility unbalanced ancient alignments and taught ethnic group members about an American core culture, it did not lead to immediate political assimilation. Social mobility produced public leaders whose base of support significantly encompassed racial, religious, and nationality groupings. In short, the impact of social and economic rewards was to sustain rather than to erode the ethnic base of public life.

4. Ethnic politics distributes material values, such as jobs and housing, otherwise denied to newcomers of divergent racial, nationality, and religious background. The story of ethnic politics as related by Oscar Handlin, Samuel Lubell, and others is told from the viewpoint of deprived groups overcoming obstacles to achieve economic and social success within a democratic system. While not denying the force of "prog-

ress" in American history, we believe, however, that one can gain a new understanding of the relation between material values and persisting ethnic political patterns by reversing the prism and observing from the top rather than from the bottom, that is, from the vantage point of politically dominant groups. These groups are most aware of ethnic politics as a threat to their positions or prosperity.

No group, including those which formerly occupied minority positions of deprivation and discrimination, has easily and voluntarily relinquished key material values. Thus, once having wrested material benefits from the Yankees, the Irish were not prone to relinquish their hold to later arrivals. Open housing drives by urban Negroes have been resisted most vigorously by groups that have themselves known previous discrimination, often central and eastern European ethnic groups. Dominant groups, often united by race, religion, and national origin, fall back along a line of prepared defensive positions from which they seek to protect power, property, social status, and core civic values from newer "undesirable," and usually lower class, elements also identifiable by common racial, religious, and (decreasingly) national origins. Within bounds, a democratic creed is a severe limitation to oligarchies. . . . The dominant group first seeks to prevent or limit the electoral power of disadvantaged groups. Thus, a propertied white Protestant elite ("Yankee," "Bourbon") sought to limit the influx of immigrants through restrictive legislation or preventing Negroes and other minorities from voting by means of economic sanctions, control of the courts, the poll tax, property requirements on the franchise, violence, and nativist agitation.

When disadvantaged persons acquire or exercise voting privileges in large numbers, dominant groups seek to retain power by offering token positions, recognition, and low-level offices to the newcomers. Thus, "Uncle Tom" Negroes, members of a black bourgeoisie living on the crumbs from the white man's table, were the first of their race to occupy ward positions in northern cities. Such recognition has sometimes meant no more than the decision of the Yankee-dominated Massachusetts Republican party to advance Italo-American Vincent Celeste as its U.S. Senate candidate in a hopeless contest against John F. Kennedy in 1958.

In time, established oligarchies withdraw from electoral prominence to civic and economic strongholds because: (a) they dislike the goals (power, not service) of the new men; (b) they dislike the means employed to gain power (urban machines, not agreement about "good" qualities of leaders); (c) they cannot win when the electoral rules of the game favor numbers over social position.[44] Attempts to manipulate electoral outcomes from economic, civic, and communications control centers are usually ineffective because new groups secure fiscal, communication, and community resources from their own supporters. Thus, New Deal urban politics and the liberal politics it supported were backed by successful members of the upper world (commerce, banking) and of the underworld (crime, shady businesses).[45]

Groups without sizable economic or civic resources, on the other hand, are especially apt to bitterly contest electoral positions in the face of invasions by other groups. The "old-line" Irish politicians who played the key brokerage role in many urban systems were examples of this tenacity because they did not have an alternative "game" to play, such as running the family bank or serving on a university's board of trustees. In short, when there are few alternative channels of advancement, ethnic competition for state and local political offices intensifies. In such situations, ethnicity remains a major factor in candidate selection, although in the long run party dominance by a particular ethnic group decreases.

In addition to electoral politics, the processes of ethnicity have applied to industrial, educational, and governmental institutions. However, no one, to our knowledge, has studied upper-class white Protestants as a "minority group," nor looked into their influence, now decreasing, within banks, universities, and zoning commissions to regulate the influx of other ethnic groups into exclusive residential areas. But as Andrew Hacker reminds us:

> It is only since 1940 that banks, investment houses, the diplomatic service, and established industries and universities have opened their positions of power and responsibility to others than those of old American stock. Twenty years ago Americans of Irish, Italian, Slav, and Jewish antecedents were simply not recruited, admitted, or welcome.[46]

Outside groups seeking entree are particularly likely to perceive occupational barriers in ethnic terms. According to Louis Lomax, in New York the Negro sees Italians as the dominant powerholders in the construction trades, Jews in communications, and the Irish in local politics. Tensions between Negroes and liberal Jews and Catholics in trade unions and private industry often concern control of key executive positions. Similarly, in suburban school systems of the Boston metropolitan area, where Irish and Italian teachers have worked their way up local promotion ladders, resentment is voiced at recent products of the Harvard School of Education, often Protestents and Jews, who enter the Boston school system at high levels. In New York, Jews predominate as school principals and bear the brunt of Negro complaints that there are few Negro principals.[47] And Negro writers manage to publish savage attacks on white society in publications owned and run by Protestants and Jews.

A society that lacks full employment and has differential racial employment rates faces ethnic political conflict. In our society, which has exhibited these characteristics to a degree, Negroes have often been barred entry to apprentice programs in craft unions which are often run by distinct ethnic groups (Irish, Polish, Italian). In addition, the "last hired, first fired" pattern has been particularly severe among workers of color in many American unions. The onus of poverty and inadequate work skills has led ethnics to seek political redress throughout the political history of urban America.

PSYCHIC GOALS: THE ESTEEM OF THE VICTIM

Although the American creed still places the onus of poverty and material success on the individual, the ethnics "could feel, as the working classes never could, that their lack of status was due to discrimination. . . . For the ethnic failure to achieve status, one could blame a discriminatory society."[48]

While concerned with the pursuit of material goals, ethnic politics has also stressed compensatory efforts to acquire honor, dignity, respect, and self-esteem. Low social valuation feeds low self-valuation, which often produces results inimical to a democratic polity. One response to low self-esteem is to withdraw from politics, cultivate studied apathy, and create social situations in which one is esteemed despite his ethnic affiliation. Among ethnics who have attained material success, those viewed as socially invisible and unesteemed may socialize their feelings of rejection through social conventions such as those used by the Negro middle-class in a period of intense social segregation. The social masks and avoidance of political issues provide a defense against the gnawing doubts about one's self-worth:

> Despite the tinsel, glitter, and gaiety of the world of make-believe in which the middle-class Negroes take refuge, they

> are beset by feelings of insecurity, frustration, and guilt. As a consequence, the free and easy life which they appear to lead is a mask for their unhappy existence.[49]

Ethnic group members cannot always retreat to such collective solace. Antagonisms among members of different ethnic groups contribute to the low self-esteem of minority members in communities riddled with ethnic tensions. One's self-esteem is supported by the positive evaluations of others in face-to-face relationships. When these relationships are laden with group and individual rejection because of race or religion, the social fabric of the individual is under heavy pressure. Such is the situation described by Morris Rosenberg in his documentation of low self-esteem characterizing other "minority members" living in New York City neighborhoods dominated, respectively, by Jews and Catholics. Members of ethnic groups who have been socialized to expect some discrimination within the larger society are likely to find release by using overt or subtle social controls against members of other "minorities" within their own neighborhoods. Thus, an ethnic may be denied the esteem normally forthcoming from his fellow group members.

Another psychological mechanism for dealing with self-doubts about ethnic worth is to identify with the aggressor or superior power while placing blame on one's own kind. Consider this case of Jewish self-hatred and identification with the Nazis:

> The German Jews spoiled things in Germany. . . . You cannot put all the blame on Hitler because the people wanted him in there since the Jews were getting the upper hand in everything and they thought it should be stopped. The Jews spoiled everything themselves.[50]

Another nonpolitical means of handling problems of group self-esteem is to institutionalize anxieties within organizations seeking to enhance the group's public image. Wallace Markfield's comment on Jewish "defense groups" in contemporary America suggests that psychic reassurance is an important aspect of ethnic group activities:

> I linger and linger over the smooth, bland, untroubled faces that preside over installations and elections. Sisterhoods and Brotherhoods, fashion shows and theater parties. Something, something is amiss in these faces, but what and why? For in six thousand years has there ever been so large, so powerful and prosperous a Jewish community? What needs

> are there yet to meet, what anxieties remain to be created? What tensions, what anxieties lie behind the surveys and statistics of the social worker and human relations expert?[51]

Thus, withdrawal, the expression of aggression, self-hatred, and organized defensive rituals are some of the nonpolitical ways in which ethnics cope with the problems of group and individual self-esteem. However, ethnic psychic goals often take a more explicitly political form. "If this election is decided on the basis that 40,000,000 Americans lost their chance of being President on the day they were baptized," said John F. Kennedy to the Greater Houston Ministerial Association during the 1960 campaign, "then it is the whole nation that will be the loser in the eyes of Catholics and non-Catholics around the world." Yet, the best estimate indicates that, in the enlightened year of 1960, Kennedy lost about 1.5 million votes because of his religion. It is clear that politics often involves an emotional consensus that places great strains on the politician as a broker of such salient forces as racial and religious distinctions.

The potentialities of translating low ethnic self-esteem into political action are kept in mind by political leaders, especially whose who themselves have experienced conflicts among rival ethnic groups. These politicians have become sensitized to ethnic politics somewhat like the Jewish woman in a Philip Roth story who can recall only the Jewish names on a list of airplane fatalities. In the politics of James Michael Curley's Boston and Adam Clayton Powell's Harlem, political organization has provided an avenue for the stormy expression of psychic rewards, acute ethnic resentment, and the longing for recognition of one's human worth. Witness how experiences with external hostilities are shaped into a particular pattern of politics in these words of a second generation, middle-aged businessman residing in an eastern city:

> A Jew personally is never liked by nobody. He is liked on the outside. But that is as far as it goes. The Jew is hated all over the world, in fact. That is why he is liberal in politics. That is why I am for giving the Negro better things in this city and in this nation.
>
> You see the Jew is liberal because it kills the poison of hate from him. That is why he wants to help other people. Not because it is going to get him any thanks for it. No, because he would not get it from some anyway. He is liberal because when you know you are doing good by other people, you don't feel the hate so badly.[52]

In this case, the feelings of ethnic deprivation are not used to punish an alien enemy or to blame one's co-ethnics. Feelings of self-deprivation are channeled constructively into political attitudes that seek to deal directly with the causes of ethnic problems.

As well as serving as a channel for the public expression of ethnic resentments, politics also provides ethnic groups with a means of seeking recognition. The tensions of marginality that play on the ethnic group member often mean that he retains positive associations with co-ethnic successes long after he has passed through the ghetto stage of immigration. Political recognition of individuals, that is, the granting of public respect by a larger society, is useful to the whole group because it shows that some co-ethnics are accepted, judged favorably. The politics of recognition is especially important to the most psychologically insecure members of an ethnic group. For instance, New Haven Jews who saw themselves living in a somewhat hostile, Gentile environment were concerned about the prospects of a co-ethnic holding public office; however, they were most worried lest the group representative endanger the group's external relations by a poor public performance.[53]

There is other evidence that ethnocentric group members are most likely to infuse their psychological concerns about group and personal valuation into political choices. For instance, ethnocentric and insecure individuals are most likely to have unstable political party identifications and to be highly influenced by a candidate's ethnic background. In addition, the politics of group recognition among ethnocentrics is positively reinforced when most of their fellow workers and friends are co-ethnics. The political expression of ethnocentrism is supported by the social isolation described by two students of the Jewish community in Minneapolis:

> One of the obstacles to the achievement of satisfactory social relations is the third generation's propensity for associating on the basis of shared ethnic origin, encouraging continued and exclusive interaction with Jews. Not many have yet developed interests that transcend the Jewish community, interests that identify individuals independently of any local community.[54]

The translation of such associations into the politics of ethnic recognition, therefore, is often a search for confirmation that public officials will listen to ordinary people, and thus it has symbolic value to group members.

Psychic claims are usually less difficult to satisfy than are political claims on a dominant group of power and material objectives. But when the old ruling stratum is threatened with a substantial decline, or when psychic and material goals are closely associated, the probabilities of political conflict increase.[55] For instance, white opposition to Negro claims seems strongest when there is a question of sharing both psychic rewards (social status, recognition) and material rewards (jobs, property values). Many of the same whites who readily approve of, and grant recognition to, the Negro entertainer or baseball star oppose open housing covenants and legislation, job integration, and school integration. This opposition appears despite the usually more supportive positions of political, labor union, educational, and church leaders. The material interest expressed in the fear of losing a white clientele, as well as status anxiety, may explain the reluctance of businessmen to support public accommodation acts. Voter opposition in the mid-1960's to ordinances prohibiting discrimination in housing and public accommodations in such cities as Seattle, Tacoma, Washington, D.C., Kansas City, and Milwaukee reflects opposition to granting psychic *and* material benefits. In these cases, opposition was based on a preference for segmenting Negro demands rather than combining recognition politics with the allocation of concrete housing and other benefits.

Moreover, when threats are both material and psychic, they may lead to political opposition in well-off communities. For instance, in the 1964 Wisconsin primaries, Governor George Wallace of Alabama received his greatest support from the most affluent areas of the state's metropolitan southeast corner (Milwaukee and vicinity), regardless of party affiliation. Every Wisconsin county and the 4th, 5th, and 9th congressional districts within Milwaukee County were rated according to income and educational, occupational, and property attainment. The party inclination of each unit was based on voting in the 1960 Wisconsin gubernatorial election. On these bases, the Wallace vote exceeded 23 per cent of the 1964 primary total most frequently in the affluent Republican *and* Democratic units. Although the Wallace vote was not limited to middle-class citizens, a Milwaukee businessman's comments are fairly expressive: "If it has to do with giving the colored civil rights down South, fine, sure, I'm for it. If it means giving them more rights here [in Milwaukee], I ain't so sure."[56]

CIVIC VALUES AS ETHNIC POLITICAL GOALS

On rare occasions, ethnic political behavior has changed basic American civic values, that is, the root ideas about the structure and purposes of government itself. Such critical changes fly in the face of a core culture interpretation that holds inherited political values as sacrosanct and enduring. Thus, in Saul Bellow's *The Victim*, the Gentile protagonist chides his Jewish alter ego about a study of early New England history written by a professor with a Jewish name, because the protagonist believes that someone with *that* background cannot possibly do justice to the subject. The protagonist understood the existence of a core culture with appropriate civic values, but he did not favor the adaptive abilities of ethnics to interpret them, or worse yet, to reorder fundamental beliefs.

Nevertheless, a function of ethnic politics has been to contribute to the creation and rejection of certain core American civic values. Two major examples are the cumulative opposition to ascriptive elites, leadership groups based on personal traits, as public authority figures, and an unprecedented emphasis on government as an agency of collective benefits and public welfare. Although America has never had a ruling class as Marx or Mosca understood the term, public deference was paid to an *ancien regime* united by breeding, wealth, and region. "From Henry Adams to Woodrow Wilson to Dean Acheson, the old-stock leaders have assumed [their prescriptive rule]. Never did they ask the forbidden question: Why should men follow me? Me of all people."[57] Since the critical presidential election of 1928, ethnic-derived urban blocs have opposed the ascriptive, old-stock elite and its eastern seaboard hegemony. In the politics of the popular man, Suzanne Keller's remarks about the Boston Brahmins have wide application to established political institutions of law, diplomacy, and the military during the 1950's and to the social types who ran them, namely, men such as Welch, Acheson, and Stevens.

> Their snobbish exclusion of the Irish and Italian immigrants, their aloofness and indifference to people with alien customs and tastes, deprived them of their role as dominant status models of the community. With fewer people to imitate them and look to them as dominant social arbiters and exemplars of distinction, their demise was inevitable. The rejected Irish and Italians, producing their own models and social codes, pushed the Yankee blue-bloods aside.[58]

In addition, the ethnic contribution was one of several factors underpinning the concept of collective economic and social responsibility inaugurated by the policies of the New Deal. While federal governments and proponents of the social gospel had previously contained elements who believed in both sorts of responsibilities, it required the major thrust of urban, ethnic forces to legitimize as a core belief government's duty to secure the individual's economic and social welfare. In this process, the experiences of ethnic, urban America fostered a new interpretation of political problems, one that emphasized the relation of political events to the workings of a broader social system necessitating collective political action. In no small way, this interpretation of socio-political phenomena derives from the ethnic experiences in metropolitan America and their cultural legacy. A statement often applied to Jewish culture—namely, that a cosmopolitan political culture can be viewed as a culture mobilized for the prevention and, that failing, for the healing of the ailment of body and mind—has wider validity in this development. The use of government to enhance social healing was derived from the cumulative struggles of American ethnic groups.

In conclusion, the persistence of ethnic elements in political choices is understood by clarifying the multiple functions that ethnic politics serves. Ethnicity is a marginal device for imposing rationality, congruity, and consistency on political choices made by ordinary citizens who have relatively low investments in normal political activity. Thus, ethnic politics contributes to the stability of the social environment. Ethnic politics also functions to secure and protect material and psychic values especially with regard to the group's comfort and recognition in the society. Beyond these functions, ethnic politics leads to collective changes in core civic values and is a means by which new groups implement their beliefs about the acquisition and uses of political power. The critical contribution of urban, ethnic groups to the denial of old-stock ascriptive political authority and the expansion of governmental welfare services to serve an ameliorative social order are cases in point.

PART TWO

Pattern of Ethnic Politics

Any general effort to account for ethnicity's persistence in American politics raises the question of the dominant forms ethnic politics has taken. The variety of ethnic political behavior and the diversity of forums in which it has developed make it unrealistic to account for every minute pattern. Nevertheless, we can develop three dominant responses of American ethnic groups, namely, *accommodation*, *separatism*, and *radicalism*. Each pattern represents an attempt to secure certain values under certain structural and cultural conditions with certain political consequences. What follows is one way, although certainly not the only way, to analyze the profusion of evidence about ethnic politics in America.

Religious, racial, and nationality communities, those entities we call ethnic, are fixed membership groups with durable characteristics. These characteristics may include marriage rules that operate rather rigidly against the admission of outsiders, cultural values that are expressed in individual and collective behavior, and common psychological perspectives on the relation between the group and the larger community. In the absence of enduring racial and religious views of politics, most ethnic political affiliations are derived from the social composition of the ethnic group.

Each of the three patterns is significantly influenced by the cultural framework of ethnicity and the availability of political institutions to express ethnic claims on the polity. One ethnic group may strongly desire to accommodate itself to prevailing political styles, but it may be rejected. Another group may have strong cultural traditions tending to keep it separate, but readily accessible political institutions may provide the means of rapprochement whereby the group and the polity can unite.

Most ethnic groups have both wanted and been able to accommodate themselves to American politics, for the pluralism of the American political system is suited to take heed of minority claims. However, separatist and radical political responses have also occurred, raising issues about the relationship of politics to cultures and life styles not normally found in America and placing major strains on a system essentially devised to cope with incremental politics based on bargaining and accommodation. Therefore, an analysis of separatist and radical politics draws attention to the saliency of emotion and ideology in American political life.

Each pattern of ethnic politics is also an account of value choices made collectively in urban and national politics over more than 70 years, since the great migrations of the nineteenth century. Choices in favor of material welfare values available from the national political economy or an urban party system lessen the political saliency of ethnic groups as cultural tribes with distinct customs and values of their own. Group values are either discarded or expressed nonpolitically in the variety of fraternal societies, welfare organizations, and cultural associations that have figured so largely in urban immigration and adjustment. If a group decides to maximize its cultural values, it confronts the necessity of strengthening the ethnic community at the expense of broader, and more intense, political effectiveness. This is the response of separatism.

There is a third critical response, namely, the fusion of ethnic group claims with those of a radical political movement or ideology. The appeal of the Communist party to some Negroes and Jews in the 1930's has numerous similarities to efforts in the 1960's by certain civil rights leaders, such as the late Dr. Martin Luther King, Jr., to fuse the issues of civil rights and the war in Vietnam. In both cases, ethnic benefits are broadly defined, a forensic ideology evolves, and an effort is made to develop broad-based coalitions transcending specific ethnic group objectives.

The dominant politics of accommodation, evaluated in Chapter Four, requires that political benefits be available to assuage ethnic demands. The nature of these benefits is an important consideration in the adoption of this as opposed to the separatist or radical political alternatives. The reader ought not come away with the idea that ethnic claims are always accommodated. Some claims are met, others are side-stepped or given only symbolic recognition. When the claims are not met, either fully or at all, the other alternatives come into play. For its part, ethnic radicalism may stress ideology because the promises of the existing ideologies have become hollow. Separatist groups may promote cultural and psychological values because these are ignored in the political accommodations arrived at by dominant institutions. If the quantity of political response were the only factor, most ethnic politics would have withered away under the impact of the New Deal and Kennedy-Johnson programs. Yet we have already seen the tenacity of intangible factors, such as status and identification, in ethnic political choices. The satisfactory accommodation of ethnic group demands depends, rather, on the *appropriateness* of political responses, and it is from this perspective that the "deviant" patterns of ethno-political separatism and radicalism ought to be assessed.

CHAPTER THREE

The Organizational Base of Ethnic Politics

The persistence of American ethnic politics can be traced, in part, to the activities of organizations capable of mobilizing ethnic sentiments for political objectives. Indeed, without the existence of ethnic-based organizations, it is doubtful that ethnic politics, as we know it, would have been with us for so many years. These organizations have historically provided forums in which group members could exchange political opinions and formulate plans for political action. Moreover, American ethnic groups have been ingenious in converting their associational ties into political vehicles. For instance, the use of the southern Negro church structure by Dr. Martin Luther King, Jr., and the Southern Christian Leadership Council in the early 1960's provides a dramatic recent example of organizational mobilization in a political struggle. Therefore, we must examine a variety of organizations, including ethnic political associations and churches, in order to more fully understand the political significance of organizations for ethnic group members. First, we will investigate the maturation of the ethnic political association and its eventual inclusion within basic American political institutions, such as urban party machines. Second, we will examine the mobilization by religious organizations of deep-seated sentiments and identifications, in so far as this mobilization influenced the political process. In both cases, our attention will be focused on the collective resources and the limitations of organizations in the sustenance of American ethnic politics.

FROM ASSOCIATION TO PARTY

If ethnic politics is based on strong group identification, then it is to ethnic associations that we must look for the initial development of these identifications. The first political impact of diverse fraternal societies, churches, and patriotic groups based on common ethnic ties was in the formation of an ethnic consciousness that would later burst forth into American politics. Responding to the needs of uprooted individuals, the ethnic associations provided renewed strength for the common ties that had been loosened in the migration from eastern Europe, the American Southland, and other areas.[1] The need for fraternity and social contact was paramount in the minds of the immigrants. The primary appeal of the *landsman* society to the eastern European Jew was identical to that of the First Baptist Church to the southern Negro, namely, that of a place in which common associations could be forged to help in coping with the bewilderment of urban life and its political processes.

The men who thus acquired new modes of fellowship to replace the old ones destroyed by immigration earned thereby some sense of security. But their efforts, no matter how strenuous, could not forestall changes. The whole of American society was changing, and the little immigrant islands within it could not withstand the trend; the immigrant societies, too, were bound to change. Their organization had been spontaneous, but once set up they drifted out of the control of the mass of their members. With growth, a select leadership appeared; it took skill beyond the capacity of the ordinary laborer to manage the affairs of an insurance association, edit a newspaper, or direct a theater. And the interests and points of view of the leaders were not always the same as those of the followers. Indeed, the upwardly mobile men who became ethnic group leaders were quick to see the advantages of the political contacts and the ethnic identifications nurtured by the organization's existence and its activities. It was significant that immigrant associational activity drew its direction from men who somehow stood apart, from men who had in common that they were concerned with using their positions as ethnic leaders to make an impact upon the general society. Among them were those unique marginal men, products of two cultures, who saw in the associations the political base for their own influence. Thus, group consciousness was quickly turned into group "nationalism" and political loyalty. The sons of the immigrants had no memories of the Old Country places, no recollection of the villages or of homeland ghetto solidarity. It was through membership in the group and participation in its activities that they realized that they were Irish, German, Jewish, or Italian.

Ethnic associations were especially important in facilitating these group references in the early phases of ethnic politics. Lacking a wide range of social contacts, and unaccustomed to the prevailing political style of the natives, the immigrant rapidly acquired the rudiments of an ethno-political consciousness by extensive participation in organizations that attracted his own kind.[2]

The associations formed by nationality and racial groups laid the framework for ethnic politics in a second way. The heart of the ethnic association was in the provision of mutual aid and welfare. That welfare might be spiritual, as in the devout Boston Irish community, but it most often included a sharing of material benefits. Thus, the politics of reciprocal benevolence had its roots in the fraternal societies and welfare agencies constructed by successive ethnic groups, for the fundamental concept of the ethnic association was private welfare, and it is but a small step to perceiving politics itself as a device for the trading of favors. Organized without surpluses of wealth or social recognition from the larger society, the ethnic associations became the prime vehicles for the organization of self-interest and the exchange of goods and services.

Over time, the variety and specialization of ethnic organizations increased in step with the organizational profusion in American society.[3] The politics of the parish and the fraternal association was explicitly related to local politics and the fortunes of local politicians. The transformation of the leadership from affective to professional in character and the use of new professional skills in national pressure group politics marked important changes in the evolution of ethnic organizations and in their political impact. Instead of face-to-face group influence, there developed "professional elites," whose values influenced ethnic political behavior.

The professionalization of ethnic political organizations helped to solve a basic problem of the ethnic leader who had obtained political influence. Within the informal association, the ethnic leader's influence depended upon his ability to personify and represent collective group sentiments. He was co-ethnic, united by common blood or belief, with the power to secure political favors. Yet, his growing political and social stature tended to set him apart from his fellows. His power and prestige had to be played down in order for him to retain the fraternal goodwill of other ethnic group members.[4] However, the social status capital of ethnic groups could be tapped when a system of political exchange developed that rewarded ethnic leaders and followers on the basis of their ethnic group prestige.

The urban political machine rationalized immigrant needs within a system of ethnic-based politics. It met three basic needs of ethnic members, providing social welfare, political privileges, and alternative channels for social mobility. Thus, ethnic leaders were able to perform their roles knowing that their status benefits were congenial with the benefits to be derived on a broad basis by other group members. Without the distribution of valuables, the machine had no rationale for existing. But, for example, when job advertisements read "No Irish need apply" or "No Irish or Negroes wanted," mass need for benevolent organized ethnic politics was created. The Irish Americans were particularly adept at using the party machine to advance ethnic claims. Within the immigrant period, the Irish are described as:

> . . . prisoners of the vicious circle that was to hold them social captives until well into the twentieth century. Spurned as lower-class menials and discriminated against as Catholics, they were caught in the economic and social conditions that prevented them from improving their material circumstances and changing their social style.[5]

In most American cities, the political machine began with the Irish politician, and the contest for immigrant votes had the effects of breaking down the social separation of immigrant communities and making their members active political participants. In return, political participation and social achievement fostered recognition within the community's economic and social spheres. The long-term advantage of ethnicizing political organizations, such as party machines, was that it provided a ready base of local support and a criterion for distributing political benefits. Ethnic consciousness became an integral aspect of party loyalty and organization, as a study of Democratic party politics in Detroit makes clear:

> The Democratic party's subcoalitions (Negroes, Polish, Irish, labor members of each ethnic group) revealed considerable political self-consciousness. . . . Those who claimed to be "loyal" Democrats generally were much more self-conscious and attached to their own coalitional subgroups than those who were only lukewarm party enthusiasts. . . . An analysis of the party loyalty of Democratic precinct leaders indicates that while manifesting significant self-consciousness as members of a subcoalition, they were, at the same time, revealing above normal party loyalty.[6]

RETENTION OF INFLUENCE WITHIN THE PARTY

The integration of ethnic loyalties and needs into the party machine involved the perfection of such techniques as the ethnically balanced ticket, group representation, and party rewards in proportion to the contributions specific ethnic groups made to the party ticket. However, ethnic groups varied in strength and purpose, and the ethnic-dominated and organized party often exaggerated the influence of the major ethnic group within the party. Although the machine accommodated the claims of newly emerging ethnic groups, domination by Irish Americans has often been noted:

> Irish domination of government made it more difficult of course for later immigrants, particularly Italians and East Europeans, to climb the socioeconomic ladder by pulling themselves up with the help of white-collar patronage.[7]

Ethnic control of a party has usually produced a time lag in the recognition of newer groups. The dominant ethnic group has normally retained power more than commensurate with its actual voting strength. Even when party tickets have been balanced according to ethnic candidates, it has been the existing party structure that has determined the meaning of that "balanced representation." Moreover, party control by a previously excluded ethnic group has been a symbol of achieved community status in an increasingly competitive ethnic group situation. The Irish, for example, unlike the New England Yankees who could fall back on acquired social and economic strength, have tended to conceive of the party as a defensive weapon to protect hard won advantages that cannot easily be replaced.

The ethnicization of party organizations over time is revealed by examining historical cases of ethnic succession that show a lag between the time when the dominant ethnic group represented a numerically dominant political group and the time the group actually relinquished control of the party machine. For instance, the significant Irish immigration into New Haven began about 1840. In 1857, the first Irish alderman was elected. By 1880, about half the New Haven wards were electing Irish aldermen. The first Irish Catholic mayor was elected in 1899, and since then every successful Democratic candidate for mayor of that city has been an Irish Catholic. Thus, about 20 years elapsed before Irish entry into minor office; 20 more years passed between the advent of the

Irish as a major electoral power in 1880 and their takeover of the New Haven political system, as evidenced by the election of the first Irish Catholic mayor. The political control established by the Irish was not easily dislodged, however. Indeed, by 1933, the Irish, although a distinct minority in the city, held over half of the jobs in the city government. And as late as 1959, they held 29 per cent of the city's major offices, although they then comprised only 11 per cent of the total population. In the process of gaining and consolidating power, the Irish also managed to gain temporary control of the New Haven Republican party in the mid-1930's, although by 1959 they shared control of the local parties with the ascending Italo-Americans.[8]

A similar process occurred in Providence, Rhode Island. The Irish held 31 per cent of all Democratic party ward committeemanships there in 1876, 70 per cent in 1910, and 50 per cent in 1957. During the same period, they held close to 18 per cent of all Republican party ward committeemanships. On the other hand, it took nearly 80 years before the Italo-Americans, who followed the Irish, were able to occupy positions of party influence equivalent to those of the Irish in 1876. Nevertheless, by 1957, the Italo-Americans were on their way to displacing the Yankees and winning control of the Providence Republican party, even though the Democratic Italo-Americans had manifested no gains in ward committeemanships since 1933.[9] It can be seen, then, that the tenacity of ethnic control within a party is such that the dominant ethnic group can entrench itself, thus blocking the path of subsequent ethnic groups attempting to utilize the same road to power.

Another example of entrenched ethnic political organization is found in Chicago. In 1850, only 20 per cent of Chicago's population was of Irish extraction, but by 1880 the Democratic party was so thoroughly under Irish control that it was called Mike McDonald's Democrats. In 1946, the Irish dynasty of Democratic leadership was interrupted by the Jewish leadership of Jacob Arvy. Yet under current Mayor Richard J. Daley, 32 of the 73 Assistant Attorneys General in 1962 were Irish, as were 12 of the 50 aldermen and 21 of the 50 committeemen of Chicago. In view of the fact that only 10 per cent of the Chicago population was of Irish extraction by the 1960's,[10] these Irish rewards were unwarranted.

These cases are convincing evidence of the extent to which the dominance of a particular ethnic group, in these instances Irish Americans, outlasts the numerical and electoral strength of the group in city politics. In fact, the most durable basis of ethnic political organization has been within the urban party machine —in the form of a coalition dominated by one ethnic group, as typified Detroit politics, or in the shape of an ethnically dominant Democratic coalition, as in the Irish American hegemony of New Haven, Providence, and Chicago.

The ethnically based political organization was dealt a critical blow by the New Deal and the vastly increased federal role in social welfare politics that accompanied it. The city bosses found themselves mere middlemen for federal policies. As soon as welfare began to be impartially distributed, and voting was, at least theoretically, no longer tied to the receipt of benefits, the political system could function without the party machine and its built-in component of ethnic preferences. These changes led to a drastic decline in the accommodative effectiveness of the ethnically rooted party machine and a transition from the politics of ethnic accommodation to the politics of intergroup conflict. Moreover, there was a dramatic shift from the local party as the seat of ethnic political power to the national level as the search for more modern solutions to classic political problems widened.

In addition, there were other subtle changes that impaired the organizational base of the old ethnic political groups. Politics based on accommodation within the ethnically based political machine was informal. There were explicit rules and laws, defined channels, and prescribed formulas and chains of command to be followed, but the essence of party-machine politics was the bond between the individual and his ethnic group. Despite conflicts among these ethnic groups, the politics of ethnic accommodation in the urban political machine was essentially based on the setting of informal boundaries, the devising of shifts in the informal party reward and recognition structure, and the granting of personal concessions by the party leadership. Access to the leaders was comparatively easy, and the extra-legal nature of the city party machine made that mechanism flexible.

The shift in the locus of power from the local to the national level eliminated this informal adaptation to both the conditions of power and the transitory needs of ethnic groups. The emphasis on rational and broadly gauged laws made the federal system more rigid, less flexible, and less accessible to ethnic groups than the coalitional or ethnic-dominated urban party machine. The federal system could no longer accommodate the old claims to political status that pervaded so many local governments. The declining availability of party patronage coincided with the tenacious hold, still visible in such cities as Chicago and Boston, of older ethnic groups on the last vestiges of the old party system as a reminder of the role once performed by urban immigrant groups and the leaders who directed them.

RELIGIOUS INSTITUTIONS AND ETHNIC POLITICS

The historical association between ethnic communities and religious denominations and the increasing importance of church groups in influencing national politics necessitates an effort to place religious organizations within the context of ethnic politics. Religious institutions have sometimes been used as conduits for ethnic political claims, as in the case of the promotion of federal civil rights legislation in the 1960's. National religious associations have also played a key role in ethnic politics. The organizational facilities of the National Council of Churches of Christ, for example, have been used by nationally oriented clergymen to promote legislation in the areas of economic reform, social justice, and civil rights. The Council's influence stems from its "cosmopolitan-liberal" leadership, which has, however, often been opposed by local clergymen and members of participating churches.

Churches also influence the political views of the mass membership, although, at times, the attitudes of a religious organization's leadership may differ significantly from those of its members, thus creating conflict for the latter. A study of religion and politics in Detroit found, for instance, that the Catholic clergy strongly supported Republicanism and conservative or anti-federal welfare and economic attitudes, and gave moderate support to progressive positions on civil rights and civil liberties. In contrast, most of those extensively involved in the Catholic subcommunity, that is, individual laymen, were strong Democratic partisans, favored federal welfare and economic programs, and held strongly conservative views about the rights of Negroes and the boundaries of free speech.[11]

In addition, there are other limits to the clergyman's political influence. For instance, parishioners may believe that clergymen ought not to take positions on public issues, although a clergyman's influence on his congregation may still be considerable if he manages to veil his political opinions in rhetoric thought to be nonpolitical. Such subtle political influence from the pulpit is highly effective among the least politically informed and involved members of the congregation.[12]

A more long-term influence of religious institutions on politics is involved when the religious institution itself promotes new political opinions among its faithful. For instance, the development of Conservative Judaism accompanied the improvement in status of German Jewry during the latter part of the nineteenth century. The social adaptation of the members was facilitated by the creation of religious congregations possessing more decorum in prayer and ritual than obtained in the Orthodox Judaism imported by East European Jews. The political significance of this development is found in the growing Republicanism among Conservative Jews, who see the Republican party as more suited to their economic status. Herein, the values of a religious institution, and its availability for transmitting group attitudes, facilitated a partisan shift of considerable importance.[13]

Although religious institutions provide political reference points and serve as pressure groups in this country, there are rules of the political game that restrain the religious influence in ethnic and other political activities. Core beliefs of the American political culture are found in the maxims that "religion and politics don't mix" and that a person's religion ought not to be a factor in his political choice. In this folklore, specific political decisions should be based on secular standards of merit. Such a secular standard is expressed thus by one political activist:

> Churches should stay out of politics because transportation, public education, and the like are not religious issues. Religion is a private matter and should not be the subject of controversy.[14]

It is one of the tenets of a secular society that organized religion should confine itself to general levels of moral discourse and avoid explicit political discussion in the pulpit. This secular view regards moral judgments as not highly effective in the Monday through Saturday work-a-day world where specific matters of economic and social legislation are concerned. Moreover, as Suzanne Keller reminds us, "the elites of opinion, morality, and morals, . . . once the most rigid arbiters of man's conduct and beliefs, . . . are today relatively diversified."[15] The absence of agreement on moral questions also leads to a more abstract level of discussion about general standards of public conduct in which such vague terms as "good government" or the need for "honest public officials" are invoked. One socially acceptable way for church groups to be politically active is to appeal on an abstract, moral level, as some groups have recently done in the area of American foreign and military policy. However, basing a claim for arms reduction on such an idealistic passive foundation provides churchmen with neither the knowledge about specific policy alternatives nor the status of policy experts. In the specialized secular society, governed by policy elites, a powerful case can be made that religion ought to stick to its role as the guardian of sacred symbols and beliefs.

Another restraint on the influence of religious institutions in

American politics has been the hesitation of the churches to be too active in the New World. Throughout American history, religious sects have devoted their resources to the politics of respect much as ethnic groups seeking social acceptance and political accommodation have done. Thus, until recently, American religion has not had the reservoirs of legitimacy and political acceptance that permitted the churches to take a continuous and active role in the politics of racial and nationality groups.

Public claims made by religious bodies are most persuasive when based on assertions of alleged discrimination against respectable and legitimate religious minorities. Because of acquired public respectability, the Catholic Church can deplore the second-class citizenship of parochial school parents who are being doubly taxed to support Catholic and public schools. Jewish parental and religious groups can also make a respectable claim that the presence of Christmas symbols in the public schools works a psychic hardship upon their children. A religious group that has acquired respectability can legitimately make such claims as an esteemed minority rather than on more overt political grounds. In order to acquire recognition, a religious entity must have its sacred symbols and beliefs recognized within the broad cultural canvas of major American norms. The politics of respect has served religion not only in countering persecution and discrimination, but more importantly in winning power and public standing for major faiths. As David Manwaring reminds us, the political consequences have been severe when religious sects have engaged in practices and held beliefs regarded as socially deviant. In these cases the state did not hesitate to confiscate the property of Mormons practicing polygamy or to press public health measures that violated the religious sensitivities of Christian Scientists.

> Where the sect is otherwise "respectable," the law is fairly quick to make adjustments. . . . Examples are the draft exemptions of conscientious objectors, and the affirmation permitted Quakers. Where a sect is so truculent in manner or drastic in its innovation that it is rejected by society, it lives in a virtual stage of siege. It runs afoul of old laws, and is the target of new ones, ostensibly nondiscriminatory, but carefully designed to harass. Eventually, accommodations must be made . . . a softening of public attitudes or substantial concessions by the sect . . . or the sect will die or be driven underground. Since the Civil War, three major sects, aside from Jehovah's Witnesses, have found the road to public acceptance rocky, but passable: the Mormons, the Christian Scientists, and the Salvation Army.[16]

INSTITUTIONAL VERSUS SOCIAL GOALS

The gains in public respect may produce conflicts between institutional and social goals of religious organizations, conflicts that may influence their general public behavior and their participation in the political efforts of ethnic groups.[17] Religious institutions are primarily concerned with *organizational goals*, such as policies designed to perpetuate the existence, mission, and status of religious bodies and their membership. Religious creeds have also supported the pursuit of *social goals*, namely, policies influencing the general distribution of such values as justice and wealth in society, but relatively unrelated to the benefits expected by the specific religious group initiating the policy. In general, however, efforts to influence public policies have been greatest, as measured by expenditures of institutional resources, when organizational goals are at stake. Social goals have usually been secondary despite the official statements and pronouncements of organized religion. For instance, not until the present decade has organized religion in America undertaken to act seriously on its commitment to secure dignity and brotherhood for the black American. Moreover, taking an earlier case, Protestant denominations failed to respond effectively to urban problems in the early twentieth century in part because of the conservatism of clerical and lay leadership on critical economic issues.[18] In this case, social and organizational goals were in direct conflict, and the promoting of social policies might have divided the congregations. Organizational goals, too, often restrain the pursuit of social goals, however. For instance, Methodist churches have divided regionally on the status of the Negro in society since the days of slavery. As recently as 1964, a national Methodist convention voted to promote church desegregation only on a voluntary basis.

What seem like exceptions to this general theme really prove the rule. For instance, the Social Gospel of American Protestantism did encourage the confrontation of social issues, but these confrontations probably weakened the churchly strength of Protestant denominations.[19] It was significant that the Social Gospel was strong before the challenges of competing religions (principally Catholicism) arose; this meant that some church resources could be safely allotted to public concerns. Moreover, the Social Gospel came into being within an environment of competing Protestant sects relatively secure against governmental intervention and the inroads of an established state church. Nevertheless, the organizational primacy of separate Protestant churches impeded both social action and the articulation of a workable social theory. As Reinhold Niebuhr reminds us, the Social Gospel lacked a theory of power based on its organized structure:

> The dilemma of Protestantism lay . . . in these factors; it had no will to power and in view of its positive principles could have none, for supreme power belonged only to God. . . . It had no definite idea of the end toward which it was traveling and could have none, since the future lay with the free God; . . . As a theory of divine construction the Protestant movement was hard put to provide principles for human construction.[20]

The primacy of organizational goals also arises from the difficulty of enforcing social positions taken by clerical leadership. Among most Protestant denominations, social pronouncements are merely advice to the congregations. Their effect is held to be purely moral, but it is said that they are entitled to be respected because they are arrived at by a responsible clerical body after careful deliberation. Their social impact on the mass membership is derived from the percentage of the religious body in fact represented on a religious commission rather than from the significance of a commissioner's position. The commission method of representation, typical in American Protestantism, also makes it difficult to enforce social pronouncements agreed upon by a council of representatives from several sovereign denominations. The distance from the National Council of Churches to the local congregation is considerable; it is difficult enough to enforce organizational policies with any degree of regularity, and specific social policies that make immediate demands upon the membership are likely to complicate greatly the already fragile jurisdictional relations among constituent denominations. The chief aspect of religious consensus on most social issues is, therefore, a general statement restraining innovative political action. An experienced student of church politics offers this conclusion:

> In American politics, the churches normally follow; they rarely lead. They usually react; they only infrequently seize the initiative. They have shown no sustained desire to dictate governmental policy, nor have they normally mobilized more than a small fraction of their total resources for political education. They have invested sizable amounts of money in education to affect the moral, social, and political climate of the country, but only a handful of dollars has been invested in specialists to influence the legislatures and the regulatory agencies.[21]

The politics of organizational defense may wither away so that churches may someday play a more sustained public role. It ought to be recalled that such organizational defense has provided a basic stimulant to religious institutions themselves. The Catholic Church in America, as John T. Ellis has made clear, has until recently expended most of its resources in ethnic accommodations fostering organized church goals, with little surplus capital for social goals.[22] Moreover, it was Nazism, not the injunctions of Maimonides, that stimulated intensive political cohesion among American Jewry. The politics of Jewish group and religious survival has found public outlets in suggestively named "defense groups" (B'nai B'rith, Anti-Defamation League, American Jewish Congress, American Jewish Committee). Similarly, the National Catholic Welfare Conference, the political coordinating council for the American bishops, was formed during World War I when feelings against Germans and Irish Catholics were running high. Only in recent years have Jews and Catholics formed political alliances with other religious and ethnic associations.

EXAMPLES OF POLITICO-RELIGIOUS INTERACTION

Religious bodies sometimes make unusual political alliances. Thus, Christian Scientists joined the American Medical Association in opposing medical care legislation during the Truman administration. And mutual concern about maintaining religious schools in declining urban areas led representatives of Orthodox Judaism to join with emissaries of the Catholic bishops in advocating federal aid to parochial schools during the Kennedy administration.[23]

Religious groups are most likely to commit resources to issues that bear upon internal solidarity or organizational creed, membership, and leadership. A study of the political role of the Catholic Church in Massachusetts found that the church best mobilized its political resources and membership on such issues as birth control, Sunday closing laws, and divorce legislation.[24] These issues are all regarded as matters of religious creed by the faithful, unlike candidates and party politics. Moreover, they importantly affect the cohesion of the Catholic Church and therefore its continuity as a viable religious organization. To cite another example, clergymen of most major faiths oppose interfaith marriages on the grounds that such marriages threaten the persistence and authority of religious institutions. The rigidity and inconsistencies of state divorce laws bear witness to more concerted application of religious influence upon politics than is found in the outcomes of most economic and military-defense policies.

A useful public role for religious institutions is to integrate core beliefs with the national purposes of the secular society. Prevailing religious myths and customs have always been absorbed into the broader civic culture, and at times they have acquired the status of law. Thus, Sunday closing laws have recently been upheld because Sunday is now acknowledged as a secular day of rest. One can imagine the chagrin of the Puritans to find commerce restricted on the Lord's Day as a matter of public health and welfare. Yet other such customs, formerly generally accepted, have recently been challenged. For instance, the Supreme Court has wrestled with cases involving the presence of chaplains in the armed forces and the use of prayers, even ones written by the New York Board of Regents, in the public school.

In the first case, the Court concluded that chaplains do not violate the first amendment's establishment clause:

> Spending funds to employ chaplains for the armed forces might be said to violate the Establishment Clause. Yet a lonely soldier stationed at some faraway outpost could surely complain that a government which did not provide him the opportunity for pastoral guidance was affirmatively prohibiting him the free exercise of his religion.[25]

In the second case, the Court concluded that the Regents' public school prayers did violate the separation of church and state.[26] The first case involved the united force of the United States, while the New York dispute resulted in controversy within religious bodies as a result of the suit of a nonbeliever. In truth, organized religion has most influenced public behavior when it has pursued *integrative goals*, those recognizing the interrelation of civic and religious purposes, rather than when it has fostered *divisive goals*, those seeking to place a particular religion's public claims above competing religious claims. The public behavior of organized religion commands the most support when it accords with widely held ideas about the nation's general welfare. Thus, in times of war and national crisis, organized religion has served as an integrating force, supporting secular military and foreign policies. It is this religion of nationalism that has infused an official secular piety:

> The identification of religion with the national purpose is almost inevitable in a situation in which religion is frequently felt to be a way of American "belonging." In its crudest form, this identification of religion with national purpose generates a kind of national messianism which

> sees it as the vocation of America to bring the American Way of Life, compounded almost equally of democracy and free enterprise, to every corner of the globe; in more mitigated versions, it sees God as the champion of America, endorsing American purposes, and sustaining American might.[27]

Mindful of the productive role religious sects have played in struggles for political democracy and equality, many people nevertheless feel that the lending of God for governmental purposes has enhanced the organizational and public stature of established religious bodies more than it has aided social policies designed to follow the Sermon on the Mount or the Book of Solomon.

This integrative function explains the privileged status of comfortable, organized religious bodies. Divisive goals—those that reveal differences between religious creeds and political or social practices—are often the work of specific clergymen rather than of major organizations, as a Protestant minister indicates:

> Five years ago you couldn't find a major denominational leader who would speak out on civil rights. A number of specific ministers spoke out and were received in pained silence. Today it is fashionable to spend at least one night in a southern jail protesting segregation, and all the best people feel obliged to do it.[28]

A FUTURE FOR RELIGIOUS INSTITUTIONS IN POLITICS

It is ironic that the relative decline of religious influence in directing public affairs may serve as a major catalyst in encouraging political behavior by religious agencies. Although we may be, in the words of Supreme Court Justice William O. Douglas, a religious people, secular and technological symbols are in the foreground of today's American society. In Calvin's Geneva or Winthrop's Bay Colony, the public policy influences of the churches were clear and pervasive. Contrast those situations with the remarks of a Catholic monsignor in an affluent, metropolitan parish:

> You ask me about political influence of the Church. There is very little of it. I feel very strongly about civil rights, but I hardly see my parishioners. They use this place (the church) like a shopping plaza as consumers of sacred traditions and artifacts. I don't know what they do the rest of the time. If their conversation denotes anything, they socialize, play

> golf, go to the Cape in the summer on vacation. The last things on their minds are the daily imperatives of Pope John's social pronouncements.[29]

Or note one scholar's conclusions about the quality of membership in a universal, authoritative Church with rich traditions and rituals and impressive documents in social welfare:

> The secularism of these predominantly Catholic men of Eastport is clear enough. . . . Divine intervention was rarely mentioned; the importance of dogma was profoundly minimized so that a position of religious tolerance could be easily and consistently maintained; and there was hardly a man who saw anything special about the way a member of his religion might look at political phenomena. Being a good Catholic, or a good Protestant, or a good Jew in the civil world meant simply being a good man, nothing else.[30]

Men look to government, science, and commerce for policy leads and, in general, religion has reacted to social change initiated by other institutions. At times, religious organizations have led or advanced political movements, from the Dissenters in the American Revolution to the southern Negro congregations that have played a catalytic role during the contemporary civil rights movement. More often, dominant churches with surplus legitimacy and power have resisted social changes. For instance, a 1937 study traced the growth of social material in the sermons of clergymen during the economic crisis of the Great Depression. Support of New Deal policies was positively correlated over time to the severity of economic conditions and to the low economic status of the congregation.[31] Early in the depression, and even later among high status congregations, ministers avoided potentially controversial social positions and statements. Like other institutions, churches seek to retain the defensive advantage.

What political resources are forthcoming from religious sects that are in a state of relative social decline? Urbanization has been a major challenge to Protestantism in New York and other cities.[32] The middle-class, native, and white elements of dominant Protestant denominations (Episcopal, Presbyterian) have gradually lost power to working-class, immigrant, and Negro groups. Steadily, the white Protestant portion of New York has declined, and the decline has been particularly severe among the older, most cohesive denominations. Concomitantly, Protestant political appointments, welfare agencies, and general influence have declined in the city.

Faced with these developments amidst the traditional patterns of decentralization and congregational autonomy that characterize Protestantism, a series of coordinating agencies, such as the Protestant Council of New York, have arisen to preserve the organizational and social influence of Protestantism in the metropolis. The restraints on the Council have been considerable. Not only have individual ministers been able to bypass the Council or use it for their own purposes (as Reverend Adam Clayton Powell did when he used his Council position to exert leverage on former Mayor Robert Wagner for more city jobs for Negroes), but the interests to be coordinated have been far more diverse than they were in the golden age of Protestant influence at the turn of the century. In 1895, the five largest Protestant denominational groupings bearing the Yankee ethos and composed of affluent old-stock congregations accounted for 75 per cent of the total Protestant churches in Manhattan and the Bronx. By 1961, their churches accounted for only 49 per cent of the total; the decline bore witness to the substantial growth of smaller denominational and nondenominational Protestant churches.

Until 1952, the Council usually avoided controversial stands on major public issues such as birth control. The attitude that Protestantism should retain its dominant integrative role, combined with the Council's diversity, reduced white Protestant political influence still further. Protestant positions on public issues were ignored, and political appointments to "traditionally" Protestant posts frequently went to members of other groups. Moreover, the Council did not fully appreciate the altered religious complexion of the city and thus failed to exploit coalitions with Jews and other potential allies on numerous issues. As Henry Pratt concludes:

> The data are adequate . . . to raise doubts concerning the common assumption that Protestant leaders cooperate fully with their Jewish counterparts (with whom they are often in agreement on many church-state issues). Perhaps the basic reason for the Council's unwillingness to enter into alliances with the Jews or any other group stems from a concern that this might prove an embarrassment and restrict its freedom of maneuver. Such a view apparently stems from the nonideological and noncompetitive emphasis traditional to the Council's political approach. The sense of Protestantism being a threatened minority, although perhaps widespread among the members, apparently is not sufficiently common among the Council's leaders to permit

> the basic redefinition of the group's role that an alliance strategy would require.[33]

Nevertheless, in recent years the Protestant Council has begun to sound like a threatened minority and has taken a public role in social issues. In addition, it has attempted to forge alliances with other groups, especially Negro Protestants. Thus, Pratt found that the Council was quoted in *The New York Times* during 1960–1965 more frequently and on a wider range of public issues than any other religious entity from the Roman Catholic Archdiocese to the Episcopal Diocese to the Jewish Community. Coverage by the *Times* may say more about the newspaper than it does about the influence of New York Protestantism. Nevertheless, it does indicate an attempt at political adaptation to maintain organizational values in a city that seems to have gone beyond the Protestant Ethic in search of a political ideology.

In conclusion, ethnic and religious organizations have perpetuated ethnic politics by providing identification, political styles, and core values for their members. However, the political impact of religious institutions is tempered by circumstances of organizational strength and position. Organizational resources are most readily mobilized for defensive politics, that is, when a basic tenet of the ethnic group (ultimately its survival) is threatened. Religious organizations are least likely to enjoy political impact when divisive social policies are at issue. Although affluent, high status religious denominations are generally conservative, new and divisive social policies may be supported by a secure and imaginative religious leadership. Indeed, the assets of social benefits now stored in religious institutions are also civic valuables that can nudge the behavior of pragmatic politicians. It may be that the leaders of the affluent congregations, now set free, as it were, from ministering to the economic and psychic deprivations of their followers, will more vigorously use their organizations to pursue general welfare policies designed to aid deprived groups.

CHAPTER FOUR

The Politics of Accommodation

The tenacity of ethnic factors in American politics has not been sufficiently accounted for in political analysis. Although ethnicity in politics is believed to wither away with the passage of time and generation, the fact that it persists in so many political issues makes us wary of statements that prematurely bury the ethnic factor.[1] Presidential elections, local campaigns, and efforts at urban reform have all encountered the durable quality of race, religion, and nationality.[2] The dominant accommodation thesis of political analysis holds that ethnic politics declines after the first immigrant generation becomes accustomed to American society. Obviously, however, this thesis does not tell us why ethnicity has endured in American political life well beyond the first generations of urban immigrant groups. Nor does it account for the modes of political organization that have developed to accommodate varied ethnic claims on the political system.

Three persistent methods of accommodation can be seen in American politics: divisible political rewards to the few, combined with recognition of the ethnic group; collective welfare benefits in which public resources are used to satisfy broad-scale group needs; and the awarding of political preferments and secondary gains in which enduring social, economic, and political patterns of distributing benefits are based on prior attainments of ethnic groups in electoral politics. Each process in turn makes increasingly greater demands on the political system. Thus, the inclusion of a few group members on a party slate or in the allocation of patronage is not very costly, nor is the symbolic *recognition* of the group's contribution to American life. On the other hand, *preferment* politics involves fundamental patterns of allocating human reserves. In short, recognition and collective benefit politics refer to the *means* used to distribute public benefits; preferment politics involves the *systems* of distributing rewards and honoring political claims. The selection of a party committeeman may represent recognition politics, while the construction of public housing is a form of collective welfare politics. However, decisions about the coverage of civil service in relation to the use of a party organization to distribute jobs is an example of preferment politics.

DIVISIBLE BENEFITS AND RECOGNITION

According to the psychoanalytic theories of Harry Stack Sullivan, individuals constantly seek to rid themselves of feelings of anxiety and insecurity in interpersonal behavior. Ethnic politics provides an opportunity to receive recognition and political status, and thereby greater security, in relations with the general society. The need for group recognition among members of socially insecure or deprived ethnic communities has been a constant theme in scholarly analysis. As Wolfinger concludes, "[Ethnic] appointments are often made because it is expected that voters will be happy with the recognition and will not make substantive demands as well. The appointees owe their positions to outside selection, often with the implicit understanding that they will dissuade their fellow ethnics from main policy demands."[3] In this sense, ethnic group members are psychologically rewarded by the intangible benefits conferred on a co-ethnic. In the calculations of professional politicians and in academic analysis, recognition politics is predicated on a strong psychological relationship between individuals and their ethnic group, and between group needs and the political system.

There is strong evidence that individuals strongly attached to an ethnic group are most likely to vote for a co-ethnic. However, the quality of ethnic identification is a factor in political choice. As we have seen, ethnocentric individuals, those with insecure feelings about their "Jewishness" or "blackness," are sensitive lest the ethnic political representative perform poorly and discredit the group.[4] Therefore, in the effort to conform to American values, self-conscious ethnic group members display great concern over the image of ethnic politicians. A description of Jewish candidates in Worcester, Massachusetts, indicates this concern about social acceptance in ethnic politics:

> Israel Katz, like Casdin, is a Jewish Democrat now serving his fourth term on the Worcester City Council. Although he is much more identifiably Jewish than Casdin, he gets little ethnic support at the polls; there is a lack of rapport between him and the Jewish voter. The voter apparently wants to transcend many features of his ethnic identification and therefore rejects candidates who fit the stereotype of the Jew too well. Casdin is an assimilated Jew in Ivy-League clothes. Katz, by contrast, is old world rather than new, clannish rather than civic-minded, and penny-pinching rather than liberal. Non-Jews call Katz a "character," Casdin a "leader." It is not too much to say that Jews, like other minorities, want a flattering, not an unflattering mirror held up to them.[5]

However, the content of the "flattering image" is a particularly uncertain element of recognition politics. While Worcester Jews, like many other ethnic members elsewhere, opt for a co-ethnic with the speech, dress, manner, and public virtues of the generally admired Anglo-Saxon model, in some cases ethnic enclaves have preferred representatives inimical to these dominant values. James Michael Curley, the long-time mayoralty choice of the Boston Irish, was the antithesis of the sober, respectable group leader. Adam Clayton Powell, the ubiquitous Harlem Congressman, is seen by many Negroes as a colorful figure who enjoys life, unmasks the hypocrisies of the white middle class, and stands up to "Whitey" in pursuit of life, power, and fame. Powell's censure by the House of Representatives in 1967 only convinced the Negro masses of what they had long suspected, that there is a "double standard" applied to the behavior of white and Negro Representatives.

Recognition politics is inexpensive since it confers mass psychic gratification rather than mass power and involves specific offices rather than general public policies. Indeed, except for the specific politicians rewarded, the mass of co-ethnics receive only the appearance of inclusion in the existing political organization. The difficulty of predicting mass responses to symbols and uncertainties about what a group regards as adequate recognition effectively limits the scope of such accommodation tactics. Nevertheless, the tenacity of recognition politics provides evidence of the ritualistic, and seemingly irrational, style of urban politics predicated on ethnic attachments. The techniques of the ethnically "balanced" party ticket, the designation of city wards as "belonging" to a specific ethnic group, and the elaborate apportioning of patronage rewards on the basis of the ethnicity of the recipients are efforts to impose rationality on a distribution of rewards predicated on psychological needs.[6]

The durability of ethnic politics in American life cannot be accounted for solely by the corruptness of urban machines, the ethnocentrism of politicians, or the anticipation of material benefits that flow from political life. The essence of recognition politics is a psychological reconciliation of the ethnic group to the existing political structure. In other words, recognition politics is a means of providing evidence that the political organization has honored the group and taken account of its accumulated grievances by symbolic mass incorporation into the governmental process. "Thus, politics becomes a form of collective psychiatry to assuage the sense of ethnic grievance and to yield support to the putative leader who promises to render the source of that grievance inoperative in the future. When ethnic groups do take their politics as a kind of collective psychiatry, even the most specific and divisible objectives are treated as sacrosanct and nonnegotiable while the most *outre* notions are treated as practicalities which must be delivered."[7]

The psychological function of recognition politics helps to explain why ethnic politics did not quickly disappear either as ethnic groups became increasingly culturally assimilated or as the welfare state expanded. Rather, a variety of particular ethnic interests became intertwined with urban and national politics, and politicians were sensitive to those interests.

The strength of recognition politics in the achievement of accommodation seems to rest on three factors: the presence of an appropriate political mechanism, the existence of ethnic needs that can be met by recognition, and the ability of the political economy to provide long-term material benefits. Although there has never been a classic "urban party machine," approximations of this model were ideally suited for providing ethnic recognition. Politics was regarded as a service industry allocating material benefits rather than as a mechanism for resolving ideological and policy issues. Ethnic recognition was a major means of determining the allocation of rewards based on party service, since the divisible benefits conferred were largely *positions*: elective offices, appointments, and party sinecures. Moreover, the urban party organization was itself often a coalition of distinct subgroups the basis of which was ethnic identification. More recently, a study of Detroit politics revealed that the Democratic party there was a collection of seven to nine major subgroups, including Irish Democrats, Negro Democrats, and Polish Democrats, with considerable subcultural identity and integrity. An analysis of the Democratic precinct leaders in that city indicated that they combined significant self-consciousness over their positions as members of ethnic groups with above normal party loyalty.[8] Ethnic attachments symbolized the major basis of partisanship for the mass of voters in each major ethnic group, who were represented in the party by their co-ethnics who held formal precinct positions in the organization.

Beneath the lore of old-style Irish politicians and the colorfulness of ethnic traditions, the recognition path to ethnic accommodation was essentially conservative, relying on an organic theory of recognition. The recognition strategy "took care" of ethnic claims in judgeships and mandatory political rituals (Pulaski Day dinner, St. Patrick's Day parade), without significantly involving the ordinary ethnic member in either the party or the governmental structure. This conservative impetus of dominant ethnic politics was useful in limiting competition within the party. At the same time that recognition politics limited mass participation and concern with public policies, its organizational consequence was to maintain the dominance for its leadership. Despite lip service to the contrary, no successful organization wishes to engage in extensive intraparty competition. Thus, there are numerous historical examples in which assertive ethnic leadership has been bought off by the dominant political group and, in return, has managed to suppress members of its own group who wished to act more aggressively within the party. Symbolic recognition and the judicious use of divisible benefits are cheaper coin than intense primary fights and challenges to the party ticket.

Holden cites several pertinent examples of restrained competition increasing the saliency of ethnicity and the use of recognition politics.[9] In the 1920's, the dominant Democratic and Republican leaders of Cleveland entered into a patronage contract whereby 40 per cent of the patronage went to the Democrats, 60 per cent to the Republicans, and each set of leaders promised never to trouble the other group. In the political history of Chicago, in order to avoid the costs of competition over judicial offices, Democratic and Republican leaders have often formed joint tickets, allowing for no competition. This process almost always involved a careful selection of ethnic group members to reflect the major racial and religious blocs supporting each party.

Moreover, recognition politics has been fruitful when ethnic group members have had a psychic need for political acknowledgement. The persisting strength of ethnic attachments is thus available when appropriate politicians need to draw on reservoirs of psychic goodwill. However, the availability of such goodwill depends on the need for recognition and the group's level of social and political development. Massachusetts politics has long been noted for the intensity of its ethnicity; an illustration from the politics of the Bay State is particularly pertinent to show the substance of recognition politics. In 1962, Edward M. Kennedy, the brother of the late President, sought the Democratic nomination as U.S. Senator. Co-ethnic responses of Irish Americans were strong, despite the fact that few Irish Americans were deprived immigrants and attuned to the middle-class ambitions of the group. A Massachusetts state legislator accurately portrays the importance of political respectability in the eyes of more acculturated ethnic group members:

> The Irish voter wants to be dignified. . . . He wants to be identified with clean candidates, and Kennedy projects that image. . . . The "lace curtain Irish" who have achieved some financial and social success are particularly anxious to be respectable, and I think they and the active churchgoing women members of Sodality and men members of the Holy Name Societies are particularly prone to be affected by the charges of corruption against the Democratic party, and those are the people who in my opinion are a great source of strength for Ted Kennedy.[10]

Further, recognition politics is particularly fruitful when the stakes are not too high, when there are alternative sources of economic and social rewards. The efficacy of recognition politics lies in a combination of organization strategy and psychological reward. Political organizations, especially the mass urban parties, have found recognition a cheap device for maintaining control and mobilizing potential support. However, when the means of social and economic advancement are not available on a mass scale to ethnic group members, the political stakes are raised; psychic recognition does not suffice, even though it is pursued with an intensity born of despair and frustration.

The "politics of revenge" that has so often characterized New England politics was largely based on the absence of economic and social rewards for immigrant groups.[11] When a group is systematically excluded from employment and social activities, it may use politics as a compensatory mechanism. Thus, the resistance of Irish Catholic Democrats to the political aspirations of other groups in New England was largely due to the fact that politics had become too important and had brought them too many social and economic rewards. Indeed, concrete group claims for status are also capable of being transformed into ideological politics, as occurred in the case of German and Irish support of the late Senator Joseph McCarthy's anticommunism crusade.[12] Race pride, in the form of "Black Power" or other serviceable slogans, may also outweigh claims to concrete political services. Political accommodation and the rationale of recognition politics are frustrated when psychic claims of an ethnic group become a primary rather than a side goal in the general conduct of political life.

The combination of organizational effectiveness (usually the effectiveness of the party organization), reasonably secure ethnic identity, and the presence of social and economic sources of satisfaction accounts for the success of recognition politics. The fact that most members of "deprived" ethnic groups have frequently been reasonably content with limited psychic rewards in politics reinforces the conservative function served by enduring political institutions and much of American ethnic political accommodation itself.[13]

ACCOMMODATION AND COLLECTIVE WELFARE BENEFITS

In a perceptive analysis of urban party organization, Holden formulates several basic rules of urban politics. For example, the Rule of Cloture is expressed in the maxim "hold what you've got," while the Rule of Dividends indicates that allocations are to be made on the basis of past performance and mutual obligation, e.g., "take care of your own." We have seen that the basic strategy of ethnic politics has been to more or less consistently apply these two rules.[14] Under this system, ethnic leaders are eventually taken care of in the allocation of material, divisible party benefits, while group members are psychologically recognized. Of course, that recognition implies the obligation to perform services and secure political favors, but among the consequences of recognition is that the potential for granting favors will in most cases not have to be realized. A political organization that always had to convert recognition into material benefits would soon be bankrupt.

However, the divisible allocation of positions and the collective distribution of psychic gratification are often inadequate to meet the mounting demands of ethnic groups. Divisible benefits can be multiplied by increasing the number of governmental positions, or they can be redistributed by using a "minor" party as a vehicle to fulfill the aspirations of ethnic groups excluded by the prevailing coalition. Thus, in New York and Massachusetts politics, aspiring Jewish and Italian politicians have, on occasion, found the Republican party an alternate route to that power denied them by the predominantly Irish-controlled Democrats.

The Rule of Expansion, namely, "get more benefits," has been applied by politicians sensitive to increased ethnic demands. However, it is with reference to collective benefits, the outcome of policy, rather than to policy decisions that this maxim most persuasively applies in the modern polity.[15] For example, the material beneficiaries of new judgeships usually include only the family and friends of the new appointee. Yet, it is clear that this old style of urban welfare politics, and its applicability to ascending ethnic groups, is inadequate to meet mass demands. In retrospect, it can be seen that divisible benefits were the dominant strategy of ethnic accommodation before the Second World War. Based on the political power of the New Deal and the guarantee of minimum amenities such as social security and welfare assistance, the much publicized urban patronage system actually has since provided direct benefits to a large share of the urban population.

The reformulated rule of Collective Expansion, namely, "use federal power to get more benefits," is a modern tool of ethnic political accommodation inefficiently pursued by the old urban party organization. The basic source of these benefits is federal subsidies in housing, education, urban renewal, and health benefits, and it is over the allocation of these considerable resources that most struggles in urban politics now take place.[16] It is important to note that this contemporary political situation marks a radical departure from the pattern of few divisive material rewards and mass psychic income provided by past urban politics.

The earlier strategy maximized the effectiveness of the ward boss and mayor as political brokers seeking to hold together the uneasy alliance of ethnically diverse coalitions. The new strategy is essentially a Negro and ghetto aid program, and its reliance on mass welfare benefits marks a significant departure in the history of American ethnic politics. In other words, the old accommodation strategy rested heavily on the authority of legitimate groups formally included in the dominant party organization and relied on the leadership of men who held party positions and whose grievances and agreements were primarily in the party arena. New-style collective ethnic politics seeks legitimacy for existing policies from representatives who have prestige as a result of their participation in nonpolitical activities, voluntary associations, businesses, churches, educational organizations, and community groups. In the old pattern, welfare distribution was usually guided by electoral considerations; hence the importance of elected officials and party workers in the distribution of ethnic benefits. In the politics of collective welfare benefits, bureaucratic and mass politics are more critical.

Recognition politics tested the power of particular groups at the polls with adjustments made later in specific rewards and group recognition given as a result of party performance. The politics of collective welfare benefits is usually played among existing government bureaucracies and between bureaucracies and mass protest organizations intent on altering the allocation of public benefits by the bureaucracies and their political allies.[17]

In addition, recognition politics was essentially local; local actors formed coalitions on the existing urban base. The fundamental premises of "control-reward-minimum expansion when necessary" in classic urban politics were themselves predicated on the existence of a static social order. New ethnic groups and their leaders were included within the ongoing political system, but the boundaries and rationale of the system itself were never questioned. Ideology and mass participation were usually effectively restricted to sporadic reform groups whose successes were followed by a return to political "normalcy." Although the style and rhetoric of mayors changed, the premises of an essentially self-contained urban system ministering to multiple ethnic claims were never questioned.

Collective ethnic benefits are themselves products of essentially federal policies, in which the local consequences are often beyond the control of local elected leaders. The federal origins of ethnic benefits raise problems that were seldom present in the incremental model in which the programmatic consequences of both urban government and federal policies were a minor element in political calculations.

Collective ethnic accommodation raises other complex problems. For instance, in order for a federal program to allocate group benefits on a large scale, it is helpful to have ethnic institutions, such as churches or associations, that can support or administer these programs. The availability of such agencies is somewhat limited; however, due to the acquisition of general community status by some ethnic institutions over time, some were available to administer the poverty programs of the 1960's. In some cases, the dominant community sees ethnic institutions as making valuable contributions to the whole community—a status that is useful when governmental collective benefits are distributed. An excellent example of accommodation to an ethnic concept of general welfare preceding the acceptance of the modern welfare state is provided by nineteenth-century Cleveland.[18] In the period after 1850, the Catholic Church there, which, given the Protestant base of the community, might have been expected to be a divisive institution, functioned constructively, by Protestant criteria. These criteria included the propositions that the better-off members of the community were normally obliged to provide assistance for those who were too poor to provide for their own spiritual and physical well-being, and that voluntary channels for such action were preferable to governmental channels. Moreover, the belief was that the beneficiaries of such charitable aid must show that they deserved it through moral rectitude, hard work, and respect for the law. Thus, when the Catholic Church in the Cleveland area undertook a program to provide hospital services, orphanages and homes for abandoned children, agencies for services to women, and care for the elderly poor, it earned the respect of the dominant Protestant community. Individual accomplishment and voluntary participation in good causes subsequently earned community respect for other ethnic groups and their institutions. This acquired legitimacy was useful when the politics of collective ethnic benefits in governmental policies became a major factor in the local politics.

Business associations, interfaith groups, institutes of human relations, and the military services have been other useful arenas in which ethnic and racial accommodations have been made on the benefits of mutually valued contributions to the "general welfare." The painful evolution of antidiscrimination legislation in the last three decades has caused voting and employment needs of minority groups to be incorporated into the general welfare category. Integrated service in the armed forces and the guarantee of voting and access to public facilities deethnicized the demands of minorities and helped the group members to become part of the general society. Herein, ethnic demands could be generalized and rationalized as part of federal policy in public housing and social welfare legislation.

However, the notion of collective benefits is sustained so long as the reciprocal benefits between the community and ethnic group are acknowledged. Thus, public housing was frequently provided without the realization that this act increased the residential segregation of urban Negroes.[19] Until recently, the politics of Chicago and the strength of the Cook County Democratic organization there were based on the assumption that collective benefits (housing, hospitals, schools) should be allotted proportionately to ethnic need or power within clearly defined geographic areas. Whether these were matters of explicit design is not provable, for numerous politicians, contractors, and administrators had a share in the decisions. On balance, however, the programs of collective ethnic benefits have been managed within the context of metropolitan politics that has been characterized by high degrees of racial and economic segregation. As recently as 1961, an epilogue to a classic study of Negro social life in Chicago noted that "the Chicago Housing Authority [has adopted] a pattern of building most of its new low-cost housing along the western margin of the [city's] Black Belt in an undesirable area near the railroad tracks. A five-mile rim of high-rise public housing is gradually going up as a monument to Midwest Metropolis insistence upon residential segregation. . . . Chicago stands near the top of the list of American cities in the extent to which Negroes are segregated. There is widespread concern that the Black Belt is now reaching the limits of its expansion without the danger of generating wholesale violence."[20]

For a while, the acute housing shortage of the post-World War II period obscured the need for a national long-term housing program. In more recent years, social goals have been subordinated to the desire to stimulate the construction industry in order to minimize unemployment. It is impossible to predict what the shape and character of the modern city and region might have been if the United States had had a national long-range program designed to provide housing for middle-income workers in the city and sites for industry and lower-income industrial workers in outlying areas. Surely, if the country had decided in 1948 that it wanted to subsidize high-density apartment development in the suburbs rather than lower-density home ownership, and mass transportation rather than expressways, it is unlikely that all the forecasts would now point to suburban sprawl as the pattern of the future.

The distribution of collective ethnic welfare benefits, such as public housing, must be viewed in this larger social context. As Catherine Bauer notes:

> The general past trend, however imperfectly realized, toward Everyone in His Place, in a standardized one-class, one-age-group, and one-color district, devoted wholly to residence . . . was not the result of any conscious overall plan or public decision to encourage maximum social segregation. It came about more or less by accident, as a side result of forces and policies employed for quite different and often distinctly progressive or idealistic ends, and because we were reluctant to assume any conscious collective responsibility whatsoever for the social pattern. . . . What we failed to recognize was that the powerful tools employed for civic development and home production also predetermine social structure to such an extent that there

> is little room left for free personal choice or flexible adjustment. The big social decisions are all made in advance, inherent in the planning and building process. And if these decisions are not made responsibly and democratically, then they are made irresponsibly by the accidents of technology, the myths of property interest, or the blindness and prejudice of a reactionary minority.[21]

It ought to be added that collective ethnic benefits are capable of accommodating the demands of ethnic minorities as long as the premises on which these benefits rest are not politically volatile. As long as the perpetuation or even intensification of racial segregation through public housing programs was unquestioned, and as long as dependent relations with welfare agencies were accepted as a necessary element of social service, the allocation of collective benefits was accommodating. For instance, the intense demands of racial leaders and poverty leaders cannot be satisfied, even by a strong political organization, through collective benefits. Values such as "integration" and "participation" run contrary to the ecology of party organization and to the rationale of collective benefits. For example, the efficiency of Chicago politicians in obtaining federal poverty funds in a city noted for party cohesion was enhanced by the weakness of forces urging reform and mass participation. During the first two fiscal years of the Office of Economic Opportunity's community action program, Chicago received $211 in federal funds for each family with income less than $3000 annually. Cities with weaker political party organizations and more mass participation were less effective. For instance, per eligible family funds obtained in New York City and Philadelphia were $112 and $101, respectively.[22]

PREFERMENTS AND SECONDARY BENEFITS

The accommodation of ethnic groups is most difficult and uncertain when the basic means of distributing rewards and positions are being challenged. Political institutions are valued not only because they provide power and benefits, but also because men and groups acquire a vested interest within the system and the rules it uses to reward and punish political claimants. Moreover, opportunities to have one's bank achieve public deposits or to sell one's product to the government in bulk are usually the particular province of those who have the greatest skills, political knowledge, and access to the central points within the political system. They are, that is, the province of the decision makers and those who have immediate and continuing access to political power.

If we are correct in supposing that some ethnic networks exist in the decision-making group, we may also infer that preferments regarding the norms and processes of political decision making and political reward distribution represent the capital accumulation of ethnic experiences in the political process. For to be in on the decision-making process—the formation of core myths used to justify political power—and the structuring of basic institutions is to indeed occupy a preferred political status. Preferment politics is more than who is to receive specific benefits. It concerns the fundamentals of the machinery that in large measure prejudges the allocation of political claims made within its framework.

Preferments are not likely to be shared without a struggle. Therefore, it often happens that "the probability of ethnic conflict within a party actually increases as the power groups rise in social status, acquire the resources with which to make a fight, and [gain] the political sophistication to identify what the strategic points in the system really are. It is the dynamics of the party itself which generate a further reinforcement of ethnic awareness as such groups encounter resistance from those who are determined not to yield."[23]

This sticky phase of ethnic political claims may be handled by party leaders in several ways. A major factor in stable accommodation is the extent to which the heretofore dominant groups have secured preferments outside of their political positions. If the dominant group is secure enough to yield the social and economic benefits of party preferments to assertive ethnic claimants, accommodation is facilitated; the most difficult problems are likely to arise when relative newcomers must displace others who have yet to securely reap the social and economic benefits of political preferment.

There are several examples where willingness on the part of dominant ethnic political groups to yield surplus preferments eased the accommodation of the newcomers. In commenting on New England politics, Banfield and Wilson observe:

> The native middle-class Protestant inherited from his Anglo-Saxon ancestors a political ethos very different from that which the new immigrants brought with them. The ethos of the native could not mix with that of the immigrant, and therefore the natives, who were in the minority, retired to a sphere in which they could conduct public affairs in the manner their culture prescribed. . . . The native elite withdrew to the community service organizations because these constituted the only sphere in which

> their political style could prevail. The boards of these organizations were self-perpetuating; they could not be "crashed" by outsiders.[24]

By contrast, elective offices could be "crashed" by the accumulation of ethnic political majorities. Moreover, the assets of the New England Brahmin included more than cultural norms. They also included considerable economic resources in the corporate world. Thus, the Brahmins could yield political power without drastic losses.

The same pattern of pursuit of alternative preferments was evident after the Cleveland election of 1873, which represented a landmark because it was the last time both major candidates were members of the hard-core social and economic elite. Thereafter, "most of the Anglo-Protestant elite chose ecologically . . . to follow the greater money rewards of private industry. Their withdrawal, at a time when the scope of government was increasing, automatically increased the political opportunities of the newcomers."[25] In these and other cases, the availability of alternative preferments reduced the tension that overt ethnic political warfare would have certainly entailed.

The importance of alternative preferments in ethnic accommodation can be further illustrated by cases in which groups having political control lacked rich cultural and economic legacies to fall back upon. Consider the political problems of Italo-American and Negro political claimants at different stages in the history of urban politics. In Philadelphia, the opposition of the dominant Irish ward bosses cemented Italians to a weak Republican party during the 1940's.[26] In New Haven, a similar pattern of exclusion and limited dividends maintained Italo-Republican loyalties well after the Second World War.[27] In Massachusetts, an Italo-American gubernatorial candidate was not forthcoming until 1956, and the Italian share of political positions lagged behind the Italian share of the total population into the 1960's. In these cases, Irish leaders, unlike the Yankees, lacked alternatives and so clung tenaciously to their political power. Thus, it is seen that the "politics of revenge," in which ethnic animosities are politically pervasive, is reinforced when controlling ethnic groups invest too much of their resources in politics. When ascending groups seek power, those who already possess it are unlikely to be flexible in meeting newer ethnic claims.

More recently, the urban Negro has been confronted with a similar problem. In such cities as Cleveland, Milwaukee, and Chicago, Negro political efforts have been strongly resisted by Slavic and other groups who themselves lacked alternatives to the political gains they had obtained. Moreover, the decline of the old service party organization and the acceleration of Negro political demands increased the relative scarcity of choice political preferments. These facts, combined with the considerable investments of politically dominant, white ethnic groups in ongoing political structures, have resulted in a heightening of tensions manifested in disputes about "de facto" segregation, the quality of police protection, and the political power of various ethnic groups themselves.

In no small measure, the quality of American ethnic political accommodation has rested on the availability of other social options, options that could provide rewards in nonpolitical activities. Only when ethnic groups have become frozen in their reliance on particular political arrangements that they prefer has the opportunity to accommodate new ethnic claims proved nonexistent. In this regard, the position of the American Negro is vastly different from that of earlier immigrant groups. The existence of "preferred political systems," such as party machines, enabled earlier groups to move up the social ladder. However, a major problem in Negro politics is the absence of such a system that prefers ethnic claims based on local electoral strength. By the time Negro political leaders have been able to win major local offices, the legacy of the machine and its patronage system have withered away. Therefore, alternative strategies of black power, violence and mass movements, and informal organizations have been employed in efforts to replace the political vacuum of the urban North with a set of rules and processes capable of translating Negro needs and votes into some enduring system of political preferments.

CHAPTER FIVE

The Politics of Separatism

The actions of the short-lived "Catholic Party" of New York during the 1850's, the social withdrawal of the Amish and Mennonites from the secular requirements of American society, and the emergence of Zionism and Black Nationalism illustrate sporadic deviations from the accommodation model described in the previous chapter.[1] In other words, these cases are examples of separatism, which occurs when an ethnic group turns inward, creating its own institutions to replenish social, psychological, and cultural values that cannot find fulfillment in the larger society. Extreme political separatism, the formation of distinct governmental institutions or political parties, is rare in American politics, as are extreme cases of ethnic assimilation in which the group's political identity itself vanishes.

The focus herein is therefore on the development of institutions designed to promote the psychic and cultural identities of ethnic groups. In the accommodation pattern, political institutions (such as the party system) play a major role in maintaining and reinforcing the political saliency of ethnicity. In separatist politics, distinct organizations and cultural practices are developed to compensate for disenchantment with the ongoing political and social order. From Garvey's "Back to Africa" movement to contemporary plans for black social and political separatism, social movements have grown on separatist premises. Their base is the ethnocentrism that animates ethnic group existence. Their short-term political consequence is the withdrawal of the group's support from the ongoing polity. Ethnic separatism is to a political system as third parties are to the American two-party monopoly.

The Black Muslims provide a pertinent case of separatist politics.[2] Few sects have recently attracted more attention than the "Nation of Islam," more popularly known as the "Black Muslims."[3] Obeying the messianic and authoritarian leadership of their "Messenger," Elijah Muhammad, Muslim Negroes determinedly remain apart, dressing their women in strange gowns, praying esoteric prayers, and advocating a separate nation of their own.

Because of the ostensibly revolutionary and fanatical tenets of this sect, observers have periodically denounced the Muslim movement as a black equivalent of the Ku Klux Klan, a "lunatic fringe" group, and a danger to domestic tranquility.[4] It is suggested herein, however, that the Nation of Islam is primarily striving to create a new identity for a people who have been deprived of any worthwhile self-identity. That the Muslims have succeeded in this endeavor will be shown in the following pages. Whether the new black nationalist identification is to their credit or discredit, whether it is a desirable phenomenon for American society, for the civil rights movement, or even for the individuals participating in the Muslim organization depends on one's value presuppositions and expectations.

What are the components of this new identification, and what is the interplay between individual and collective identity? What practical results and functions have emerged from Black Islam's brand of nationalism? Most importantly, by what methods and mechanisms has such a remarkable racial, quasi-religious, nationalistic re-identification been effectuated?

THE SEARCH FOR A PAST AND A FUTURE

Just as a patient on the analyst's couch, attempting to ascertain "Who am I?" and "What is wrong with my present condition?" begins a journey into his past, so do a people seeking a new identity and purpose look to their history. What is true of individual identity appears true of collective identities: To see what is wrong with our present predicament, we must rediscover the past; to decide who we *are*, we must ascertain who we *were*.[5] Few people have been so alienated from a sense of cultural heritage and historical origin as the American Negro. This alienation is described by a prominent Negro sociologist:

> Reduced to a chattel in an alien and [unfriendly locale], the enslaved Negro was not only "detribalized" as the African who has contact with European civilization, but he was annihilated as a person. . . . The enslavement of the Negro in the United States destroyed not only his family ties and his household goods; it effaced whatever memories of the African homeland that had survived the Middle Passage. The destruction of a common tradition and religious beliefs and practices reduced the Negro to a mere "atom" without a personality or social identity.[6]

The period of bondage in the United States was followed by a century and a half of white repression which left the Negro economically and socially deprived and burdened with a deep feeling of racial inferiority. Today, millions remain in this Negro *lumpenproletariat,* living in desolation and squalor, beset by every known kind of social pathology, from whose ranks have emerged the thousands who embrace Elijah Muhammad's vision of a grandeur that was Islam.

This Muslim vision bears a striking resemblance to the eschatologies propagated by revolutionary-religious and nationalistic mass movements throughout the centuries. First, there was the state of original purity and bliss: the first man whom God (Allah) created was black, indicating that "blackness" was the true expression of Allah's beauty and virtue, and "whiteness" the antithesis. Then came the fall: the black man was obfuscated and enslaved by the Devil incarnate, i.e., the white man, who is a corrupt replica of man contrived by Yakub, the evil universal adversary of Allah. But there came the Message: a Messiah and his followers, the Black Muslims led by the Messenger Muhammad, who saw through the devil's machinations and who, armed with the truth of Islam, were purged of the white man's corruption.[7] (The Message was brought by Allah to Muhammad in the person of one W. D. Fard who appeared in Detroit during the 1930's.) The Muslims were—and are—to lead the chosen from their present bondage to a terrestial paradise, an autonomous Muslim nation.[8] The black man will find happiness and redemption in a land of his own, but the blue-eyed white devil will meet his Nemesis in an Armageddon, when the wrath of Allah is delivered upon him. From then on, the black man, i.e., all nonwhites, will rule the earth.

Whether the prophet be Treitschke, Doestoevsky, Hitler, Moses, Mazzini, Mussolini, or Elijah Muhammad, the myth of the past and the illusion of the future remain a remarkably consistent, nationalistic, mass movement formula.[9] To convince an alienated people of their worth and unity, one must remind them of their sacred origin. To explain the disheartening realities of their present plight, one must convince them of their natural superiority and ferret out corruptors and devils. To gird them for the trials ahead, one must reveal a glorious destiny ordained since the beginning of time. Past, present, and future must intermingle in one expression of Divine Intent.

That such myths, be they revived from an earlier day or invented anew, are wanting in historical accuracy is a consideration of minor importance when compared with the function they serve in erecting a new collective pride and individual self-respect. However preposterous Allah and Yakub may appear to the outside observer, Muhammad's sacred tale is perhaps no more implausible than that found in Genesis and Revelations. In any case, the Muslim eschatology affords the believer an answer to the question "Who am I?" He is not "a nigger up from the Southlands," but a creation of Allah striving for redemption, an "Asiatic black," a member of that great nation of Islam whose adherents stretch clear across the world, part of that great rising tide of mankind – Allah's colored races – as opposed to Yakub's whites.[10] In this view, the roles have been reversed: The white man is now the "minority" with his back to the wall, the cursed and the misbegotten, and the black man is God's chosen. The psychological impact of this myth should not be underestimated. The ghetto Negro had never heard the likes of it before.

REHABILITATION

The Muslim myth does not serve as a battle plan directing nonwhites toward some cataclysmic confrontation with whites, although many alarmed critics have leaped to that conclusion. Its real function is a reconstruction of social identity. As Essiem-Udom concludes, after an intensive study:

> . . . The eschatology of the Nation of Islam shows the black nationalists' desire to free themselves from the exploited image of blackness and hence from the deep feeling of self-rejection, cultural alienation, and social estrangement which pervade and corrupt the personalities of the Negro masses. It expresses the nationalist's need to attach himself to something worthy and esteemed, some center of power, some tradition, and, generally, some "central ideal" capable of endowing his life with meaning and purpose. It offers hope in a future, one in which blackness will no longer be despised. In part, this vision of the future inspires the Muslims to pursue their life activities with courage and unbending determination.[11]

The practical effects of the myth have been astounding. Drug addicts, alcoholics, criminals, and despairing slum dwellers in general, many of whom social workers and community leaders had tacitly declared beyond help, have been rehabilitated by joining the movement.[12] Men who had heretofore lived shiftless or illicit lives now are employed at honest jobs (the first in their lives, for some), conscientiously marrying and raising families, obeying the law, saving money, and faithfully contributing a tithe to black Islam. In obedience to teachings of Elijah Muhammad, they abstain from drink, drugs, and tobacco, and they refrain from gambling, promiscuity, dancing, long vacations, idleness, excessive sleeping, lying, and stealing. Muslim women are devotedly domestic, thrifty, and keepers of fastidiously clean homes.[13] Muslims are forbidden to spend money frivolously and are committed to pooling their resources to help each other. The result is a relatively healthy living standard, even in the ghettoes where most Muslims dwell. The movement has, in its own strange way, repaired some "irreparable" damages and saved some of the damned.

ORGANIZATIONAL AND INSTITUTIONAL SUPPORTS

Aware that faith alone does not always work this extraordinary transformation, the Muslims buttress their belief system with a host of organizational controls and psychologically fortifying symbols. The "cured" addict or ex-convict, for example, is often thrown back into the same pathological environment that brought him to his difficulties. By the same token, the slum dweller may entertain no serious thoughts of improving his lot because he is surrounded by others similarly, and seemingly hopelessly, situated. This problem of emerging from a social milieu while being perpetually subjected to its contamination is partly solved for the person who enters the Muslim nation. Formerly unsavory companions are eschewed, and new group relationships with others living the regenerated, inspired life are established.

The neophyte is assisted, encouraged, and disciplined by an elaborate organization within the Muslim brotherhood. Frequent visits to Muslim temples are required to hear the Message from a dedicated and vigorous clergy. Temple "investigators" mediate disharmonies within families or among members, or refer disputes to the appropriate officers, while a well-disciplined elitist security force (Fruit of Islam) guards against attacks from outside enemies and heterodoxy within Muslim ranks.[14] Muslim publications, the most popular of late being *Muhammad Speaks,* filled with inspirational messages, articles on the Negro's struggle and on the activities of the organization and individual Muslim brothers, are distributed and read regularly by the faithful. There are women's auxiliaries to teach domestic skills, child care, and the woman's proper role in the home; summer camps for Muslim children; accredited Muslim grade schools; community centers for adolescents; employment training and housing agencies for Muslim families; and modest but prospering Muslim retail and service businesses. In addition, the Muslims have created their own University of Islam with Muslim teachers and texts for educating the young in standard subjects and on the virtues of the disciplined Muslim life and the black heritage.[15]

Presiding supreme over this empire is Elijah Muhammad, whose alleged messianic wisdom and strength are an inspiration to the rank and file. It is not long before the novice comes to share the admiration and loyalty his brothers express toward the Messenger and the emotional comfort and security that is associated with such devotion. Membership in the Muslim nation, then, is not something exercised in one's spare time; it is a total commitment to Islam. Every day is lived with the consciousness of one's new Muslim identification.

THE FUNCTION OF SYMBOLS

The search for a collective identity, as we have observed, necessitates a reconstruction of past, present, and future. Collective myths, however, are fortified by symbols which furnish deified objects for mass loyalty and expressions of aspiration. Every nationalistic group has its flags and its god or gods around which the faithful may rally. For the Muslims, Islam provides some of the necessary accessories: Allah, the star and the crescent, the black nationalist version of the Koran, and the Islamic tongue, which some Muslims make a determined attempt to master.

Of greater importance is the "symbolism of the self" utilized by the collectivity for the benefit of its individual members. The search for an identity is often expressed by the adoption of appearances and practices that are meant to symbolize the self. Thus, a desire to be a Bohemian may include the wearing of old clothes, long hair, and sandals, the use of a new speech pattern, the development of a taste for avant-garde arts and a Greenwich Village apartment. But these appurtenances are not merely symptomatic of the new social role; they become an important, and often the sole, means of expressing it. Symbolic appearances and practices, by becoming fortifying and substantive expressions in their own right, not only signify a way of life, but to a great extent they *are* that life. One might say there is no such thing as a "mere symbol"; for something to be a symbol, it must take on meaning.[16] In much of their practice and ritual, the followers of black

Islam may seem, at worse, cultists and, at best, laughable. However, if we keep in mind that an individual's name, appearance, deportment, and tastes are part of what identify him to himself and others, such things are symbolically functional and must be transformed and redefined for the sake of a new identity. Either by conscious design or shrewd instinct, this is exactly what the Muslims do. Here are some of the steps in that process:

> Initiation into the Muslim society is designed to facilitate and dramatize withdrawal from the "dead world," i.e., the Negro world, which means above all an eradication of labels and attributes associated with Negro stereotypy. The neophyte learns that he is not, nor was he ever, a Negro, his "real" nationality being "Muslim" or "Asiatic." The term "Negro" is rarely used by Muslims except in the expression "the so-called Negro," indicating that it is an appellation fabricated by the white slavemasters centuries ago and lacking in historical legitimacy.
>
> What is true of the group name is true of individual names. The black men in their generations of captivity lost their original identities and were given names by their masters, or themselves adopted white names when emancipated. These slave names are discarded as an important step toward independence from the "dead world," and replaced by an initial or, more commonly, by the letter "X." Some Muslims have been accorded the high honor of receiving their "real" Islamic names from Muhammad.[17] This rejection of former names and of the appellation "Negro" is of no minor importance to the membership. One Muslim minister, commenting on American Negroes who retain their "slave names," observed: "They don't even know who they are."[18] To the question "What's in a name?" the Muslims seem to answer, "A man's identity."
>
> In Islam, one's apparel is no longer a matter of personal taste. Muslim men must dress conservatively in suits, ties, and white collars. The women usually wear a headdress and a full white habit covering arms and legs. These "uniforms" have several identification functions. The disheveled or flamboyant appearance represented by the lower-class Negro stereotype is replaced by a sober neatness which both expresses and strengthens a new sense of dignity. The rather archaic dress of the female perhaps emphasizes the protected, sequestered, and obedient role she plays vis-à-vis her male counterpart. The uniformity, as in the military, heightens a sense of group cohesion and affords a readily detectable commonality. Brothers can be differentiated from others.[19]

One's appreciation of racial physical appearances also changes considerably. The Negro suffering from a "slave mentality" and a lost identity accepts Caucasian standards of personal attractiveness, but the black man who becomes a Muslim learns differently: black skin is truly the most appealing; kinky hair is "strong hair"; Negroid features are the highest human representation of Allah's beauty; nonwhites are the only desirable mates. The observation volunteered by one female correspondent for *Muhammed Speaks* is typical: "The handsomest and most beautiful and congenial people in the world are the black and brown people . . . African and Asian types. Even white policemen resent and are jealous of our men. The Islamic faithful have no need for skin bleach, hair straightener, and other cosmetic contrivances. The black man is invited to love rather than hate his own skin. What we are witnessing here is a whole reversal and reconstruction of racial esthetics."[20]

It seems, from what has been said thus far, that not only their achievements but the people themselves become symbolic. Along with the name and appearance, one's very deportment is instrumental in identity reconstruction; Muslim composure and self-control are to be maintained at all times. Boisterous behavior and displays of unrestrained emotion are interdicted.[21] Brought into Muslim company, the novice immediately grasps that he is to listen quietly to any music, and not sway or croon. Other people, including whites, are to be treated courteously, and domestic management is in contradistinction to the haphazard eating schedules and unhealthy dietary habits of many lower-class Negroes.

Of equal interest are the prescribed foods: as a true Muslim, one is divinely forbidden to touch pork, sea food, or other scavenger creatures. Corn bread, black-eyed peas, collard greens, 'possum, 'coon, and other standard southern fare reminiscent of past "slave habits" are also strictly prohibited. Hence, even in what and how the Muslim eats, he receives an answer to the question "Who am I?" His dietary laws are one more means of bolstering the new identity while eradicating the old.

What that new identity means for the rest of American society remains an important question.[22] But one thing is certain: it means that the black man is neither what the white man is nor what he has believed the Negro to be. Witness the admonition from Elijah Muhammad to "Stand yourself up and look . . . with your eyes, not the white man's," and to "get away from the idea of depending on others to do for us what we can do for self. Fear, cowardice, and laziness are our greatest enemies." In so many words, Muhammad teaches: Feeling inferior results in acting inferior, and this is the outgrowth of accepting the white man's view of yourself. Pleading for his acceptance is another way of waiting vainly for him to liberate you. Free yourself of the slave mentality. Love yourself and you will not need the white man's love.

Muhammad's greatest desire, it seems, is not racial war but racial self-reliance and separation. His "program" perhaps best sums it up. Some of its points read: "Separate yourself from the slave master. Pool your resources, education, and qualifications for independence. Stop forcing yourself into places where you are not wanted. Make your own neighborhood a decent place to live. Rid yourself of the lust of drink and learn to love self and kind before loving others. . . . Build your own homes, schools, hospitals, and factories. Do not seek to mix your blood through racial integration. Stop buying expensive cars, fine clothes, and shoes before being able to live in a fine house. Spend your money among yourselves."[23]

It is a curious fact that his "extremist" movement, which blames the whites for the downfall and enslavement of the Negro, nevertheless does recognize that blacks are at least partly responsible for their continued plight and, therefore, must take it upon themselves to better their lot, independently of the wider society's approval and goodwill. This idea that the major responsibility for betterment now rests not with the white man but with the black man is one of the less obvious points, often overlooked, that distinguishes the Muslims from most other militant civil rights groups.

As long as there are millions of Negroes among the urban poor (and the next twenty years promise amelioration but no miracles), there remains a substantial pool from which the Muslims may draw. It is this very stratum which benefits least from integration and which is generally forgotten by middle-class civil rights organizations.[24]

The Muslim movement, then, is neither faddist nor ephemeral; it is born of the deep-rooted malignancy of racial oppression; in some cases, it has helped individuals whom society has tacitly declared beyond help. Moreover, the growth of Black Power concepts indicates the appeal of the Muslims within the total black community.

LONGEVITY AND TRANSITION: FROM REVOLUTION TO INSTITUTION

What becomes of a millenarian-enthusiast movement that is too weak to achieve its dream of paradise, yet too strong and too functional to wither away? The chiliastic sects of the middle ages were characterized by inspired upsurges that either spent themselves when prophecy failed or collapsed with the demise of the messianic leader. In some cases, the devoted shared a collective death at the hands of the established authorities. The Islam movement, however, is better equipped for longevity and shows no inclination toward suicidal excesses. On this score, the Black Muslims more closely resemble those millenarian, true-believer movements, such as the early Christian Church and the early Bolsheviks, which neither burned themselves out nor just dissipated but which, by achieving stability and longevity, embarked upon a process of transformation and transition that continues even today.

Two propositions drawn from Max Weber's analysis of culture and society might guide us here. First, Weber understood that certain beliefs of a cultural system can set in motion social practices and social organization which, in turn, can eventually negate the very end values of that cultural system. Thus, Muslim worldly organization and practices, which are the outgrowth of an enthusiast-true-believer system of beliefs, lead to interests and material conditions that eventually vitiate and undermine transcendental Muslim values.

Second, in order to do justice to their mission, Weber observed, the charismatic leader and sect "must stand outside the ties of the world." It is the fate of their charisma, when coming in contact with "the permanent institutions of a community, to give way to powers of tradition or of rational socialization."[25] Contrary to the expectations of many whites, the Muslims are: (a) developing from what was potentially a revolutionary sect into a generally relatively "conservative" Negro self-improvement group, more interested in material advances than in sacrificing the life of the movement for the sake of a black supremacist doctrine; (b) developing an organizational maturity and efficacy that extends beyond, and actually modifies, the chiliastic and charismatic impulses; (c) manifesting a growing inclination toward a *modus vivendi* with larger communities, both black and white, thereby changing from a charismatic sect to an organization committed to, or accommodated within, the ongoing social system.

ORGANIZATIONAL MATURITY AND EFFICACY

The Muslims have constructed a sturdy mass organization with leadership operating via a chain of command from Muhammad through his chief lieutenants to an aggressive and vigorous clergy. Decisions are seldom the haphazard inspirational measures one might expect from a cult of visionary chiliasts.

Elijah Muhammad, in the eyes of his followers, is a messianic leader. Yet given its bureaucratic maturity and the grass-roots strength of its apparatus, his movement should not collapse like a house of cards when the leader dies. The rank and file manifest a dedication that is sustained and enduring rather than impulsive. Membership is not something exercised in one's spare time; it is a total commitment to Black Islam. Every day is lived with the consciousness of one's Muslim identification, reinforced by activities and involvements which are almost exclusively related to the movement. The movement thus promises to outlast its leader. The true problem of succession looms large, as in any authoritarian political system. It was solved once when Muhammad succeeded Fard, and it will probably be solved again, perhaps more easily, by Muhammad designating a successor. Extensive interviews with followers indicate that they are not worried about succession; they believe their sense of unity is such that almost any minister could lead them.[26]

FROM HAVE-NOTS TO HAVES

One characteristic that the millenarian, the enthusiast, and the true believer share is a deprecating attitude toward the present. The past is important because it contains the myth of a lost identity and grandeur, a lost purity and paradise, and the vision of a future when these things shall be repossessed. Placed between the myth of the past and the vision of the future, the present is often but a pale interregnum. This is true of the Muslims, however, only if one gives exclusive attention to their arsenal of historical hallucination and futuristic fantasy. Just as the early Christian rejoiced at the prospect of Armageddon and the Second Coming, and the Bolshevik of 1919 saw his future attained only by an international chain reaction of revolutions, so some desperate black man might find solace only in anticipating the destruction of the white world. He who has nothing can care little for stability and the incremental advance of self-interest. But what if, in the interim, this despised world grows ever more comfortable and meaningful?

As Hoffer observes, ". . . We are less ready to die for what we have or are than for what we wish to have and to be. It is a perplexing and unpleasant truth that when men already have something worth fighting for they do not feel like fighting."[27] Might it not be that the Muslim is willing to risk less as he acquires more? As early as 1960, Essien-Udom discovered that "an improved economic status tends to moderate the militancy of the [Muslim] members. In fact, this interest in the acquisition of wealth appears to be one of the important internal constraints on the possibility of the movement becoming politically significant or revolutionary."[28]

Muslim conservatism is not confined to material acquisitions, however. The Muslims prescribe psychological goals for those who have been severely deprived of them. Equally significant is their creation of a system of controls, responsibilities, and identifications, i.e., institutional means, that allows for the attainment of these goals. The consequences can be measured by the dramatic decline of anomie, despair, and destructive pathology among the members.[29] He who is without a self is the most ready to sacrifice himself, but he who is building a viable self-identification becomes in some ways wedded to this world. In sum, among ghetto Negroes, the Muslims appear as psychological, as well as material, "haves."

SIGNS OF ACCOMMODATION

There are several signs that the movement is beginning to accommodate itself to a larger society. The most important are: (a) its present relationship to groups making attempts at integration; (b) less emphasis on the separatist aspects of the movement; (c) the appearance of conventional interests in political life: (d) the recognition that some improvement can take place within the present political structure; and (e) the moderation of expressions of hostility toward the white man. To illustrate each of these points:

> (a) At one time, integrationist leaders were the objects of personal attacks. Martin Luther King ("Martin Luther Queen"), Thurgood Marshall ("The Ugly American"), Ralph Bunche ("The George Washington of Israel"), and others were considered the white masters' sycophants.[30] The Muslims of late seem disposed to overlook the fact that the objectives of the NAACP are diametrically opposed to their own and that whites play fairly prominent roles in that group. Integrationist leaders and white officials and professionals have been allotted full-page interviews in Muslim publications.[31] In addition, Elijah Muhammad has reserved a page in every issue of the Black Islam's official organ, *Muhammad Speaks,* for "Other People's Opinons," inviting comments and criticisms from organizations or individuals on any phase of the Muslim program or on the plight of black America. Correspondence, often critical, from other black nationalists, integrationists, and whites has appeared.

(b) To be sure, Muhammad still submits his plea for "a land of our own"; yet, one may detect a shift in emphasis and tone if not in doctrine. The call for "separation or death" is now rarely heard. A reading of *Muhammad Speaks* demonstrates this transition. Accounts of integrationist battles are now treated sympathetically rather than disdainfully, and headlines and news reports typically read like those found in any militant Negro integrationist publication: "70,000 Negroes Battle to End Second-Class Citizenship," "Jackson, Citadel of Segregationists, Under Assault," "Negro to Run for Mayor," "Danville Negroes Continue Struggle for Freedom," "CORE Unit Wants Change to Right of Self-Defense," "GI's Face Jim Crow Alone."[32]

(c) At one time, Muslim leaders discouraged their followers from voting. To participate in the political system, they argued, was in effect to condone the white corruption and dominance of that system. Yet, the Muslims never explicitly ruled out future electoral participation.[33] Muhammad, himself, set the current tone when he called for "a full-scale struggle on the political front in 1964 to elect, particularly in areas where Negroes predominate, black representatives dedicated to the struggle for the advancement and welfare of their people and to the weeding out of black political puppets used to maintain white supremacy."[34] While not exactly like the Urban League in tenor, the proposal sounds not unlike one that might be made by any interest group attempting to mobilize its strength to back favored candidates and oppose those who have not been responsive to its interests. No mention is made of separatist goals; there is merely a call for unity with the NAACP at the polls. This is not insignificant as a step toward integrating the Muslims into American political life.

(d) Unlike some Marxist revolutionaries, who anticipated a worsening of working-class conditions as the necessary prelude to revolution, and who dismissed reform as a sop designed to weaken proletarian militancy, the Muslims seem to work for incremental gains for Negroes within white society. Muhammad's "Muslim Program" promulgated in 1960 reads in part:

> We believe that the federal government should intercede to see that black men and women tried in white courts receive justice in accordance with the laws of the land . . . or allow us to build a new nation for ourselves, dedicated to justice, freedom, and liberty. . . . As long as we are not

> allowed to establish a state or territory of our own, we demand not only equal justice under the laws of the United States, but equal employment opportunities . . . now.[35]

The Muslim teaching that there can be no real justice and no real equality without separation has been significantly modified by this new demand for justice and equality within white society to compensate for the absence of separation. "White Justice" is no longer necessarily a contradiction in terms.

Nor are the Muslims unaware of the integrationist implications of their efforts. Before breaking with the Muslims, the late Malcolm X, in a revealing statement, said that, "Some whites are listening more these days to some of the so-called Negro leaders who are working for integration. They're listening to the moderates. But the white man wouldn't listen to a moderate if there were not an extremist behind him. Tom Mboya (of Kenya) wouldn't have gotten that far if there hadn't been the shadow of Jomo Kenyatta."[36] Acting as an integration catalyst apparently does not fill Muslim leaders with the dismay one might have been led to expect.

(e) Since 1960, Muhammad has toned down much of his polemics, thereby revealing his sensitivity to the charge that "he preaches hate." Little or no reference is now made to white people as "devils," and emphasis is on "black pride," rather than "black supremacy."

Eric Lincoln attributes this moderation to the Muslims' new appreciation of the weight of the forces against them and to a desire not "to antagonize the opposition so that the movement will be destroyed."[37]

To dismiss such expressions and actions as merely "tactical" is to imply that they are not a measure of the movement's real intent. But what leaders do in the name "tactics" is, after all, what they do; it is how they behave and is much of what they are. A group's unwillingness to maneuver, compromise, and retreat is usually taken as evidence of its extremism. Surely the presence of a willingness to compromise, retreat, and come to terms with reality may be indicative of the converse. It tells us in this case that Muhammad gives priority to the movement's survival as opposed to the movement's racial chiliasm. Nothing corrodes the apocalyptic vision like *realpolitik.*

We might return to Father Knox's description of the enthusiast: "Extenuate, accommodate, interpret, and he will part company with you." What an uneasy white society, abetted by mass media not noted for eschewing the sensational, has tended to overlook is that the Muslims have constantly extenuated, accommodated, and interpreted. When the Muslims' utterances are moderate, we discount these as mere words and point to their seemingly hostile behavior. When their behavior is conciliatory and constructive, we prefer to believe their hostile utterances. Such a predisposition makes any measured evaluation of the movement impossible.

CONCLUSION

The Black Muslim official credo, a compendium of fantastic racial myths, is in the tradition of millenarianism, both ancient and recent. While the Muslim appeal is viable, there is little evidence that the movement will reach its separatist goal. Neither does it promise to fade into oblivion in the foreseeable future. But this investigation, it is hoped, has been more than an exercise in prognostication; in noting the relationship of Muslim doctrine to practice, we have attempted to analyze the directions and causes of present transitions and to illuminate the relevance of the Muslims for the entire Black Power movement.

Visionary doctrine can operate as an instrument of revolution. There are ideas that "change the world" and those that crystallize and mobilize sentiments. No one knows better than the visionary how vision can inflame life. The chiliastic impulse has infused whole populations with a thirst for paradise and a willingness to risk all to win all. But eschatological doctrine may serve other roles. As indicated earlier, Weber demonstrated that ideas may generate consequences that create the very conditions which negate the ideas. By working at a calling for the glory of God, maximizing and rationalizing all efforts to cultivate God's vineyard for God's majesty, the Puritan unleashed secular forces in industry, commerce, and science that eventually undermined the very values he sought to propagate.

Weber's thesis, in all its paradoxical nature, seems to find confirmation in the Muslim movement. Black Islam's fantastic eschatology does not serve as a battle plan directing blacks toward some cataclysmic confrontation with whites, although many observers have hastened to that conclusion. The real effect of Muslim doctrinal belief is simple and powerful: blackness is given a superior, majestic, and even magical status, and the black man is thereby rescued from the condition of suffering from a missing heritage and lost identity. In being thus doctrinally infused with a zeal, a confidence, and a sense of means and goals, the Muslims fabricate the wherewithal to overcome racial defeat, despair, and self-destroying self-hate. This accomplishment, even though it is impelled by fantastic tenets, leads the Muslims away from the separatist myth and closer to the existing social system. "The impossible," as Mannheim suggests in his discussion of chiliasm, "gives birth to the possible."[38]

Rather than being possessed by ecstatic and revolutionary impulses, the Muslims have set about, in response to their new-found race pride, to uplift and transform themselves from *lumpen-proletariat* Negroes into practitioners of a law-abiding, middle-class Protestant ethic, from have-nots into haves interested in securing a better communal, material, and psychological existence for themselves and for other Negroes. Hence, the action born of the beliefs of racial desperadoes produces racial reformers.

Closely related to this is Weber's postulate that the charismatic inspirational sect, coming into contact with the permanent institutions of this world, must eventually become of this world. Here again is a paradox. The achievement of organizational stability and longevity, designed in part to strengthen and solidify the inspirational message, can be secured only at the expense of the impulsive and charismatic. Thus, the messianic zeal and magic which give rise to the institution become modified by the exigencies and structure of institutional life. The necessities of *realpolitik*, the desire for a wider appeal, and the sheer fact of longevity and organization commit the Muslim leadership to the growth and survival of the movement and of all its meaningful functions in a manner that far outweighs any fixation on separatism or black cosmic futurism.

It would seem that the purity of the millenarian movement is endangered by only two things: destruction and survival. In the case presented herein, and in most cases of American ethnic separatism, the emphasis is on the distinct cultural and psychological problems of the ethnic group. These questions of "life style" may be converted into a politics less pragmatic and incremental than the pattern of welfare accommodation we have explored. If so, they are likely to produce high tension politics that cannot be coped with by conventional political institutions. But since the goals of organized separatists, from Zionists to Black Muslims, are so exotic, large-scale political activity can but dilute the bonds that animate the separatist impulse.

CAVEAT AND PROSPECT

The thesis of this chapter ought not to obscure certain unpleasant realities of separatism and the Black Muslim movement.

Since the Muslims organized themselves, violent racial conflicts have engulfed urban America. Within the Muslim movement itself, these conflicts have included the presence of violence, power struggles, and even murder.

The Black Muslims, and other separatist groups like them, are definitely not romantic ethnic communities, nor are they modern versions of traditional ethnic associations created by white immigrants. Yet the remarkable thing is that the Muslims have been able to create *any* measure of personal and political accommodation for their members. The point is that Muslim methods and ideology have provided the structure of identification and behavior so often lacking in the black man's family and history. The so-called breakdown of the Negro family and social organization often noted by urbanologists has been dealt with by the Muslim movement, whatever one may think of the means employed to create substantive social life out of ghetto chaos. Therefore, the thrust of this chapter stems from the fact that viable social and political institutions have seldom been present in the black, urban environment.

The root problem of separatist politics, dealing with life styles not easily accommodated by conventional politics, has been met by the Muslim culture—at times by promoting paramilitary and fascist actions. This is not to say that paramilitaristic and fascistic organizations will, or should, become the mode of black separatism. But it is intellectually important to distinguish between the generally conservative economic and political *functions* performed by the Black Muslims in their early history, and the exotic *culture* they developed out of ideas and practices seemingly bizarre in the eyes of the dominant society.

The psychic and social identity sought in separatist politics must be balanced against the parochial and antidemocratic tendencies of separatist groups. No ethnic group can truly withdraw from American society, because the heart of social and political power lies within major institutions. Thus, the separatist path may be one of conflict based on efforts to shake the system with the accumulated passion of common blood, belief, and grievances. In this regard, the Muslims have provided a model that other Black Power groups may use in defining both organic notions of the black community and their relations with white America. In the past, such separatist ethnic groups were functionally absorbed into the society and their cultures (nationality, religious practices) given recognition. Whether the history of Eastern European Jews, Italian Catholics, and others will be repeated for the black man heretofore attracted to the Muslim movement depends on the interplay among key institutions in the immediate future.

CHAPTER SIX

The Politics of Radicalism

> The society of losers may grow in number and power with increasing rapidity. If this pool grows to substantial proportions, if it gives vent to its resentments and frustrations . . . power will meet power, the power of a mass movement confronting the power of the machine. The discard heap the machine created may arise to devour its progenitor.[1]

TWO STYLES OF RADICALISM

Entry into the American political system is normally achieved through existing institutions. For many decades, ethnic groups have pressed their claims in the country's two major political parties, state and local governments, and the federal behemoth in Washington. In the long run, most of these claims have been recognized and accommodated in some measure within the polity. As we have seen, the accommodating strategy is a restrained form of politics in that basic substantive policies are seldom examined and the essential metaphysics of the American system are taken for granted. Even when collective benefits replace recognition politics, the assumption is that the allocation of more resources can itself assuage the divisive potentialities of ethnicity.

A separatist strategy can provide some tangible benefits. It can help an ethnic group rebuild its communal base and reconstruct the institutions of family, work, and sociability that may have been eroded by a cruel history. Above all, a separatist effort can replenish the psychic and cultural resources of group members who may have lost the belief in their own political efficacy. The short-term consequence of most separatist movements, such as Zionism or Black Nationalism, is that they detach group members from learning experiences in the normal workings of the American political system. Yet, in the long run, the communal solidarity achieved in the ethnic parish and fraternal society may prepare individuals for more enduring and self-confident participation in the larger polity. The goal of the separatists is—or should be—group reconstruction rather than the alteration of the dominant political machinery.

The radical strategy provides yet another option for politically inclined members of a disadvantaged ethnic group. In fact, one ought to speak of radical *strategies,* for either organized, coherent political ideas or the diffuse passion of ethnicity itself may fuse ethnic political responses into a new movement. The differences between politics of ideology and politics based on passion per se are considerable, and each response, although commonly outside the usual boundaries of pluralist politics, tells us much about the relations of an ethnic community to the political system. The point to emphasize is that diffuse passion replaces ideology when the requirements of an ideological system no longer conform to even potential political realities. Thus, it is far more difficult for a political regime to cope with unrestrained passion rooted in race, religion, or nationality than to combat the legacies of such ideologies as Marxism and socialism, which have influenced ethnic politics in the past.

OLD-STYLE RADICALISM: THE POLITICS OF FORENSIC IDEOLOGY

Just as a Marxist orator could exhort workers to prepare to revolt by telling them that they had nothing to lose but their industrial chains, so could the radical agitator attempt to persuade the foreign born, the Negroes, the victimized Jews that they could overcome discrimination only by uniting in a coalition or third political party outside the dominant political institutions. The advantages and appeal of this political option ought not to be minimized in assessing ethnicity's impact on American political history.

It must be said, however, that radical movements have not always called public attention to the plight of ethnic groups in

America. Until after World War I, the American Socialist party, for example, did nothing special to better the position of Negroes and other minorities in America. Torn between a commitment to the position of the established white working guilds and the solidarity of all men of labor, regardless of color, the Socialist party vacillated for many years about its responsibility to unpopular minorities. Finally, however, the need of all radical organizations feeding on a futuristic ideology for the skills of men subtle in intellectual and philosophical analysis came to the fore. American socialism, as has every other form of ideological politics in the United States, found men with such skills among the middle-class intellectuals. The ascendency of these radical intellectuals in the Socialist party forced a pronounced change in party attitudes toward minority groups. The Intercollegiate Socialist Society and the League For Industrial Democracy, founded after World War I, redefined worker solidarity to include unpopular ethnic minorities. Although few Negroes joined the Socialist party, the Negro was more fully represented among the group's leadership between 1920 and 1940 than in most other American political institutions.

At the same time, numerous "foreign federations" provided white minority groups with forums to absorb and transmit socialist ideology and to apply it to the problems of unionism and poverty.[2] Unlike separatist ethnic organizations, the federations sought to unite co-ethnics into a broad political coalition with a common political creed transcending specific ethnic claims and identifications.

Despite the fact that its policies responded to the dictates of the Soviet Union, the American Communist party, too, performed an important function in dramatizing racial and religious discrimination in America.[3] Indeed, that group's indirect impact on democratic institutions was probably greater than were its organizational successes among the American Negro population. Thousands of Negroes joined the Communist party during the first thirty years of its existence, but only a fraction of them made any kind of permanent identification with the organization. Thus, the National Negro Congress, although the largest and most effective organization developed by the American communists to deal with race issues, had a life span of less than four years before the Second World War. Numerous efforts by the communists to revive the organization after the war failed dismally. In short, while the communist impact did affect the evolving pattern of American race relations for more than three decades, it had meaning only under certain conditions. For instance, other institutions were obliged to meet the social competition advanced by the communists. The real impact, often overstated in the past, developed for the most part only when the communists joined in, rather than initiated, demands for equal rights and racial justice. As Henry Lee Moon concludes:

> It is a matter of record that the communists have generally fought for full recognition of Negro rights. They have carried on this fight through their own organizations and through those organizations in which they exert influence. They have pushed the Negro to the forefront in party work. They have constantly nominated him for office on the party ticket. They have dramatized his problems. They have risked social ostracism and physical violence in his behalf. They have challenged American hypocrisy with the zeal, if not the high principle, of the abolitionists. In all this they have performed a vital function as an irritant on the American conscience.[4]

The communists also left their mark on the Negro press. While few Negro journalists were party members, they frequently found that much of the more dramatic material on Negro protest derived from the various struggles of the party to secure Negro rights. In this regard, communist demands and agitation were headline material and grist for the editorial mills.

Another important, albeit indirect, influence of the American Communist party was its effect on moderate protest and betterment organizations. While it periodically alienated such organizations as the National Association for the Advancement of Colored People (NAACP), it also forced such occurrences as the increased identification of the NAACP with the labor movement, which dates back to the early 1930 s and which can be viewed as having happened partly as the result of communist pressures. The growth of internal democracy within the NAACP was also a gratuitous by-product of the communist threat to the existing administration. Moreover, the party's role in making the question of Negro rights an intraunion political issue subsequently forced noncommunist trade unions to take practical cognizance of the issue. Thus, the communist irritant, despite the ouster of party leaders from the union movement, contributed to the pioneering efforts to combat racial discrimination developed by the Congress of Industrial Organizations' national leadership and by forces within the United Auto Workers. Moreover, the communist support of Henry Wallace's Progressive party campaign in 1948 contributed to the adoption of the first strong civil rights plank by the Democratic party and the growth of Negro influence within the majority party.

The yields from the ideological radical alternative are further illustrated by a third historical case, the development of Jewish community leadership. Between 1890 and 1920, the urbanized and intellectual American Jewish community frequently assumed an ideological posture rare among the leadership of American ethnic groups. As one settlement worker in a Jewish district of New York put it, "the real university of the East Side was Marx's *Capital.* Read like the Bible, with faith, like the Bible it formed the taste and moulded the life of its readers. Socialism as an economic theory is one thing, as an education it is another. It is what we are excited about that educates us. What the East Side was excited about was socialism."[5]

The socialist influence also pervaded important trade unions, the Yiddish press, and Jewish social activities such as the socialists' Workingmen's Circle. From their experience with socialism, the Jewish communal leaders of three decades quickly acquired the political skills and style that influenced the American trade union movement (witness, for instance, the International Ladies Garment Workers), the development of American intellectual life (through the numerous academic and political accomplishments of "ex-radicals"), and American national politics (note, for instance, the critical role played by New York's American Labor party, and its successor, the Liberal party, in the elections of Franklin Delano Roosevelt in 1936, 1940, and 1944).

THE LIABILITIES OF IDEOLOGICAL RADICALISM

An ideological movement that cannot locate the sources of resentment in the existing social order constitutes an impotent political force. Thus, when the ineffectiveness of the appeals of radical ideologies to the masses of foreign-born and Negro citizens at times of major social distress is noted, it is not surprising to realize that though American Jews did play a significant role in the leadership of the American Communist party during the 1930's and 1940's, the overwhelming majority of American Jews have consistently opposed communism. Moreover, a number of surveys confirm the finding that even during the national hysteria about communist influence in Washington, only a small minority of non-Jews were even aware, or critical, of Jewish contributions to the American communist movement.[6] In short, ethnic factors were not of major import in ideological radicalism.

The appeals of American communism to Negroes yielded a low degree of hard-core black support. By 1964, only five per cent of the Negro rank and file and only two per cent of sampled Negro leadership accepted the communist claim that there was no racial discrimination under communist systems.[7] Among the predominantly Catholic and peasant-derived ethnic groups, ideologies such as socialism, fascism, anarchism, and communism played little part in political maturation. For example, before World War I, the American Alliance of Polish Socialists sought support among Polish Americans for the adoption of socialism by Poland when it achieved nationhood. But this group's membership was infinitesimal compared to that of the Polish National Alliance, a fraternal organization that rejected leftwing politics. Subsequently, the Alliance became fragmented, and those interested in American socialism joined the Polish section of the American Socialist party.

The roots of this lack of attraction to radical politics among most ethnic group members are not difficult to uncover. Available religious orientations, principally the strong affiliation with Roman Catholicism, provided for many ethnics a traditional and secure source of emotional support in coping with a strange environment in urban America. Moreover, the longing for social acceptance encouraged ethnic members to seek access to conventional social and political institutions rather than strike out on their own in novel political organizations not fully in accord with American values. It must be remembered that an explicit and militant political ideology rooted in concepts of social justice and promising to reveal the contours of a preferred future order requires the energies of men who will bypass the immediate, practical needs of an ethnic group in search of tomorrow's promises. However, the social and emotional needs of the foreign born do not usually resist available gratifications for the sake of the ideologue's long-range blueprints. For these reasons, the infrequency with which the radical strategy has been blessed with a mass following has made political accommodation easier for the two-party system and other persisting American institutions. The dominant accommodation strategy was strongly facilitated by the social and emotional conservatism of ethnic group memberships. As we have seen in accounting for the persistence of ethnicity in individual political choice, the economy of traditional choice is one important factor in sustaining individual attachments to the ethnic group and its supporting community. In addition, an ideological commitment requires some basic political skills and interests, and these have previously been lacking among the less educated and less informed ethnic members.

IDEOLOGY AND POLITICAL CONGRUENCE

The ideological alternative causes or at least portends the creation of broad political coalitions based on common views of society that are beyond the scope and claims of any single ethnic group. It may lead to some remedial action by governmental institutions fearful of ideological movements and their ability to alienate political support from the existing regime. On the other hand, the radical option may lead to political isolation, bizarre views out of step with the requirements of the political culture, a deepening sense of self-alienation that merely feeds, rather than assuages, the sense of resentment based on racial, religious, or national discrimination.

The task of the radical ideologue is to convince ethnic members that future rewards outweigh the benefits from the present system. His success is partly determined by the value ethnic members attach to the social and economic rewards they are presently reaping from American society. The ideologue must also convince ethnic masses that attachments based on principle are more important in the long run than short-term satisfactions obtained from membership in ethnic fraternal and social associations. Further, an ideology requires some degree of political awareness, and the response of most ethnic group members has varied from low to moderate political interest. Moreover, the ideologue must persuade men bound by common bonds of "blood and believer" that they will receive more personal recognition within his political movement than within the circles of ethnic attachment and identification.

Despite the difficulties of these tasks, the ideologue faces an even greater job, that of promoting the ideological premises themselves. While accommodation politics promises increments in tangible benefits, and separatist politics yields the emotional ties of group identity, the radical option puts its stock in a set of ideas explaining the individual's position in relation to creeds of justice, the prevailing power distribution, and the preferred outcomes to be achieved when the ideological promise bears fruit. In order for an ideology to be salient, the ideologue must convince masses of men that his option is worth the price to be paid in possible social ostracism, deferred gratifications, and schisms with those co-ethnics who are not persuaded to become ideological co-believers:

> Even the most abstract ideology, the most utopian scheme, has an empirical content that must be squared with the small world of experience of the individual confronted with the problem of finding meaning to his world. And even the most facile devices for squaring particular experiences with incompatible interpretations . . . such as a "long run" inconsistent with any observable short run, the idea that whatever happens is "willed" by some vaguely outlined authority, the view that there is an inscrutable

> reality beyond all appearances, . . . even these must eventually fail to protect men from the abrasions of reality.[8]

Reasons for the lack of congruence between the beliefs of American workingmen of recent immigrant stock and such full-blown ideologies as Marxism and socialism are found in the hard core of the American experience. Consider the disparities between the Marxist ideology and the common experiences of the American ethnic, at least among the white segment of recent European antecedents:

> The empirical world described by Marxists does not fit the world experiences of American workingmen. Government devotes much energy to increasing the gross national product and meeting needs for housing and welfare. The view of an executive, capitalistic committee of the ruling class is difficult to square with these realities.
>
> The time dimensions and references of Marxism (and other ideologies) are long-range; for instance, the notion of a long era of struggle leading to a proletarian dictatorship and the international brotherhood of workers. By contrast, the tendencies of ethnic industrial associations, and probably urbanism as well, have been to plan for individualistic unreflective men who focus on their local communities and the needs of their families and friends.
>
> The causal explanation of Marxism (and other ideologies) employs a dialectic based on the manipulation of intellectual abstractions; it often involves a search for a conspiracy and always attributes problems to moral causes, such as the evil of existing leaders.
>
> The causal explanations of the American political culture learned by most ethnic group members are pragmatic, based on a real if vague moral order relying on adjustment and understanding through such devices as education and personal contact. Ideologies are based on major premises; compromises on the "facts" and group interests in specific cases. Ideologies encourage men to avoid uncongenial information; pragmatic problem-solving requires an approach to new facts useful in *ad hoc* solutions.
>
> Ideologies (such as Marxism) offer future identity with a solitary group, social conflict in pursuit of "justice," and psychic security for the hostile and dependent in return for disassociation from the present social context. American political culture, learned by the immigrants and their de-

> scendants, is contextual with the existing adjustments and security highly valued at the expense of long-term social plans and evaluation.[9]

Therefore, the ideologically radical option holds out little appeal to those groups and individuals being "leveled up" in the American social system and for whom the amelioration of ethnic and interpersonal relations has provided secure grounds for self-appraisal. Moreover, the variety of ethnic associations and organizations, including those created in response to a distant, ancestral ideal, form a sturdy social anchor not easily dislodged by ideological appeals. In fact, the success of American ethnic group life and the achievement of a variety of political accommodations probably reinforced the "conservatism" found among the foreign-stock population and quickly eroded the basis of full-blown ideological appeals.

The situations of white immigrant groups and the American Negro differ markedly in this regard, however. First, the Negro was in the northern city often long before the initial masses of ethnic immigrants arrived. Second, the foreign immigrant rose in political, economic, and social stature and found his way out of the ghetto, while the Negro generally maintained a low social position. Unlike the foreign immigrant, the Negro has inherited a political legacy of "outside people," that is, people who cannot be fully integrated into the American urban political system. These two points are related to a third factor which increases the appeal of ideology to black people, the sociological reality of group visibility. The white immigrant and his immediate descendants could climb out of the ghetto, change or modify their names, and blend into the population, disassociating themselves reputationally and physically from the more recent immigrants. The Negro, on the other hand, was associated with the slaves or with the uneducated members of Southern immigrant groups, no matter how affluent or cultured he became. Color visibility has probably had more bearing on the slow political and social assimilation of the American Negro than any other single factor.

The net result has been that the immigrant's need for ideology has been low because he has been able to do what others before him had done, namely, climb out of the ghetto. The Negro, however, as a result of and in reaction to the discrimination he has encountered and the segregation that has been forced upon him, has had a greater stake in ideological positions that can explain his unjust fate. Thus, one of the essential features of ethnic and racial conflict is not merely conflict of material interest, but the minority group's perception of a diffuse sense of insult in the community. Politics, or any other activity or interaction with the dominant community, provides a symbolic vehicle for asserting group worth. But when this fails, an ethnic group such as the Negro community has several options. One is to refine tactics leading to rewards within the political system, as the accommodation thesis propounds. Another option is to use violence and other conflict behavior to achieve group ends—in which case, a full-blown ideology explaining one's position and public mission is critical.

NEW-STYLE RADICALISM: PASSION AND ANOMIC POLITICS

Despite their vast differences, the accommodating, separatist, and ideologically radical political options share certain similarities. All three approaches convey some guidelines relating ends to means, some probable estimate of the political outcomes to be achieved by group effort. All three are based on an articulated relationship between the ethnic community and the political order, and all three include some calculations about the probabilities of success, the psychic and social resources of the group, the importance of political ideas and action, and the locus of power within the American political system.

However, a fourth option, the politics of passion, which encourages ethnic nihilism, is based on the absence of an ethnic community possessing sufficient political and intellectual resources to further its goals effectively. It is also based on the belief that none of the other options will work. In other words, the politics of ethnic passion has no "strategy" other than that of violently removing the real or imagined sources of its frustrations. The phrase "Burn, Baby, Burn" conveys the depths of despair of a group which feels—and possibly fears—that its problems are beyond political redress.

Considering the depth of discrimination and personal abuse suffered by American Negroes and other minorities, it is remarkable how infrequently the politics of passion has plagued American politics. Paradoxically, apathy and alienation, potentially the stuff of political volatility, also produce little interest in politics. In the usual case, political activity requires individuals who possess ample social and psychological resources. Consequently, the politics of passion, or "new-style" radicalism, is not the politics of normal times. A number of factors, in particular the politicization of the deprived Negro in the urban North, encourage resorting to passion when other strategies fail or are deemed not relevant to the personal situation. The new radicalism is emotional rather than ideological. It is based on a preference for action rather than for cognition and polemics. And it is fed by the convergence of particular conditions in contemporary American society.

THE ANOMIC PERSONAL SITUATION

When they first arrived in America, the members of every immigrant group acutely felt that they had lost their bearings in a new world and were cut off from the stable relations they had enjoyed in the past. Such a feeling of anomie is one of the most painful conditions for both individual man and men collectively joined by common blood or belief.

> Anomie is the feeling that the world and oneself are adrift, wandering, lacking in clear rules and stable moorings. The anomic feels literally demoralized; for him, the norms governing behavior are weak, ambiguous, and remote. He lives in a normative "low pressure" area, a turbulent region of weak and fitful currents of moral meaning. The core of the concept is the feeling of moral emptiness.[10]

Anomic feelings result when socialization and the learning of norms are impaired. Some impediments to learning are social, but others are deeply personal and psychological. Thus, persons whose cognitive capacity is for some reason deficient are likely to view society as disorderly and bewildering and to deplore the incoherence of its value system. Persons strongly governed, for whatever reason, by anxiety, hostility, and other adverse motivational and effective states suffer not only from impaired cognitive functioning but also from a tendency toward distorted perceptions of social "reality." For example, 42 per cent of all low-income northern Negroes and 40 per cent of lower-middle-income northern Negroes questioned in a national survey felt that Negroes would not lose in a showdown with whites despite the fact that Negroes comprise only a small minority of the total population. By contrast, only 17 per cent of the middle- and upper-income northern Negroes and 12 per cent among a panel of Negro leaders interviewed subscribed to this view.[11] Although the survey does not tell us how much personality or residence in a heavily black area contributed to this distortion of political reality, it is likely that a combination of personal and social situations, uniting to produce anomie among the poorer respondents, governed their unrealistic perceptions. Moreover, anomic individuals accommodate themselves poorly to social change, complexity, and ambiguity, and through the projection of their own anxieties, fears, and uncertainties perceive the world as hostile and anxiety-ridden. These personality dispositions have the secondary consequence of reducing their opportunities for effective interaction and communication, hampering further their ability to learn the norms and achieve a more coherent sense of how society works.

For our purposes, the genesis of anomie is less important than its potential consequences for extreme ethnic politics. Whether because of cognition of social reality, personality, or a combination of both factors, deprived individuals united only by common location and color are likely to view normal, accommodating politics as chaotic and meaningless.

THE WEAK SOCIAL BASE

Personal anomie among ethnic group members would not be so politically potent were it not built into enduring social relations. The traditional meaning of a strong ethnic community extended not only to the help and comfort that an ethnic could find in his religious, educational, and fraternal associations; it also connoted a source of opinions about the political world and provided agencies through which new or alternative political claims could be formulated. The "conservatism" of most American ethnic politics was rooted in the extension of family, clan, and/or association into the urban political structure. Connections with existing party leaders and elements of the community power structure, however limited in value, strengthened the social state of ethnic members in the existing political order. Such connections also enabled ethnics to perceive more accurately the norms and processes of ongoing politics.

Personal anomie is likely to produce politics of passion when the individual's frustrations are not screened by a social mechanism. Thus, it is of no small consequence that "the first and most important feature of Negro social structure is the predominance of a lower class lacking a strong sense of community. And a second feature is the relative inability, or unwillingness, of the middle class to identify with the lower class and to provide leadership for it."[12] The history of isolated social groups reveals their susceptibility to mass movements and an extreme volatility in behavior. This was true of isolated farm and factory worker groups in the populist and labor movements. The politics of radical ethnic passion need only find the proper incubator for its extension.

THE GOVERNMENTAL PRESENCE

A third element in the propensity toward extreme ethnic responses, or new-style radicalism, is the broad and direct intervention of federal institutions in the core urban areas. Partly because they were entering a communal void, the enormously expanded federal programs in welfare and related fields are the most important new element in the politicization of ethnic anomie. Accommodation politics took place in an arena where the activities of the federal government were limited; separatist politics emphasized the cultural qualities of co-ethnics, regardless of formal political arrangements; and radical ideologies have always stressed the relations of professional politicians and community leaders to the downtrodden. The politics of passion, however, occurs precisely at a time when federal governmental initiatives have had major impacts on the heretofore autonomous domains of local education, housing, and urban renewal. Thus, it may be that the new role of the federal government will be the catalyst in the emotional radicalization of ethnic politics.

In the old accommodation model (and to some extent in radical politics based on a specific ideology), the impetus for social change comes from *ethnic group demands* made within the party and local governmental system. Collective ethnic benefits, as noted in Chapter Three, provide the means of expanding the scope of accommodation in order to maintain political stability. Suppose, however, that the ameliorative and punitive impact of federal governmental agencies increases enormously? It can be persuasively argued that the enlarged role of the federal government and the extended activities of the police, the welfare agencies, and the Office of Economic Opportunity have shaped the politics of the Negro ghetto more than have racial leaders and community notables.

Moreover, the nationalization of ethnic politics often leads to political tactics encouraging ideological and passionate political activity. The development of political leadership and mass media skills, each contributing to the effectiveness of the other, contributed to the rise of the Negroes as a national pressure group. The charismatic leadership of Dr. Martin Luther King, Jr., in the December 1955 Montgomery, Alabama, bus segregation boycott established the style of the modern Negro revolt in the federal era. Nationally recognized leadership, no matter how apparently fragmented and splintered, is the key to the development of unified Negro action in reaching the federal government.

Although many have attempted to become widely known racial leaders, it is only since the advent of sophisticated mass-media reporting and interpretive reporting that a Negro leader has been able to become known among many populations. It is important not only that the presence of a Martin Luther King, a Stokeley Carmichael, a Roy Wilkins, or an H. Rap Brown, who reasons or rants and raves, give a voice to the otherwise disconnected pockets of Negroes in the nation; it is also important that a Negro leader be known to the groups he is attempting to influence, in this case, the members of the white establishment and the federal government. The expanded use of the media has influenced the development of the Negro's particular political style. Rather than developing a highly personal two-way relationship with many individual clients, as did the old ward bosses, the Negro leader must establish among his followers an identification of him as their representative and their spokesman, a one-way relationship facilitated by the use of passion and ideology to strengthen the national leader. Organizational skills, although always substantial at the local level, must be expanded phenomenally on the national level in order to influence the upper-level national political leadership, which makes so many critical decisions. Herein lies a major problem of the Negro movement, namely, the need for coordination and funding on the national level. Herein, also, can be seen some reasons why the new ethnic leader must be media-oriented and may be inclined to practice the politics of passion. Only media coverage can provide a leader with the broad base of associational support and the sense of unity he needs to direct and support a nationally oriented organization. One man presenting a petition signed by several thousand Negroes may be received by a mayor, but let Martin Luther King, Jr., lead a march of only several hundred Negroes to Chicago's City Hall to present a petition to Mayor Daley, and *The New York Times* covers the story on its front page. A contemporary Negro leader is, of necessity, a publicity-monger, for this is the basis of the unification of his movement to deal with government.

Federal politics is associated with a sense of national immediacy and cause. Shown on the same page, an incident involving Negroes in Memphis and another in Chicago cannot help but be associated in the newspaper reader's mind, whether they are in fact related by either planning or mere chance. A sense is created of *Negro* unrest, of a unified *Negro* feeling or purpose, and the reader begins to wonder whether it may be valid to assume that a group viewed as a whole will eventually associate and react as a single entity.

The media play a further role in the politics of group passion by publicizing the existence of crises, which, if significant enough, could trigger federal responses. For example, the riots of the past few summers have caused individual local crises and have collectively led to a sense of national crisis, triggering a concern about the accommodation and political style of urban Negroes. The riots are more than manifestations of discontent with a system that has condemned so many to live with so little. Evidently, they are also indicative of the distance, the impenetrability, the imperviousness of the formal channels below the federal behemoth to isolated group demands. If the federal government will only take notice when a crisis occurs, eventually a crisis will happen. This does not imply planning or Machiavellian manipulation to coordinate the riots. They are better seen as spontaneous, contagiously spreading examples of the politics of passion triggered by failures in local political accommodation. The riots put pressure on the federal system, which in turn acts to energize the sprawling local governments.

Negro demands, although often blocked on the local level, are rechanneled, through leadership and the creation of crises, to the national level. This shift in the level of political involvement is accompanied by the use of media, ideology, and passion characteristic of mass movements operating without local checks and restraints. Thus, even federal efforts to mitigate poverty and to salvage victims of discrimination may actually intensify the tensions within local politics.

In an urban situation, the convergence of anomic individuals who lack both meaningful social institutions and a sense of group accomplishment and an unprecedented federal governmental presence intensifies the probability of minority-group violence in dealing with local governmental institutions. (Feeling against local governments has risen greatly in recent years as expectations of federal aid have raised expectations about local governmental performance.) One of the unintended consequences is to create a forum for mass politics in which there is a direct confrontation between public authority and individuals who lack, for a variety of reasons, a sense of commitment to and anchorage in the local political community. Public institutions operating on the local level, such as schools and law enforcement agencies, become primary targets for pressure activities stimulated by the national political crisis. On one hand, local government seeks to implement the generally liberal policies of the federal government. Thus, a city's educational system may attempt to make improvements and stimulate additional programs with federal funds. On the other hand, the local community functions as the keeper of a set of dominant norms and institutions that are protected by city agencies. In this regard, the police, for example, may tighten their procedures against loitering and demonstrations in order to curb the passions aroused by new expectations and demands.

Unfortunately, the accelerated governmental response, on all levels, is frequently confronted by the social consequences of the "vicious circle" phenomenon in which whites, on the basis of learned prejudice, discriminate against Negroes. As a result of this discrimination, Negroes are forced to adapt to deprivation in ways that serve to perpetuate the status quo, e.g., by dropping out of school to seek employment.[13] What seems to be required is for one generation of Negroes to sacrifice its adaptations and plunge ahead as if there were no prejudice and discrimination, e.g., to obtain an education even though the "payoff" for being educated will not be forthcoming. Another option would be for a generation of whites to refuse to fall into the trap of stereotyping Negroes and other minorities as "stupid" or backward, even though these groups sometimes do demonstrably achieve at lower levels in some schools.

The difficulties in effecting one or the other of these sacrifices (accomplishing both simultaneously is probably a near impossibility) are attested to in the emergence of new views on race relations. Where once the Negro self-development view of a Robert Park or the white initiative thesis of a Gunnar Myrdal dominated, a more pessimistic view of racial politics underlies the growth of recent radical politics. This view is centered in a "vicious circle" outlook in which one generation's pathological adaptations are compounded and spiral in the next generation.[14] Things get worse instead of remaining stabile. Unemployment leads to welfare and, ultimately, to welfare dependency; family instability and illegitimacy lead to inadequate socialization of children and, thus, to a perpetuation of family instability and illegitimacy.

It is with respect to breaking the vicious circle that the massive "liberal" welfare programs of the Kennedy and Johnson administrations made their major appeal. What was—and is—ignored is that when the politically involved within the ghettoes confront the institutions of law and order, they carry with them the legacy of the vicious circle, namely, antagonistic models of white society, of which the representatives of public agencies and institutions are the most visible members. The stored resentments and sense of rootlessness unwittingly find visible targets in the massive political institutions that, to the majority, represent the sacrosanct foundations of the governmental system. The political consequences of the vicious circle thesis are most obvious in confrontations with law enforcement agencies:

> The issue of police brutality and police malpractice in the ghetto cannot be disposed of by checking a sociologist's statistics or the records of police review boards. It remains an unrecorded fact that lurks in unlit ghetto streets, in moving police cars, in the privacy of police stations. It is recorded in the eyes of the young Negroes at Black Panther rallies who do not even blink when the speaker talks of "executing

> a cop"; it is as if every one of them has at least one memory of some long unpunished indignity suffered at the hands of a white cop.
>
> To these young men, the execution of a police officer would be as natural and justifiable as the execution of a German soldier by a member of the French Resistance. This is the grim reality upon which the Panthers build a movement.[15]

As we have seen, the massive welfare intervention of the federal government and the use of the media to stimulate crises have produced some results that might have been expected in anomic situations. Efforts are made to "play the system" while emotionally disengaging from it. This has been a time-tested response of marginal ethnic members who nurture deep animosities toward the prevailing system. Of more serious consequence is the difficulty of providing participation in and identification with, and winning support for governmental agencies engaged in, ameliorative welfare efforts to deal with the vicious circle problem. The usual governmental response to the politics of mass passion is accommodation and recognition. But efforts to accommodate cannot succeed without an intricate structural rapport among the dispossessed people, their leaders, and the political institutions. Neither mass federal support nor political repression can break the vicious circle of political anomie. Only the inculcation of genuine political identification and motivation can yield the necessary support for governmental programs among people with a history of frustrations and newly acquired social expectations. We have not overcome the problems of participatory democracy, which permits government to function while integrating mass populations into the political system. The failure has been the inability to establish long-term political structures that can provide welfare *and* participatory values. The most meaningful long-term impact of governmental agencies may be the creation of forums for group politics such as are no longer available through the old ethnic association or the party machine.

An analogue to the impact of political institutions on anomic or disadvantaged groups is provided by James Coleman's study of the relation between racially integrated schools and quality education:

> For children from disadvantaged (nonwhite) groups, achievement or lack of it appears closely related to what they believe about the environment: whether they believe the environment will respond to reasonable efforts or whether they believe it instead merely random or immovable.[16]

The task of public officials and governmental agencies is to provide continuing and positive support of the aspirations expressed by disadvantaged ethnic groups. Since these "aspirations" are sometimes expressed in an unacceptable manner, i.e., by political hostility or violence, it is often difficult for officials to respond positively, even if they know what to provide. Yet, punitive responses by authoritative institutions only serve to compound the sense of resentment and alienation felt by the ethnic society.

The political situation surrounding ethnic nihilism is almost the opposite of that under "White Colonialism," the term used by Marxists to describe imperialism. The colonial power is primarily concerned with extracting valuables from the subjugated land with as little harm as possible to life and property, and colonial "native uprisings" are put down by the imposition of brutal or subtle power. On the other hand, the government, by massive intervention in American cities, has attempted to foster relations that would better the conditions of the resident population. The motives and behavior of federal officials, white students, and police officers in sophisticated community relations programs are often commendable. The critical point is that victims often behave in the spirit of their victimization, dramatically confronting public institutions with the legacy of normlessness.

The long-term dilemma is that if public institutions do not grant some power and recognition to deprived groups (thus filling the role of the old ethnic fraternal agencies), the nihilistic option of violence and disorder is unlikely to abate. Few institutions gladly share power with nonmembers, especially when the outsiders have deepseated resentments against all authoritative institutions. Yet, it is the federal presence in a hundred new programs and projects that has fanned the hopes of the ghetto Negro and aroused his passion when expectations have exceeded realities. If the federal attempt to break the vicious cycle does not effectively provide some sense of political identification and attachment, the anomic legacy will continue to strain American politics with outbursts of political passion whose volatility taxes the patience of even the most sympathetic members of the white community.

PART THREE

Varieties of American Ethnic Politics

There are certain limitations in reviewing the political characteristics of specific American ethnic groups. One of these is a tendency to distort the complexities of any group's behavior by concentrating on visible themes: the political perseverance of Irish Americans, the contemporary militancy of Negroes, the relation of crime and marginality to an Irish-dominated Church in the evolution of Italo-American politics.

The notion that particular ethnic groups develop cultural values that produce significantly diverse politics in common circumstances has often been advanced.[1] So, too, critics have frequently retorted that the ethnic contribution to local political institutions and specific public policies is difficult to substantiate amid the influence of class and regional factors shaping a community's "political ethos."[2]

Aware of the ambiguity of cultural interpretation in ethnic politics, I have attempted to tie the politics of each of three ethnic groups, Jews, Irish Catholics, and Negroes, to a critical issue of American politics. The three chapters that follow relate the politics of ethnicity to three dominant matters of political discourse. In each case, there is persuasive evidence for the congruence of the major question at issue and the group under investigation. Concerns about political liberalism have been often noted in studies of Jewish political behavior in America; the legacy of clerical and social conservatism has major significance in the contemporary analysis of Irish Catholic political responses; and the problem of democratic participation, a classic concern among political scientists, is particularly pertinent to the course of the Negro revolution in America. In each case, a dominant political response is challenged by new conditions and significant changes in the American political culture. In each case, the emphasis is on the degree of political adaptation to the new course of politics and its evolving distribution of power and valuables.

CHAPTER SEVEN

Liberal Political Culture and the Jews

Probably the most significant contribution of the Jews in America, observes Nathan Glazer, has been the generations of energetic and gifted young people they have supplied to the arts, to radical politics, and to the labor movement. Many of these young people were able, in the 1920's, '30's, and '40's to find challenging and satisfying environments that were politically liberating. Thus, Jewish culture, ethnic attitudes, and values have pervaded Jewish politics in America, making it distinct. Now, the question of future stimulants to Jewish creative life, important to the future of political liberalism among American Jewry, is becoming relevant:

> One wonders about the supply of such young people in the future. . . . Will they emerge from this comfortable middle-class group? One also wonders where they will go. They certainly find little in the Jewish community of today that attracts them.[1]

Jewish political liberalism has combined a productive culture with a sense of marginality in American society. The fruitful tension between these two elements explains much of the historic Jewish presence in the American liberal coalition promoting social welfare and civil rights advancements. In part, this emphasis can be accounted for in the tenets of Judaism, as some scholars have indicated:

> Of Franklin Roosevelt it was said that he was partisan to protect and uphold the rights of the weak. He did not lead from sympathy for the weak, he spoke for their rights. Judaism knew no charitable concept which meant that generosity and goodness of soul induces men to help the weak. It knew *tsedokah,* righteousness, not charity. Righteousness means the rights of men. It was said that Roosevelt was partial to Negroes. So he was. They were the weak. . . . It was said that he sided with the oppressed people. So he did. . . . Roosevelt shared the prophets' faith in the rights of the weak.[2]

However, the religious heritage only partly accounts for the distinctiveness of Jewish cultural values in fostering a particular type of political liberalism.

SOME DISTINCTIVE ELEMENTS IN JEWISH POLITICS

The distinguishing qualities of Jewish political behavior include long-term attachments to the presidential wing of the Democratic party, a generous view of federal power as a tool in the amelioration of social ills, and an unusually wide participation in voluntary organizations and the opinion-forming networks of American public life. Jews have been found to favor distribution of economic power to lower-income groups to a significantly greater extent than other individuals in comparable financial circumstances.[3] Thus, guaranteed employment, extended welfare services for the poor in federal government and politics, and the use of federal tax funds to aid inhabitants of poorer states have been heavily supported by Jewish voters. Jews have also been found to be more internationalist and to favor a broader view of American commitments than others of similar education. Moreover, there is consistent evidence that Jews support racial integration in schools and other public facilities to a greater degree than do Gentiles in comparable economic positions.[4] The synthesis of a decade's research supports the proposition that the core of Jewish political values is the ameliorative use of federal and other governmental power to enhance the educational, social, and psychological well-being of the individual.

Jewish altruistic liberalism has led to the support of candidates committed to the expenditure of funds and other resources on ameliorative public policies. This liberalism has also been important in political reform movements based on the employment of educational and professional skills in pursuit of general (community) principles of social reconstruction:

> The reform movement in politics has already been one of those areas in city life in which people of different backgrounds, from different groups, come together not as representatives of groups, not to bargain for group rights and positions, but to work in a common task as individuals. . . . The fact that it happens in politics, where the common end is a general good, is a cause for satisfaction. This is after all the only real basis of "integration" . . . common work in which one's group characteristics are not primary and therefore of no great account.[5]

Since the early days of the New Deal, the Jewish community has been prominent in developing social services, promoting political reform, establishing the civil rights coalition, and furthering the defense of intellectual and civil liberties in American politics. An analysis of the sources of this liberal bent on the part of the Jews is revealing to the extent that it informs us about a dominant characteristic of modern political culture. In addition, the "political assimilation" of Jewish liberalism within the context of the social welfare state raises some critical questions about the future of distinctly ethnic politics.

THE SOURCES OF JEWISH POLITICAL LIBERALISM

The particularly strong impact of Jewish cultural values on modern American politics can be traced to the convergence of Jewish group qualities with structural developments in the American society. As Gerhard Lenski points out, Jewish entrepreneurial skills, especially those developed in urban, European cultures, were particularly well suited to the dynamic, capitalist economy in early twentieth-century urban America.[6] Had the American economy by then developed to its present complex organization of skilled private and public bureaucracies, the marginal capitalists of the Jewish economic tradition would have been socially redundant. By the same token, had the dynamics of the positivistic, welfare state not been present in the New Deal, the political phenomenon of Jewish liberalism would not have continued to fascinate us.

The foundation of Jewish altruistic liberalism was a strong

emphasis on personal achievement. That the Jewish subculture markedly facilitated the rise of its members in the American capitalistic system is borne out by many long-term studies of economic mobility.[7] Thus, the rapid attainment of middle-class rank by a large portion of American Jewry is notable, whether social class is measured by income, occupation, education, area of residence, or any combination of these indices. One review of Jewish demography found that every private survey of the Jewish population since the 1930's showed that Jews were most concentrated in the clerical and sales fields at first; later in the positions of managers, officials, and proprietors; and, most recently, among the professions.[8]

Many rankings of groups in American society indicate that the median income, education, and occupational attainment of Jews are higher than those of any other ethno-racial category.[9] One source of this strong Jewish motivation to achieve is the family constellation that combines incentives with mixed degrees of support and anxiety. The supportive nature of the Jewish family can be seen in Jewish concerns about well-being, mental health, and familial affection. Indeed, a major study of urban mental health found that, when compared with members of other ethnic groups, Jews most often functioned at a "mild impairment" (or anxiety) level that provided enough tension to achieve without causing major functional disorders within the individual.[10]

Obviously, the achievement propensities of American Jewry and the economic fruits that these propensities have reaped would not have supported altruistic and liberal politics were it not for other elements within the Jewish ethnic experience. The achievement of economic and social success often brings with it a lessened concern for disadvantaged groups in society. This is especially likely when a group's economic success is based upon independent effort and achievement. Jewish liberal political attitudes were formed despite the strong impact of such economic and social discrimination:

> Barred from employment advancement in many business firms dominated by Gentiles, Jews have been forced into occupations where they are not dependent on the goodwill of others. Despite these limitations Jews have been extremely successful. . . .[11]

A critical element in the liberalism of American Jewry was the organizational development of the Jewish community. Mediating between the Jewish family and the political order was a variety of social organizations that provided Jews with the opportunity to acquire political skills and produce meaningful collective responses to prejudice. Of all American ethnic groups, the Jewish community developed the broadest, yet most specialized, organizational structure . . . [including] welfare agencies, trade unions, political clubs, and fraternal associations. The critical pivot in this social development was the Jewish professional, who applied to ethnic concerns those skills and educational techniques most suited to the needs of the modern welfare state. The Jewish professional internalized modern liberal values in the use of collective resources to heal social and political ills. By achieving a position of prominence and acquiring social skills, the Jewish professional was able to shape Jewish political attitudes about the distribution of economic and social goods.[12] The organization of the Jewish community around agencies based on professional competence prevented the entrenchment of economic conservatism among Jews who had achieved a high level of social and economic affluence. Because of the strength of the organized, socially oriented professionals, the myth of the rugged, self-made individual was never part of the modern Jewish community's experience. Moreover, the combination of organizational skills and professional capabilities thus developed was devoted to the myriad of service and defense organizations that characterized the typical Jewish community.

Achievement orientation and social organization supported the socialization of Jews to contemporary American politics, but those factors do not account for the emphasis Jewish cultural values have led Jews to place on the reduction of discrimination and deprivation among deprived people. Fuchs accounts for the unique Jewish view of discrimination by citing the reinforcement that Jewish values received from social and economic discrimination directed against Jews:

> Although discrimination against Jews was a factor in the development of [liberal] cultural consciousness, it was not the prime factor. The primary twin elements of such consciousness are emotional nationalism (Zionism) and humanitarian socialism. The sensitivity to discrimination among Jewish youth is increased because of the image of a just society which is at the back of their minds.[13]

The importance of social discrimination in accounting for the liberal response of Jews to party and policy choices is reiterated by Seymour M. Lipset:

> The fact that the Jews, who are one of the wealthiest religious groups in America, are shown by survey data to be most Democratic is probably due . . . to their sensitivity to

> ethnic discrimination and their lack of effective social intercourse with the upper-status groups in America.[14]

Nevertheless, feelings of discrimination and estrangement do not necessarily encourage the support of political policies designed to benefit other groups and deprived individuals. Rather, such feelings are likely to encourage indifference to the plight suffered by less fortunate people. That this did not occur with the American Jews, can possibly be attributed to certain evidence that it is a particular attitude toward ethnicity, rather than feelings of discrimination, that supports Jewish liberalism.[15]

In accounting for the relation between his own ethnic situation and the situations of others, an individual may either draw on the cultural values of his group, designed in part to compensate for discrimination, or he may emphasize his feelings of rejection because of his insecure ethnic status. A sense of ethnic involvement or identification does not by itself provide an adequate basis for the strong political influence of ethnic factors. Merely to say that an individual is ethnically involved fails to indicate the extent to which he feels that his ethnic membership relegates him to a subordinate position within the American society. For instance, two Jewish Americans may be highly involved in their ethnic subculture, but one of them may feel that he occupies an inferior social status because of his ethnic affiliation, while the other may not even relate his ethnicity to social status. In fact, Jews who feel subordinate because of their ethnicity are significantly less active in politics and feel less politically effective than Jews who do not feel socially and psychologically subordinate. Moreover, feelings of subordination lead directly to the weakening of cultural liberalism. Thus, Jews who do feel socially and psychologically subordinate because of their ethnic affiliation are the least likely to be tolerant of political nonconformists and are least altruistic toward other ethnic groups.

The closeness of an individual to his ethnic group does not, per se, appear to be a potent factor in accounting for ethnic political behavior in general or for Jewish liberalism in particular. A high degree of ethnic involvement may sensitize one to political phenomena but it does not predispose him to react to most of these phenomena in any specific manner. Indeed, ethnically determined political responses are most directly based upon the individual's perception of the social climate in which his ethnic culture is located. A climate that is not seen as hopelessly discriminatory aids the development of altruistic group values that can help overcome the external situation. On the other hand, feelings of social subordination based upon perceptions of ethnic discrimination and hostilities weaken the individual's sense of control over his environment, and this, in turn, diminishes his sense of participation in the affairs of the remote and overpowering world "outside." Feelings of minority status reduce both the sense of effectiveness in external political affairs and the amount of political activity engaged in on behalf of others. It is only when ethnic identification is based on positive self and group qualities, and when these are supported by the ethnic community, that ethnicity supports liberal attitudes.

However, if the source of political effectiveness is diminished, altruistic and liberal political attitudes toward other groups will be lacking. If ethnicity is viewed as a source of personal deprivation rather than as a cultural strength, illiberal or nonliberal politics results. The mental ghetto called "ethnic subordination" diminishes feelings of political tolerance and altruism precisely because the sense of social deprivation negates the basis of personal security from which tolerance and altruism often flow. In fact, concern about ethnic discrimination per se increases fears about making the ethnic group appear politically conspicuous (let alone politically liberal) in a potentially hostile environment.

An individual's personal view of his ethnic situation, whether he focuses on group values or subordinate status, is closely tied to the way an ethnic group responds in the political arena. It was not discrimination or the absence of social intercourse with dominant Gentile civic and economic groups that bolstered Jewish liberalism. Rather, the critically supportive element was the Jewish subculture, with its variety of ameliorative institutions, which mitigated resentment at past discriminations.

Paradoxically, the marginality of Jewry to dominant American social and economic institutions created a vacuum that was effectively filled by Jewish communal organizations, which inserted altruistic and welfare-enhancing political attitudes within the Jewish community. The Jewish community's social structure focused much of the individual's sense of ethnic subordination in collective agencies that dealt with problems of discrimination and prejudice. Moreover, the Jewish community and social service agencies functioned like a "welfare state in miniature" by supporting liberal policies that led Jews to the social and economic liberalism of modern federal policies. Unlike most other ethnics, the Jew had a collective, organizational identity that assuaged his personal resentment toward ethnic subordination and provided him with constructive ethno-religious values based on social responsibility toward disadvantaged members of American society. Such collective beliefs supported the Jew's inclination to express feelings about his own experiences with prejudice in altruistic terms:

> A Jew personally is never liked by nobody. He is liked on the outside. But that is as far as it goes. The Jew is hated all over, all over the world in fact. That is why I am for giving the Negro better things in this city and country. You see, the Jew is liberal because it kills the poison of hate from him. . . . He is liberal because when you know that you are doing good for other people, you don't feel the hate so badly.[16]

THE FUTURE OF JEWISH LIBERALISM: ABSORPTION, ADAPTION, ANTAGONISM

The Jewish political style has usually combined pragmatic awareness with a sensitivity to the injustices suffered by others. The activities of Jewish organizations in the defense of intellectual freedom, the promotion of the civil rights movement, the protection of free speech, and the enhancement of justice are cases in point. However, the distinctiveness of Jewish political liberalism is currently challenged by developments stemming from the currents of political change.

Jewish political liberalism is now part of more widely held attitudes about the purposes of governmental activities in an advanced, secular society. Consider the parallels between Jewish political style and the premises of the modern welfare state:[17]

1. (a) The politics of the welfare state rests on the premise that there is an economic surplus, continually replenished in a productive society.
   (b) The expectations of a liberal, affluent polity are initially supported in the permissive and achievement-oriented Jewish family structure. In the same vein, the achievement of middle-class and professional status by an affluent Jewish community blends in with the development of welfare liberalism in the larger society.
2. (a) The complicated politics and administration of the contemporary welfare state requires the intensive and continuing use of scientific knowledge and advanced education in order to make possible rational public choices.
   (b) The emphasis of the Jewish community and its acquired value system is supportive in this regard. The broadening respect for "policy intellectuals" in the American culture has been anticipated by the traditionally strong Jewish emphasis on education and learning. The love of learning is a basic tenet of Juda-

ism; the cultivated tradition of German Jewry and the position enjoyed by Talmudic scholars in the Orthodox Jewish communities provide historical evidence of this passion for education, which has also often been documented in Jewish intellectual performance, rising admission rates to the best American colleges and universities, and the high accord paid the intellectuals by the Jews.[18]

3. (a) Welfare state politics and administration are seen as resulting from the application of skills to the progressive amelioration of social ills using all available resources.

   (b) An ameliorative society is also a well-educated, charitable, and pleasure-seeking society. The nonasceticism of American Jewry is attested to by the Jewish contribution to the de-Puritanizing of America. The special place of the Jews in Hollywood, in the legitimate theater, and in fashion testifies to the strong sensual element among the sect. An expansive, humanitarian culture is willing to provide resources for the eradication of social deprivation. In this sense, welfare politics is seen as an extension of Jewish cultural values insofar as power is used to heal society's ills and to expand the distribution of power and affluence.[19]

Although none of these welfare-supporting attitudes has ever been limited to the Jewish community, it is clear that they have been disproportionately supported by Jewish cultural values. The cosmopolitan thrust of American politics, with its recent emphasis on amelioration, social and professional skills, and cultural progress has tended to erode the distinctiveness of Jewish political behavior, however. This distinctiveness was greater before the qualities of political modernity were so widely distributed on the American social scene.[20] Thus, in support for civil liberties and racial integration, college education has become more critical than specific ethnic affiliation.

At the same time, the American Jewish community and its professional organizational structure may have lost some of the creative tension that formerly marked its relations with the larger society. The absorption of Jewish cultural values by the larger society may parallel the decline of these values within the Jewish community itself. What will the Jewish "defense" groups defend in the absence of religious and racial discrimination? What will promote the social consciousness of Jewish communities now that secularization has become so extensive and federal welfare policies so pervasive? The analysis of the "gilded ghetto," the home of prosperous, secure, middle-class Jewry, raises disturbing questions about future sources of the empathy that has so long produced concern about racial and religious discrimination.[21] The tendency, understandable among a group so long aware of discrimination, is to enjoy the fruits of affluence and to leave social problems to the government and its policy experts.[21]

Yet, society's absorption of Jewish political liberalism does not *necessarily* negate the Jewish cultural tradition. In American politics, the better-off groups of every ethnic composition have usually—and possibly uniquely—supported liberal and innovative policies designed to improve the distribution of social justice.

Another factor in the withering away of Jewish liberal responses is found in the failure of organizations and institutions, that in the past successfully fought injustice, to adapt to new challenges:

> When Jews were poor, it seemed reasonable that they should try to become rich; as they emerged from poverty, it seemed desirable that they should remain liberal and sympathetic to the needs of those who were still poor and deprived and those who came after them. But a hard look at the Jewish situation today reveals a number of disturbing elements. . . .
>
> Jewish liberalism, which is sound enough perhaps from the perspective of an American nation that is still in many ways remarkably conservative and bound to old slogans, is, in the context of New York, not quite as sound as it should be. There is much self-congratulation on the struggles and successes of the past. Jewish socialists and intellectuals played a great and important role in the building up of the labor movement in the 1930's, but they seem to have been struck dumb by the problems created for the city by the rise of a new proletariat of Negroes and Puerto Ricans. . . . One must acknowledge that the great tradition of social reform and social engineering that was identified with the Jewish labor unions and the Jewish labor movement in the city seems to have been unable to make any serious impact on the problem.[22]

One reason for this apparent inability to adapt is that Jewish professional organizations have their greatest stake in terms of influence and prestige in precisely those areas of education and social service where the Negro revolution has made its most intensive demands. Moreover, the professional skills of the Jewish agencies and their rapport with middle-class groups make it difficult for them to adopt new techniques. The essence of professional skill lies in the assumption of a rational social order amenable to change and reformation. Thus, attacks by Negro groups on "white liberal" control, often Jewish, in civil rights organizations, educational institutions, and certain trade unions are in large measure attacks on established middle-class institutions constructed under different circumstances. The inability of these institutions to adapt to the conditions is based partly on the vested interests developed by every successful enterprise. For this reason, *inter alia,* the largely Jewish United Federation of Teachers resisted autonomous black control of the Ocean Hill-Brownsville district of the New York City school system.

The difficulty of reconciling the power position and integrationist goals of Jewish community organizations has led to increasing frictions in Jewish-Negro relationships. The latter, recognizing the organizational skills and liberal tradition possessed by Jewish groups, have consistently demanded more from Jewish trade unions, educational institutions, and political agencies than from other ethnic entities, whose members and leaders are historically less sympathetic to Negro demands. In addition, Jewish-derived agencies and their professionals are most adept at dealing with the *individual* educational and status problems of middle-class Negroes attempting to use education and other social valuables as means to further achievement.

However, from the view of lower-income Negroes and Negro leaders making broad racial claims on the system, the array of Jewish-led commercial, charitable, and social service institutions is not symbolic of either aspirations or benevolent white liberal agencies. Rather, these institutions sorely indicate that in the areas of education, health, and economic valuables, Negroes are denied power by the affluent and organized Jewish community. The problem facing Jewish welfare agencies in coping with militant Negro demands is that the demands are not easily met within the existing structure of the Jewish welfare establishment. First, any organization is more adept at dealing with individual claims for resources than it is at coping with mass claims organized around racial solidarity. Second, the relationship between professional and client learned in the Jewish welfare experience makes it difficult to adopt the notion that it is the "clients" who will determine the scope of their claims and the political adjustments required to obtain them. Herein, the expertise, goodwill, and power position of policy and service experts is profoundly challenged.

Despite their liberal rhetoric, Jewish organizations and liberal Jewish professionals often find themselves involved in superordinate-subordinate relationships with Negro mass-action groups. This power relationship, and the challenge made to it by

"Black Power" demands, provides a most severe test of the legacy of Jewish liberalism. The essence of that attitudinal set herein called Jewish liberalism was in the relationship of a group to an individual or in intergroup relationships. Jewish liberalism, and the cultural value system sustaining it, were never prepared to cope with collective demands made upon social institutions run by or largely influenced by Jewish professionals. Nevertheless, the new federal presence, the role of Jewish community institutions, and the problem of evolving social techniques to handle collective ethnic demands do not fully explain the schism between the Jewish liberal tradition and the new drive for social and political equality. Indeed, the progressive and ameliorative core of Jewish liberalism had led to positive expectations about the consequences of ameliorative policies:

> The ultimate irony in American race relations may yet be that the bitter insistence of the Negro revolt will have provided the initial impetus for basic social and economic change for all Americans. Having gone beyond morality to power in order to achieve its aims, "the movement" may have begun to create a society in which morality will be the normative principle in action.[23]

This is an outcome strongly supported by the Jewish tradition of cultural liberalism. Sporadic anti-Semitism among Negroes and other minority groups and the economic presence of Jewish shopkeepers in Negro neighborhoods are only minor aspects of the problem. The core problem is that what is looked upon as legitimate militancy by some Negroes is seen as intolerance, nihilism, and extremism among some legatees of the Jewish cultural tradition, which has emphasized civil peace and political negotiation. Questions of power relations between ethnic groups have never been solely quantitative matters. They have always involved a qualitative component that defines in subtle ways the mutual expectations about how ethnic power and recognition is to be sought and brought to public attention.

The very achievements and "liberal" values of the Jewish community and its political tradition make the resolution of this core problem particularly vexing. Ethnic group interrelations are usually most antagonistic when there is widespread competition for social and economic valuables among the members of the groups. In general, the incidence of such overt competition between Jews and Negroes in the United States has not been extensive. Perhaps, this is partially due to the fact that, somewhat paradoxically, overt competition between ethnic groups is sometimes more amenable to political negotiation than are basic value differences. The recognition strategy of "classical" American ethnic politics was a serious attempt to resolve or to mitigate group differences on a pragmatic level. However, the crisis of Jewish liberalism in response to current Negro demands is more a matter of basic cultural, e.g., nonmaterial, values.

The chief and probably decisive question of ethnic politics in this context becomes that of political conditions, the conditions of power in which group identity is held. How dominant or how dominated is the group to which the individual belongs, and how, therefore, is he able to bear himself in his relations with others? This is probably the cardinal question, and it is essentially a question of politics or power. The central crises of identity and achievement marking the emergence of lower class Negroes from long-term positions of subordination increase the salience of questions about their group identity and its consequences for political behavior toward other groups. Thus, the core cultural values of Jewish liberalism, and beyond that of the politically cosmopolitan groups in American society itself, become *the* central issues in the chorus of demands made by less well-off, militant Negroes.

The Jewish response to militancy, anger, and rejection of previous support is in one aspect similar to a general white liberal response: "After all we have done for you, you reject our goodwill and our traditional institutions."[24] Reflecting the strain of a vastly different social and economic situation, the identity stage of Negro protests does not call forth many positive responses from Jewish liberals. After all, the Jews contend, earlier Jewish "nationalistic" behavior, primarily Zionist and radical socialist, never resulted in the *physical* use of power to make claims against dominant American institutions. Verbal revolutionary activity in the form of Marxist dialectics and polemics is one thing; overt behavior that seems to physically threaten the existing political order is another.

Amelioration means gradual change, hopefully leading to eventual progress. It means faith in the ability of the extant system to gradually improve things. The application of urban and professional skill is persistently tied to the core of the Jewish tradition of liberal politics. The rejection, or at least the questioning, of this core represents the major problem facing Jewish liberalism. In fact, the major demand, at times the only one, made by altruistic liberalism is that those it aids must reciprocate by embracing those values and behavioral norms deemed central by the altruistic group. Finding a creative response to a new situation in which Black Power and a partial redefining of politics and values are at issue taxes the resourcefulness of the Jewish liberal tradition. The vast differences between the Negroes and the Jews on such matters as tolerance of heterodox opinions, contextual versus emotional responses to political issues, civil liberties, a bargaining style versus a mass style of political adjudication, and support of core political institutions are not likely to be easily overcome, but they must be overcome if political moderation is to be achieved or maintained.

In the past, Jewish political liberalism has been devoted to efforts that enlarged the integrated sphere of opportunity for Negroes. Funds donated by Jews to civil rights causes, emotional support of racial integration, and the cultivation of attitudes supporting the dignity and self-esteem of the black man were predicated on a notion of a generous and civilized society. The symbols used by Jewish liberals in civil rights activities were largely based on their own norms acquired in professional, middle-class white society. Mass movements designed to sharply alter the distribution of power and the control of major institutions were never part of Jewish liberalism. Nor were styles of political behavior emphasizing violence, mass action, and authoritarianism. Jewish liberalism has been grounded in the enlightenment of the progressive, secular state since the French Revolution and the Age of the Enlightenment. The Jews became part of the American establishment because of the relatively gradual acquisition of skills and status. Negro political claims formed in this position, however, are deeply colored by notions of prior deprivation and powerlessness. Many Negroes see no future in following the Jewish path to power and status. Thus, political and social reciprocity has not been forthcoming in many aspects of contemporary black militancy, and this is important in understanding the limits of future Jewish-Negro cooperation. Jewish liberalism promoted the concept of the "inclusive society" insofar as race and religion were concerned. Now it must cope with the political questions of how Negro claims are to be made and secured, not simply with questions of the creation of more opportunity to enjoy legal and social rights. It remains to be seen whether Jewish liberalism and Jewish liberals can tolerate resentment and cultural rejection from a mass movement, black or white, and whether the liberal style will continue as a creative and psychologically congruent Jewish response to discriminatory experiences. It is clear that the Jewish community can no longer play the major role it assumed during the integration phase of the Negro revolution. Yet, there is the hope that another aspect of the Jewish legacy, namely, the skills in mediation and persuasion, will enable it to play a constructive role in working out the vast cultural and political differences between the ghetto Negro and the middle-class white. The next decade will determine whether or not the Jews will be able to act as brokers among competing political and cultural values within a modern society, as the Irish did during the immigrant period.

CHAPTER EIGHT

Irish Catholics: The Politics of Adjustment

Various Irish Catholics have functioned as radicals, machine politicians, and reform-minded chief executives, respectively, within American politics. Therefore, to speak of *the* Irish adjustment to American politics is to select certain key problems within the changing Irish Catholic community. Although the Irish were often the natural political brokers of urban politics, there has always been a sharp division between the forces shaping their political behavior and the liberal, secular assumptions that underlie the modern period of American national politics. The heart of Irish Catholic uniqueness in American political life stems from the interplay of family, church, and communal values designed to defend group integrity. In the era of Know-Nothing fundamentalism and nativist bigotry, the devout Catholics were subjected to pervasive discrimination because of the "alien" nature of their faith. The result of these discriminatory experiences was a tenacious clinging to available opportunities in social and political life and, more recently, in the American corporate structure. It was this tenacity, coupled with the resultant problems in adapting to the noneconomic dimensions of liberalism within the modern state, that determined the major characteristics of Irish Catholic political behavior.

PATTERNS OF POLITICAL LEARNING

The two most important facets of this behavior have been sustained Democratic partisanship and strong opposition to many noneconomic "liberal" policies, even though these policies have often been products of the Democratic party's liberal coalition. Party identification is one of the most enduring features of political life for most groups. In fact, only under the most dramatic conditions will a mass shift in party identification take place. With the important exceptions of the Eisenhower triumphs in 1952 and 1956, American Irish Catholics have overwhelmingly supported the Democratic party.[1] The impact of the Korean conflict combined with relaxed enjoyment of post-World War II affluence to cause many Irish Democrats to vote for General Eisenhower.

The persistence of Irish Catholic partisanship has impressed political analysts. For example, despite Republican dominance in most suburban areas, Catholics, particularly those of Irish descent, have been found to retain their Democratic partisanship when moving from the central city. In short, partisanship has been "transplanted" in spite of the social transition.[2] The combination of clerical and communal solidarity further sustained Democratic identification among Irish American Catholics, even when the party was advancing "liberal" policies that were anathema to many of the faithful:

> The main effect of the New Deal in the upper reaches of the Irish community in New York was to reveal to its members that while they had been rising socially and economically, the Democratic party as a whole remained an organization of the masses. It rarely occurred to the Irish to stop being Democrats because they had become bankers, or whatever. The party was an ethnic and religious alliance, as much as an economic one. . . . Irish businessmen hated Roosevelt much as did other businessmen, but with the special twist that they felt it was their own political party, overcome by alien influences, that was causing the trouble.[3]

The cohesive psychology of ethnicity has also played an important role in sustaining political loyalties, as evidenced by the finding that Catholics are particularly likely to perceive, and vote for, a co-ethnic on the ballot.[4] Moreover, the relations among the family, the Church, and the Catholic community have produced a particularly intense investment in partisanship and in the established ways of conducting politics. Each has contributed to Irish political partisanship. The Irish stake in urban politics produced a general inability to respond to noneconomic issues requiring broad political perspectives and led to intense ethnic political conflicts when other groups in turn pressed their demands for political benefits and recognition. Ironically, this ethnic resentment often involved Catholic co-religionists. Thus, to establish their own place in politics, Italo-Americans in New York and New England and Poles and Czechs in Cleveland and Chicago had to overcome the tenacious Irish American hold on the Democratic party.[5]

The adaptation of peasant-derived groups to urban circumstances has had a causal relationship to both broad political and noneconomic inflexibility. Organized about the mutual personal obligations of family and clan, recognizing the need for a party hierarchy in order to make practical decisions, yet hardened against appeals of urban reformers, the Irish Catholics clung to party positions. In New Haven, half the wards were electing Irish aldermen by 1880, and beginning with 1899, every Democratic mayor was of Irish persuasion. In 1959, 29 per cent of the major political offices remained in the hands of Irish descendants, although the Irish share of the population had shrunk to only 11 per cent. Between 1910 and 1957, the Irish percentage of Democratic party ward committeeships in Providence, Rhode Island, decreased from 70 to 50, yet the Irish were still a primary factor in the politics of that area. The Irish controlled the Democratic party of Chicago in the 1880's when the city's population was only about 20 per cent Irish. By 1962, the Irish comprised only 10 per cent of the total population, yet under Irish Mayor Daley, they still clung tenaciously to their Democratic party power base. In fact, 32 of the 73 Assistant State Attorneys (most of them from Cook County, where Chicago is located), 12 of the 50 Chicago aldermen, and 21 of the 50 Democratic committeemen in Chicago were of Irish extraction at that time.

The consequences of this long relationship between the Irish and the party machine have been a singular emphasis on the politics of organizational solidarity and a collective conservatism in responding to new ideas. Irish politicians acquired an inability to conceive of politics as anything other than the distribution of welfare benefits based on prior personal and group loyalties. Nor could the Irish- and Italian-led organizations of major American cities often conceive of collective benefits as a new basis for making decisions in the public interest. Indeed, a collective, public political style was poorly and slowly learned by all major Catholic ethnic groups. In Chicago, for example, a study showed that while low-income renters voted more favorably for broad-based public expenditures (such as parks, a county hospital, a courthouse) than did middle-income homeowners of the same ethnic group,[6] within the same economic class ethnicity made a striking difference in support for particular projects. Thus, low-income Negro renters were much more enthusiastic than low-income Polish or Irish renters about broad community public expenditures, and middle-income Negro homeowners were more enthusiastic about the same proposals than were middle-income Polish or Irish homeowners. Despite the fact that they are commonly the chief victims of land clearance programs, Negroes were two or three times more favorably disposed toward urban renewal than were comparable Polish and Irish voters.

How much these values have been a consequence of ethnicity (for instance, the result of early Irish American socialization to America), and how much of religion remains a matter of scholarly debate. Nevertheless, in those states where ethnicity has been politically influential, Catholics have usually opposed party reform and urban renewal; moreover, their religion has led to conservative positions about such issues as dissemination of birth control information and reformed divorce laws.[7] It must be noted, however, that the politics learned in ethnic tribal enclaves has more recently been increasingly ineffective against the onslaughts of high-powered reform groups using the skills of modern education and communication.

In general, though, the traditional political style of many urban Irish Catholics ran counter to the course of modern politics in many policy areas. First, the experiences of immigration produced a set of clerical and communal norms that tended to oppose the general drift of American liberalism after the early period of the New Deal. When political "reform" currents ran through major American cities between 1945 and 1960, many Irish American politicians found themselves defending their hard-won positions within the urban party machine. When American foreign policy elites appeared friendly with Soviet Russia and other communist countries during and after World War II, prevailing Irish Catholic opinion was dismayed, and the "softness toward communism" issue was effectively used by Senator Joseph McCarthy and others among urban Irish Catholic populations. When a renewed emphasis on intellectual and economic achievement led to a thaw in the Cold War posture of the Eisenhower-Dulles years, most Irish Catholics continued to stress bipolar Russian-American antagonisms and to believe that American communists represented a major domestic threat. It was probably only the ascendance of a co-ethnic, John F. Kennedy, to the presidency that tempered strong Catholic feelings about the need to act tough with communists wherever they appear. When the problems of modern urban life and the American Negro called for novel responses, Irish Catholic politicians, with notable exceptions, continued to act on the premises of the accommodation model they had learned in the wards and precincts of immigrant politics.

Those acquired experiences produced a rigid style of coping with public affairs beyond the practical realities of the urban machine. One consequence is reflected in Irish attitudes toward civil liberties, especially where the freedom of speech and press of communists, fascists, and other political groups who desire to destroy the traditional structures of American society is concerned. Part of this Irish Catholic conservatism stems from the threat of communist tenets to the teachings and power of the Church. Some of the coolness toward civil liberties can also be traced to the status anxieties of an ethnic group which has proved its Americanism by stoutly affirming orthodox civil creeds. A still more compelling source of Catholic opposition to political heterodoxy is found in the slowness with which middle-class Irish Catholics have accepted the norms of civil diversity, norms that have been most strongly espoused by the educated and affluent middle classes. To cite a typical finding, in 1961 middle-class white Protestants were from one quarter to one third more likely than middle-class white Catholics to adopt a liberal position on civil liberties, and the difference in views was most apparent among the college-educated members of the sample.[8]

Moreover, Irish Catholic conservatism in the area of civil liberties can be traced directly to a religious orientation stressing rigid doctrinal orthodoxy. These religious preferences seem to have had a direct correlation with low support of civil liberties, although this may change, as the sway of orthodoxy is now under attack within the Church. Heretofore, however, there has been much evidence that freedom of speech, freedom of the press, the right to a fair trial, and other fundamentals of political democracy not fully supported in the United States, despite the fact that they are embodied in a written Constitution that is taught in every secondary school and despite the general acceptance of "democracy" and "freedom" as essential characteristics of American society, have not had the full backing of religiously orthodox ethnic groups such as the Irish Catholics. This lack of support for libertarian ideas can be attributed to persons of an authoritarian personality. In other words, those adhering to a doctrinal orthodoxy have exhibited a restrictive life view.

Thus, the theological tenets of fundamental Catholicism (especially among its Irish immigrant adherents), and fundamental Protestantism as well, have impeded support of political heterodoxy in America. It is probably for this reason that consistent church attendance among Catholics has been strongly and negatively correlated with support of civil liberties. That this connection between religious doctrinal orthodoxy and political orthodoxy is both real and significant is also supported by findings that the mean scale of political dogmatism is highest for Protestants and Irish Catholics and lowest for Jews and those who express no religious affiliation. In other words, religious orthodoxy has had a major influence on the political views of Irish Catholic—and certain other—opinion leaders.

THE CRITICAL TRIAD: FAMILY, CHURCH, COMMUNITY

The persistent opposition to civil liberties characteristic of the traditional American Catholic community is fostered by the group values defended by family structure, clerical orthodoxy, and the Catholic subcommunity itself.

The particular heritage of the Irish immigrant family, which led to a greater emphasis upon values of security and affection and a lesser stressing of independence and personal achievement, has left its mark on the social mobility of the American Irish Catholic. Most studies indicate that Irish Catholics have not advanced over time on socioeconomic indices. What is more, there is a strong tendency for Irish Catholics to select as their employers those corporate and governmental bureaucracies in which career lines are predicated on gradual and orderly personal advancement.[9]

There is strong evidence that white Protestants are more upwardly mobile than are Catholics. When white Protestants were compared with Catholics who began life at the same point in the social class system, it was found that the former rose to (or stayed in) the ranks of the upper-middle class more often than did the latter. At the opposite extreme, Catholics wound up in the lower half of the working class three times more often than did Protestants. Furthermore, increased Americanization and urbanization appear to increase rather than reduce differences between these two major socio-religious groups. There is also significant evidence to indicate that an even more striking and important difference exists between white Protestants and Catholics of similar social positions in their attitudes toward work. Among white Protestants, positive attitudes toward work were more frequent among men holding more responsible positions than among men in less responsible positions. As Lenski summarizes the evidence:

> It appears that Protestantism is conducive to more positive attitudes toward those positions in society which are more demanding (and also more rewarding) while Catholicism is conducive to more positive attitudes toward the less demanding (and hence less rewarding) positions.[10]

The consequences of family "pull" on achievement orientation among American Irish Catholics have often been noted:

> There may be some kind of lower-middle or lower-class orientation among them to anchor Catholics in the lower socioeconomic groups and which limits those who do achieve higher education to certain fields which appear to offer more security albeit less prestige and income. . . . It seems that Catholics creep forward rather than stride forward in American society, and the position of American Catholics in the mid-twentieth century is better, but not so much better, than it was a century ago. Neither is it as high as one might expect from such a sizeable minority with a large educational system and reputed equality of opportunity in a democracy.[11]

The combination of cultural values that offer an alternative to work and the structure of Irish Catholic family life underlies these findings. Family choices are the major deterrent to high work achievement, and there is much to support the notion that the extended Irish family has enhanced this tendency to play down the importance of personal responsibility and achievement. Strong family ties combined with the concept of extended kin loyalty to reduce significantly the potentialities for personal achievement in a mobile society. Moreover, in local politics, the civil service, and the trade union movement, where early Irish Catholic occupational successes were recorded, the demands of work were less intense than they are in careers pursued in contemporary large-scale institutions. In fact, the Irish Catholic immigrant group "chose" those pursuits least likely to be at the core of a modern political economy. Moreover, the reconciliation of work and family demands was easiest within the confines of the political clubhouse, the union fraternity, and the service-oriented occupations.

Hence, the "bureaucratization" of American family life in compliance with the national demands of corporations and government undoubtedly placed a major strain on the Catholic family structure, a strain that probably contributed to the salience status politics held for Catholics during the McCarthy era and the major role Catholics played in the anticommunist movements wherein "traditional" family values stressing nationalism and religiosity were vigorously defended. The long-term effect of this "bureaucratization" on the Irish Catholic family structure, however, has been to adjust political and social attitudes to the prevailing norms set by the major institutions in the American political economy.[12]

The second unique influence on Irish Catholic political attitudes has been that of the Church. The propensity to "defend the faith" in a predominantly Protestant and constitutionally secular society undoubtedly retarded Catholic socialization to middle-class norms supporting tolerance of heterodox thought. In view of the fact that these norms often included some freedom to attack both religion and the support of civil rights for "Godless" communists, the clerical impact on the civic attitudes of the laity is understandable. Moreover, the emphasis on doctrinal orthodoxy and strong hierarchical control in traditional Catholic structures slowed the learning of norms promoting the toleration of political heterodoxy. These defensive efforts of the Church were most apparent when the civil liberties of American communists were at issue, but they have also influenced Catholic political attitudes on such issues as "American foreign aid to nations who are not as much against communism as we"; those Catholics with strong group identification most strongly opposed aid to neutralist countries.[13]

Commenting on the political outlooks of predominantly Irish Catholic men in an Eastern city (this may not be true in other parts of the nation), Lane notes that most "have cast off their peasant metaphysics and robed themselves in the pragmatics of an urban democracy."[14] The metaphysics of the Catholic Church are not much in evidence in political studies, nor do studies of Catholic education often find that attachment to democratic principles is weakened by the exercise of clerical influence. The main influence of the Catholic Church, however, probably lies neither in the production of authoritarian attitudes nor in the exercise of political influence. The Church's principal influence is in the cognitive structuring of political thought as a process based on deduction from logic, tempered by only modest exposure to conflicting empirical evidence. A tendency toward dogmatism or close-mindedness must already exist within the personality structure, but its growth is certainly fostered by the example of formalistic reasoning toward knowledge by an unquestioned, authoritative source. It is only in the realm of political knowledge that "adversary thinking" toward nonconformists manifests itself. However, many Irish Catholic intellectuals are beginning to dedicate their efforts to the elimination of such cognitive rigidity and its political consequences:

> The great Protestant and secular thinkers of America are not just men who made mistakes like the "adversaries" of the scholastic manual. They have positive things to say to those American Catholics who have neglected the search itself. The partial segregation of Catholic life from that of the general community adds difficulty in that respect, but further defensiveness concealed under lethargic self-satisfaction is hardly an adequate response to the situation.[15]
>
> There is one state of mind, fairly common, that is confident in the possession of the ultimate answers to life's mysteries and does not see the need of seeking anxiously for the proximate answers also. There is another state of mind, also common enough, which is convinced that God saved the world without science; therefore prayers, sacrament, and sacrifice are the things to be concerned about.[16]

The impact of the clergy on the political opinions of co-religionists is not all inclusive, however. Three major factors tend to reduce it. First, the major accomplishment of the Irish American Church early in this century was to accommodate other distinct nationality groups professing the Catholic faith. One of the costs of that enterprise was that it strengthened autonomous ethnic associations. Thereafter, the Church tended to limit its political dictates to the "faith and morals" domain. Although previously a major accommodating institution to a complex, secular polity, the Church soon found that it lacked relevance to the new experiences confronting the faithful in the industrial order. From then on, even the most devout Irish Catholic had to seek political guidance outside the parish or the Holy Name Society. The basic strategy for preserving the Church's secular and spiritual strength in a new environment made it an even less important reference on many political issues. The reason for this was that in large measure, the prevailing theology of the Catholic Church had been shaped in a precapitalistic feudal and aristocratic society; it had drawn very little upon its few large-scale experiences with socialism and capitalism. Thus, the successful accommodation to life in America increased the social diversity among American Catholics while reducing the potential for religious influence on large segments of Catholic political behavior.

Second, the lessening of direct Church political influence can be at least partially attributed to the diminishing importance of those issues in which religion was a ready political referent. The ascension of the Catholic Church to a prosperous position occurred at the same time as the intensification of the Cold War during the 1950's. In this regard, it must be remembered that beyond experiences with anti-Catholicism, it was the disagreement of the Church with national policies toward communist nations that sustained the partial political apartheid among American Irish Catholics. In fact, the dominance of the conservative elements within the clergy was further sustained by the seriousness of external and internal communist threats. In retrospect, it can be seen that McCarthyism gave a new lease on life and power to the politically and religiously fundamentalist wing of the Church. An authoritative Church is politically relevant when it can attach its doctrine to sweeping ideological issues of major moral import. The decline of "communism in government" also eroded the immigrant-based influence of the old-line Irish clerics.

A third factor involved in reducing the political impact of the Church is the fact that fundamental doctrinal and organizational changes have been undertaken by younger and more progressive Irish Church leaders. These social adaptations have followed the professionalization of the clergy and the increased specialization within the Church itself. Although the common notion of Church "hierarchy" as a structural entity extending from the parish priest to the Cardinal and the Pope was never completely based in fact, traditional Church authority placed little reliance on specialized experience. The process of adapting to American and European society, however, forced the Church to make extensive use of intellectuals and specialized professionals. Demands for more autonomy and social involvement among younger clerics required the Church to adopt new organizational techniques, such as the cooperatively administered urban parish in the hands of several socially involved clerics. Hereafter, purely theological learning would no longer suffice in the seminaries, nor would the practical methods of bishops raised in working-class neighborhoods. Thus, specialization and professionalization provided increased independence for Irish Catholic clerical intellectuals in their relations with both conservative parishioners and "traditionalist" clerical authorities.

Recent organizational and social adaptations within the Church have pregnant consequences because they affect relations within each parish and diocese. The potential costs of organizational change are great, in that the support of parishioners, so vital to the organizational stability of the urban diocese, can be lost if the modification process is badly handled. The importance of these urban dioceses would not be as significant if the Church's relationship to the urban center were not significant. The modern adaptations among the clergy, often spearheaded by socially conscious young clerics, are particularly important when related to the otherwise fragmented or tangential positions of other urban institutions. Even after deflating exaggerated statements about the Church's hierarchial power, it is nevertheless true that few local institutions can match the vigor of the Church when it decides to invest its resources and energies in a social issue. Urban government, for example, is almost always fragmented government lacking executive control over most political and economic resources.

Moreover, the Church has the leadership and the resources to sustain a social policy once it has been initiated. An ironic characteristic of most urban politics is that the most powerful institutions are of, but not socially in, the local community. Thus, a nationally oriented university, a farsighted foundation, or a socially conscious corporation may initiate social reforms, but all lack the local political base to sustain their efforts. The Church, on the other hand, has long experience in diocese and parish organizations that deal directly with ethnic groups and formal city government. In addition, organizational change within the Church has been enhanced by conciliar reform and the ecumenical progress of the modern Church.

The future is not without pitfalls, however; changes in society and among parishioners have created a crisis within the Church. It will require a long-term undertaking to heal current schisms over such issues as birth control and Church authority. The essential ingredient for this long-term effort is skilled and dedicated leadership. Here again, the Church has a distinct advantage over other major institutions endeavoring to deal directly and consistently with the problems of the cities. The extent to which a leadership corps will use its energies in a particular area depends on the dominant norms of accepted leadership behavior. (While a businessman maximizes profits and a politician enhances his stockpile of political influence, the clergy normally emphasizes the pursuit of spiritual values.) A number of fortunate circumstances have coincided to translate clerical objectives into concerted social action designed to deal with urban problems. First, the Church is now secure and affluent; it possesses sufficient surplus social capital to invest in problem areas. Second, as previously noted, the Church often finds itself in a political vacuum as one of the few institutions with the goodwill and strength necessary to hammer out more or less satisfactory bargains signifying social change in the cities. Third, the timing of the Church's new role enables it to draw on a continuous supply of leadership emerging from the seminaries, for it is in the current seminary training that one finds the zenith of a new social consciousness in the aftermath of ecumenical reform. The "new theology" and pragmatic social action are legitimized in the new curriculum offered the seminarians.

The major problem facing the Irish politicians who ran the

old urban political machines was that of dealing with the demands and needs of other white immigrant groups. The current Irish American leaders in clerical and community leadership positions face the major responsibility of coping with the Negro revolution in the metropolis. Although papal encyclicals on racial questions were issued some years ago, it is only recently that they have prompted response from vigorous Irish Catholic leadership in the cities. The recent increase in clerical and lay leadership prone to intellectuality and social concern is needed because the impact of civil rights movements has been especially intense among urban Catholics. This is so because the major ethnic groups coping with Negro educational, housing, and political demands are usually of the Catholic faith, for Jewish and white Protestant congregations are seldom concentrated in those marginal areas where the allocation of public valuables constitutes a serious political issue. Under the auspices of the conciliar movement, a new generation of Irish American bishops—men like Wright of Pittsburgh, Cousins of Milwaukee, and Hallahan of Atlanta—have moved to enhance the Negroes' position. In some cities, the Catholic Church has played a key role in facilitating accommodations between assertive Negro demands for school integration and jobs, and the political structure within the white community. While Jewish and Protestant clergy did participate in the civil rights movements, the presence of Catholic clergy and Church resources had more significant long-term implications. In many cases the Church represents the most powerful ameliorating institution within the white communities of our major cities. In brief, its hierarchical structure, long experience in running parochial schools and welfare programs of considerable magnitude, and unideological approach to American politics enhance its role in dealing with the complex racial issue.[17]

Nevertheless, all of the traditional Irish skills in political accommodation will be required to meet the impact of the Negro revolution on the Church and its communicants. The immigrant need for sociability and mutual affection produced solid Catholic communities based on co-ethnic parish life. Although the new Church has become more specialized and cosmopolitan, Catholic communal life has retained much of the traditional value system emphasizing doctrinal orthodoxy, familial attachment, and the social proximity of co-religionists. Such attachments are quickly registered in political behavior when group status is threatened.[18] The efforts of progressive churchmen and laymen to respond to the Negro revolution have emphasized the division between the liberal and fundamental wings of the Church itself and of its faithful. The defensive solidarity that once cemented the Irish Catholic community is restored when Negro advances are perceived as threats to the urban lower-middle class. In areas where modernist elements direct the Church, long-term Catholic communal (and sometimes religious) ties are under severe strain. Having been asked to "defend the faith" for so long and having evolved ways of behavior to differentiate group members from "outsiders," many Catholics, both clerics and laity, are strongly at odds with some contemporary Church policies to advance Negro political and social interests.

It is with respect to social consequences that the major tensions between "fundamentalists" and "liberals" arise in the American Catholic community. Differences of doctrinal interpretation were not critical so long as they could be attributed to the mistaken zealousness of young priests. The authoritative use of Church resources in pursuit of a liberal interpretation of Catholic beliefs is a different and far more serious matter. In addition, because the new social policies have upset the everyday lives of urban Catholics by threatening to change the racial composition of the neighborhood and the educational system, the devout do not find it easy to separate their feelings about these immediate problems from their feelings about the Church.

It is in this sense that the social views of American Irish Catholics have in recent decades been modified without traditional socio-religious supports provided by the Church. The strain upon the contemporary Church can be best appreciated by comparing current internal social ferment with the problems faced by American Protestantism during its "social gospel" period during the mid-twentieth century. In both cases, a major effort was directed toward the reformation of urban social problems. In both cases, progressive clergymen came to the fore and wrested certain amounts of power from older conservatives within the most insular (in one case rural, in the other ghettoized) areas of religious orthodoxy. In both cases, a major reinterpretation of religious doctrine was set forth within Church organs and institutions. The competitive aspect of Darwinism was changed by the Protestant social gospel; the defensive aspects of a rigid Catholicism were abandoned by many contemporary Catholic leaders.[19] However, the social similarities end at that point. Protestantism never altered its individualistic base, and its social energies were always based on a voluntary, fragmented effort. By contrast, the social awakening in the contemporary American Catholic Church has led to the *collective* utilization of Church resources on behalf of numerous progressive policies.

As a result, a major, traditionalist segment of Catholicism has been left with a set of collective values and institutions that

Church leadership no longer deems appropriate to current conditions and social needs. It is from this sense of displaced solidarity that fundamentalist and parochial politics have emerged. Confronted by real economic and social problems made manifest by the "threat" of Negro militancy, some Catholics have activated existing communal norms to block racial integration, stall the implementation of open housing legislation, and otherwise frustrate the integrationist efforts of the cosmopolitans within the Church.

Despite these actions, it ought not to be concluded that Catholics have behaved any worse than other Americans in these matters. Indeed, given the social proximity of large segments of the Catholic population to non-Caucasian minorities, on balance there has been a good deal of support for the new democratic ends the Church is pursuing. Nevertheless, the current schism in the Church is less a matter of income, education, or occupational differences than of religiously based social policies. The Church has always been skilled at coping with social and ethnic differences. However, it is with regard to future political actions by its fundamentalist supporters that the Church faces its most severe test. Indeed, the evolving distinctions between segregationist communal stances and integrationist Church efforts are most likely to shape whatever further developments distinguish American Catholic politics.

Here, as in the past, the political sagacity of Irish Americans will be required. It is difficult to predict the future mood of a group of people whose behavior has provided so many legends and literary portrayals of political life. The broad scope of urban patronage and power is a thing of the past. Yet, the signs in the reform movements and in current American politics point to a continued Irish American influence on the reconciliation of the sacred and secular realms in the search for the well-being of the political community. As a Marxist student of a wise Jesuit might have said, it is no accident that in the autumn of 1967 a devout Irish Catholic Democratic politician found that his education caused him to raise the moral question of American policy in Vietnam in a presidential campaign. The background to Senator Eugene McCarthy's decision was conveyed in these words:

> When McCarthy came to Washington as a freshman Congressman in 1949, the works of Thomas More came along too. He lectured on More at Newman Clubs around the country, quoted and analyzed "Utopia" in articles he contributed to Catholic intellectual monthlies, kept pondering More's life and writings, and kept contemplating that bas-relief portrait (in his Senate office), and now, quite clearly,

> McCarthy has found the moment to act upon the inspiration of "the man for all seasons" . . . such as it is given to him to understand.[20]

In the restless age when modern secular political beliefs no longer have the capacity to inspire, perhaps the stage is set for the ascension of the Irish Catholic as reformist cleric and intellectual politician, who combines the acquired political sagacity of urban life with the contemplative strain that has always marked the more submerged and aesthetic side of the Irish heritage in American life.

CHAPTER NINE

The Negro Revolt and Democratic Participation

It is doubtful if the politics of any other ethnic group has received the amount of scholarly and popular attention that has recently been paid to the Negro American's bid for political power. Yet, amid the deluge of inquiry, an important issue of democratic theory has not received the attention it requires. That issue is the nature and quality of the political participation possible for an ethnic group painfully and obviously inexperienced in participatory "civic training." The story of the American Negro's political oppression, his disenfranchisement, and the scars he bears from slave and ghetto life need not be recounted here. Suffice it to say that the present struggle of the American Negro, and the efforts of other poor groups, seriously tests the viability of democratic theory.

The progression of the civil rights movement of the 1960's squarely raises the issue of "political participation," an issue that until recently was thought to have been settled in the American polity. In the area of Negro politics, our attention is directed toward the consequences of "unconventional participation" for democratic life and theory. What were the expectations of and concerns about mass participation among political analysts? What critical assumptions about the nature and quality of participation ill-prepared us for the political issues raised by the Negro protest movement? What new formulations about participation and political stability are useful in examining how group participation can mesh with democratic practices in the future?

THE CONCERN ABOUT MASS POLITICS

An interesting picture results when we place the emergence of the Negro civil rights movement in the context of our accumulated knowledge about the qualities of political participants in America. Coming after at least a decade's empirical investigation into American political habits, the passion and scope of the Negro rights movement was totally unexpected.

It would be difficult to find a group more characterized by the syndrome of passivity than the American Negroes. Are politically apathetic people often characterized by cognitive impairment and inattentiveness to the norms of the prevailing political order? The Negro, cut off for so long from the levers of power and from the dominant norms of white, middle-class society, has little historical experience to guide him in the acquisition of the skills required to participate in pluralistic politics.[1] Further, the absence of these skills can be traced to the qualities of family, work, and school relations dominating Negro life, relations that figure significantly in determining the extent of citizenship competence:

> Almost every Negro adult . . . not only his organizational leaders . . . has been schooled in ways to get along in superior-subordinate relationships. Moreover, the picture he has acquired very commonly puts him in the latter role. The extent to which the mental outlook of oppressed people tends toward fantasies, childlike incompetence, and passive dependence is hard to measure; available evidence suggests that a pervasive pattern of such behavior has historically laid its imprint on Negro America.[2]

Does effective participation in politics require rich social experiences in interpersonal relations and political learning? The Negro American has had few opportunities in the past to acquire the social prerequisites of democratic participation. Is successful political participation almost always strongly associated with such positive psychological qualities as self-esteem, ego strength, and basic trust in human nature and human institutions? The Negro experience is almost a laboratory experiment in the inculcation of antidemocratic qualities, namely, alienation, authoritarianism, and misanthropic views of political leaders and of mankind. Does the propensity to participate in group politics usually rest on extensive membership in several, overlapping reference groups that cut across social and economic boundaries? Such membership certainly provides the opportunity for enriched and subtle perceptions of the problems faced by other political actors. But the social, economic, and psychological isolation and dependency of the urban Negro has provided few opportunities for social heterodoxy and the acquisition of tolerance of diverse social and political opinions.

Political analysis is not an omnipotent guide to political events, and an appropriate modesty of social scientists is deepened by the fact that events in the real political world do not always follow the lines of predicted trends. For instance, by every index of the qualities required for political participation, the Negro civil rights movement and the subsequent involvement of the Negro masses in northern cities ought never to have come about. Yet, the poor correspondence between the actual politicization of the American Negro and the predictions which evolved from the research about political participation, research that makes such mass involvement seem highly improbable, is only part of the story. The remarkable disparity between what the "experts" thought they knew about political participation and the actuality of the Negro protest movement is great. The Negro movement has durable causes that center about the meaning of political participation itself. In democratic theory and practice, political participation has a rich and optimistic legacy. Active and widespread political involvement has always been a major instrument by which ascending groups have made new claims upon the polity. There has also been a consistent effort to relate political participation to human development, in that civic activism has also been a therapeutic technique designed to provide men with attachments to a political order in which they have felt some sense of belonging and in which they have been able to exert some political influence. Concern for the well-being of deprived groups has also supported emphatic consideration of the scope and breadth of popular participation, for it has been through popular action that the quality of political debate and action has been determined. The availability of local and national political forums for popular discussion and grassroots decision making have been major items of concern to democracy.[3]

It is ironic that the well-springs of this concern had dried up at about the time that the Negro thrust for justice and equality became a matter of national concern and a prime factor in determining the ability of our central cities to survive and prosper. By the time the civil rights movement had moved into high gear, a drastic modification of the concept of "political participation" was becoming quite widely accepted among American scholars. Subtle redefinitions of "political participation" were developed, and the empirical research guided by these concepts fundamentally influenced the analysis of mass politics. Underlying this development was a basic concern with the potential threat mass movements could pose to the stability of a political system.[4] The basis for this concern was a fear that individuals inexperienced in democratic politics, individuals characterized by antidemocratic and authoritarian attitudes, would undermine the order and stability of existing political institutions. Moreover, it was thought that volatile outbursts of mass participation might impede the ability of democratically trained elites to bargain and govern in the imperfect world of practical politics. The ideas of the New Deal had been transformed into the governmental system of the postwar era. The intellectuals, sensitive to the complexities of political negotiation, became disturbed by sporadic anti-intellectual and antidemocratic outbursts (liberal intellectuals were profoundly influenced by their bitter experiences with McCarthyism) and distrustful of ideological politics.

Although seldom applied directly to the Negro movement, this deepening concern about the mobilization of the politically dispossessed had particular relevance for the politicization of black Americans. A central idea of those worried by mass movements is evident in variations on the dominant theme that popular participation ought to be carried out within established political institutions. Concern about the irrationality of the masses and a newly acquired faith in the professional competence of political elites led to narrowly prescribed limits on participation, limits that allowed activity only in such areas as the political party system, the representative system, and interest-group lobbying for pragmatic, legislative ends. According to this position, the qualities needed for electoral and representative participation are central to the stability of an ongoing democratic regime. Thus, in thie view, *electoral* participation is the core criterion for mass involvement. Herein lies an important clue to the failure of social science to anticipate the political activation of American Negroes: it was assumed that voting was the critical process for articulating the concerns of the socially dispossessed.

This conservative reinterpretation of political involvement has had several variants. The most conservative holds that political apathy is not merely an empirical reality of modern politics, but in fact strengthens the political system. The politically uninvolved serve as stabilizers and balance wheels for the political order. By contributing functional passivity to the body politic, they curb whatever inclinations to extremism might exist among the active (and more democratically trained) political elites. Thus, the feared excesses of political extremism and volatile attacks on the existing order are restrained, political apathy is legitimized in the name of the system's stability and the ability of its political elites to govern without mass intervention.[5]

However, the legitimization of political apathy diverted attention away from the relationship between political participation and other facts of public life. Since the economic and racial have-nots in American society became its most passive members, their small share of society's rewards made participation and its relation to public policies an important public issue. This occurred because political elites in general bear the responsibility for articulating those issues that take into account the needs of the silent electorate. In this view, articulation of such issues as poverty and racial discrimination provides the previously apathetic with a new stake in the extant political system, a system that expands its legitimacy as conventional participation is extended. Yet, this traditional concern with the semi-sovereign nature of American politics, i.e., with the muted and indirect voice of the apathetic in their government, failed to conceive of participatory processes outside established party and interest group channels. The major emphasis remains upon the political wisdom and responsibility of existing elites; it is they who are to be wise enough to promote policies reducing the frustrations of the apathetic. These conventional defenses of limited participation are of little help in understanding the effect of unconventional mass participation on the structure of a democratic society and on the well-being of its most deprived groups.

A third approach to the problem of mass involvement of deprived ethnic group members is an absorptive strategy employing participation. Herein, group leaders, supposedly representing a mass following composed of critical groups, are given specific "recognition" in the form of political appointments, jobs, and other benefits. The group leaders, those most socialized in the forms and style of pluralistic politics, bargain on behalf of their mass following, to whom symbolic participation is granted through the recognition of the leadership. This technique, critical in accommodation politics, profoundly limits the possibilities of mass intervention in the political process. Indeed, the appointment of representatives of the poor to established agencies and the election of candidates from distinct ethnic minorities are techniques that were developed partly to control the impact of such mass participation. Under this plan, the group leaders, socialized to established politics and few in number, do not constitute a threat to the system's stability and its normal methods of political adjustment.

In each of the major variants of the interpretation of political participation reviewed here, the scope of democratic activity allowed for is narrow, encompassing only the politics of party and group operating within central public institutions. Mass action of the type seen in the Negro civil rights movement and in other, related protest movements falls outside the cognitive structure of participation theorists. Perhaps the closest analogue to mass protest contemplated under the conventional theories is the role of a third party in a two-party system. A third party is an appropriate device for organizing and dramatizing discontent with the existing system. It expresses ideological commitment, a desire for social change, and the articulation of passion in politics: the three enduring elements of mass political action. However, the analogy is faulty because even many of the most radical third parties that have sprung up heretofore have been primarily concerned with *electoral* politics based upon a solid party base and were unlikely to make broad demands on the polity between elections. It is the intensity and scope of mass participation between elections that characterize the Negro revolution on the fronts of housing policy, educational structure, and the administration of justice. These mass efforts often reinforce the concern of conventional democratic theorists about the volatile nature of unconventional and untutored mass participation. To them, the politics of direct action, exemplified by such efforts as rent strikes and school boycotts, appears as a basic threat to the system's stability. Any new evaluation of civil protest and popular participation with respect to democratic practices must be sensitive to these consequences.

ASSUMPTIONS ABOUT PARTICIPATION

The traditional emphasis on participation within major existing political institutions bears testimony to the concentration on the organization of politics, for in fact the major concern of the conventional participation theorists has been the criteria by which leaders can govern effectively. To understand the new varieties of participation, three important considerations, the responses of mass groups with certain, limited resources, the new direct relation between participation and governmental policy, and the lack of clarity about the precise relationship between mass action and democratic order, must be examined.

In a curious way, the leadership of the civil rights movement during its early legalistic phases acted explicitly on the premises and empirical evidence advanced in academic studies of participation. Aware that their mass following lacked many of the social and psychological resources needed to participate effectively in institutional politics, in the politics of party organization and representative government, they nevertheless evolved the techniques of mass protest and direct action as rational responses to the problem at hand. Using the resources of spirit and numbers possessed by southern Negro congregations and abounding in the urban ghetto, the northern Negro protest movement effectively redefined the qualifications for political participation in terms of its own potentialities. The seemingly endless bargaining sessions, the skill in verbal compromise and accommodation, and the organizational skills of mass communication were beyond the capabilities of the mass following. By contrast, the techniques of boycott, rent strikes, and demonstration could be learned and used effectively by most citizens. The civil rights movement therefore redefined the skills of political involvement, relying particularly on expression and action rather than on cognitive knowledge. However, it managed to enlarge its mass base of participation and link it to the action program in community politics that conventional theorists had in mind, in which support bubbled up through the party machinery and the representative system.

The broad approach to participation that developed in the civil rights movement took cognizance of the fact that the power of implementing public policies had shifted in part from a mélange of local and state agencies to the innovative agencies of the federal government. The civil rights movement in many ways developed a direct dialogue between the governors and the governed, making the rhetoric of a Jeffersonian or Thomas Paine primer about direct democracy strangely real in the middle of the complex twentieth century. Here again, it is important to contrast the perspectives of the conventional participation theorists and those of the civil rights leadership. The conventional and more conservative view of participation was formed at a time when government was not structured to respond broadly and directly to mass policy demands. The direct action phase of the civil rights movement operated in a political culture vastly different from the condition that faced previously excluded groups. In essence, the recent movement emerged in a period of unprecedented governmental initiative. The strategy of creative protest, involving nonelectoral politics, was designed to force substantive changes in the operation of political agencies that did not exist when other ethnic groups were entering the system.

The third element in the new definition of participation is the use of "creative disorder," as Waskow terms it, as a major strategy of direct action.[6] Creative disorder, by nature, goes beyond the limits of traditional political behavior, but it does not involve the use of violence. As practiced in the sit-in, the rent strike, the economic boycott, and the demonstration, creative disorder was often designed to change the behavior of key actors in the power structure. Here the difference in perspective between the participation theorists and the civil rights activists is most dramatic. While the theorists were primarily concerned with the behavior of the dispossessed and the threat they posed to the existing political system, the activists' attention was directed to the behavior of men who controlled critical decisions about the allocation of such human valuables as jobs, education, housing, and the allocation of political power itself.

THE RECONSTRUCTION OF DEMOCRATIC PARTICIPATION

The development of the civil rights movement, despite its limited resources and frequent failures, suggests that democratic theorists had too narrow a view of "democratic participation." Thus, it can be concluded that participation theory should be reconstructed so as to find positive value in what may be seen, from the narrow perspective of organized, middle-class electoral politics, as disruptive behavior. First, the scope and scale of "normal participatory channels," such as the party system and organized interest groups, have increased enormously. So, too, have the number of skills and amount of resources needed to make successful political demands within the organized electoral system. Second, the American polity now strongly influences the allocation of human valuables in education, jobs, health, and the entire span of human existence. It has become more difficult for minority groups lacking professional skills to make effective use of modern political research and bureaucratic organizations. Moreover, this political impact is manifest in every sphere of organized life, from big business and education to the structure of local community power. In this context, the gains from electoral successes lack the meaning and significance for the ghetto Negro that they had for white immigrant groups who used electoral strength to accommodate themselves to local politics. In the old accommodation model, disruptive behavior was usually limited to shady election tactics and the actions of demagogues who based entire campaigns on racial and religious animosities. While urban riots have many causes, they are most directly related to the low level of general human accomplishment in the securing of education, job, and other critical valuables. White immigrant politics emphasized the representative phase of political life, while contemporary Negro politics most fundamentally raises the issue of distribution in a society where the federal government is the key to the distribution of valuables.

In large measure, the implications of representative politics extend well beyond the grievances of a particular social minority and the durability of the American electoral system. The core political issue raised by the Negro revolution revolves around the mass use of activism to secure more social and economic resources from governmental and private institutions. This question has not been forcefully raised in American society since the activist phase of the trade union movement in the early days of the New Deal. At that time, the development of the mass industrial unions involved use of political techniques, such as collective bargaining and a variety of strike tactics, outside the major institutions of the polity. The union movement thus raised all the questions of violence, preparation for effective participation, and disruption to the ongoing political economy that have been raised anew about the Negro revolution. However, the essential issue for the trade union movement has never been the representativeness of worker-management organizations or the direct control of private industry by the mass of workers. The main goal of the American union movement was to mesh labor demands with the capabilities of the major distributive agencies of the political economy, namely, private industry and the social welfare agencies of federal and state governments. Herein evolved the variety of collective bargaining techniques and organizational structures, such as the National Labor Relations Board, that institutionalized the new policy of the early New Deal, which, in essence, was that labor's share of the economic product was henceforth to be included within the American political economy.

Despite numerous advances, it is clear that the Negro revolution has not yet created new structures within the American political economy capable of providing long-term payoffs in social benefits commensurate with the intensity of feeling and action that has characterized civil rights activity. There is no shortage of proposals that would link Negro demands to the growth and development of the political economy. For instance, the Freedom Budget proposal of A. Philip Randolph and Bayard Rustin represents a direct effort to integrate participatory efforts with structural changes in the distribution of such scarce values as jobs. As Rustin articulates the plan:

> We are confronted in 1967 by a nation which has neglected to meet the basic needs of its entire population and

> which has most grievously failed in providing for the needs of Negroes. It is beyond the resources neither of human ingenuity nor of the national treasury to formulate and act upon a plan for doing what is necessary. It remains to be seen whether it is beyond the resources of the national will. The goals are clear. First, full employment. Second, a $2 per hour minimum income for those now dependent, through no fault of their own, on welfare.[7]

Just as the union movement initiated mass participation to guarantee a more generous distribution of health, skill, and income resources to workers, so the Freedom Budget plan seeks to tie Negro mass needs and activity to welfare policies of the American political economy. However, the problem of democratically effective participation is raised when we consider important differences between the labor and Negro movements. First, the union movement was probably better organized after the reconciliation of the American Federation of Labor and the Congress of Industrial Organizations than is the contemporary mélange of Negro protest groups, black militants, and integrated combinations of moderate Negroes and white liberals. A major factor in the variation of organizational effectiveness was the special interest nature of the labor movement, that is, its ability to concentrate on practical "bread and butter unionism" while ignoring the divisive social and religious identifications of its mass base. By definition, race is a primary social factor to the Negro movement. The documented pervasiveness of racial discrimination in the obtaining of education, jobs, skills, and other human valuables means that Negro participation is related to the impact of politics upon the entire life situation of American Negroes.

A second critical difference between trade union and Negro mass movements is found in the nature and location of the opposition to the broad changes in the distribution of valuables within society sought by the respective groups. The trade union movement effectively isolated the conservative business and financial communities within the political arena provided by the New Deal and the Democratic party. Moreover, the cohesive organization and common interests among the economic and fiscal decision makers made it possible for the New Dealers to adjust to the new realities of collective labor power. Indeed, the impact of Franklin Roosevelt's description of "American economic royalists" facilitated a flexible series of modifications in economic conservatism that allowed the nation to live with the collective demands exerted by union leaders. For instance, American industry effectively blocked worker efforts to control primary industry policymaking by adding to its stockpile of pension and profit-sharing plans, thus incorporating the workingman within the American political economy. On the other hand, Negro demands have drawn intense opposition from sizable elements within the broad national coalition created by the majority Democratic party. White ethnic groups, trade union members, and the elderly living on a fixed income have not been in the forefront of the civil rights movement; at best, they have begrudgingly accepted the liberalized housing and employment measures urged by the powerful biracial coalition of the early 1960's. This opposition is less flexible than the conservative resistance of the 1930's because it is poorly organized and because its proponents often view broader distribution of status and jobs to Negroes as a direct threat to their own precarious status. Therefore, the types of restraints to structural changes that would benefit Negroes seriously impair efforts of liberal leadership, both white and black, to implement broad changes in the way people (such as welfare recipients) are rewarded.

Mass participation is directed toward changes in *collective* distribution of political and social advantages rather than toward the individually merited achievement and recognition that characterized both accommodation politics and much civil rights legislation in the early 1960's. Such collective changes in the distribution of human valuables come about more readily when there are dramatic changes in the symbols and myths that underlie a people's acceptance of proper efforts and rewards. Anchored to the American creed's insistence on individual rewards for individual effort, the members of white ethnic groups and trade unionists do not readily accept the notion of "special advantages" to a group within the American society. Thus, the problem for policy makers and communications specialists is how to blend "Negro subsidies" with the underlying premises of the American political economy. One possible, though certainly only partial, answer is the negative income tax which would aid the poor within both the white and black communities. Such efforts require more political and intellectual impact than administration liberals were able to muster during the productive Johnson emphasis on poverty and racial injustice, however. Unless a politically viable way is developed to absorb the political, economic, and psychic costs of massive aid to the ghetto Negro, the intense participation of civil rights militants will not bear fruit in the form of those enduring political institutions and policies that have resulted from successful protest movements.

In retrospect, the quality of democratic participation may lie in the ability of a polity to absorb demands in the creation of viable institutions that distribute human resources more effectively and more justly. American politics of the 1960's has seen the reenactment in modern form of the classic debate between Edmund Burke and the French populists about the scope and consequences of mass participation. The modern Burkeans are quick to point out the excesses and unrealistic expectations of political passion exerted by people without experience in political compromise and negotiation. However, in their emphasis on individual behavior and traditional electoral procedures, they have missed the crux of the matter, namely, the effort to translate participation into more favorable policies for distributing jobs, housing, education, and other social valuables.

Neither earlier types of mass movements nor the more recent civil disturbances within urban America have exhibited all the possible relationships mass participation may have with the enduring polity. Moreover, there is no substantial evidence to support the notion that unconventional participation and the infusion of other than political elites into the political process by themselves necessarily subvert the political structure. In this regard, conventional participation theorists may have unwittingly overlooked demands for effective governmental power in order to more broadly distribute valuables in society with basic challenges to the authoritative nature of the political regime itself.

A persuasive case can be made that the absence of mass participation and the failure to evolve new and effective methods for making the citizen's relations with his government more productive do, in fact, increase that sense of frustration producing breakdowns in the political system and violent outbursts against the regime. Therefore, we should not continue to rely solely on electoral involvement and the social norms supporting it as evidence of participation and attachment to particular policies. Indeed, the diverse perceptions of conventional participation theorists and civil rights activists mask a fundamental, although ancient, question of political analysis, namely, the extent to which politics is merely a device for determining the composition of the governing entity and the extent to which it is a device for evolving new and durable mechanisms for distributing more fully the social goods of a society. It ought to be recalled that the electoral processes so highly valued by the participation theorists were themselves means of accommodating earlier ethnic groups to the practices and opportunities of the American political system.

Despite its difficulties and failures, the modern civil rights movement has provided new support for the populist theme that political participation is important in the determination of the qualities and quantities a political system will underwrite for its citizens. Despite the dangers of frustration and alienation present in any mass movement, it is unlikely that mass Negro involvement per se represents the kind of basic danger to democratic stability envisioned by participation theorists. The failure of the policy elites to channel participation into creative institutions producing more social valuables in tax, welfare, and employment policies will produce the violent outbursts that undermine polity and the aspirations of its disadvantaged members. Nevertheless, it may be that when the results of the Negro Revolution for freedom and justice are weighed on the scales of calm reflection and historical judgment, as one can now do when considering the important social precedent of the trade union movement in America, the restoration of broad popular participation to the forums of American politics may prove to be its single most constructive accomplishment.

CHAPTER TEN

Ethnic Politics in America: Retrospect and Prospect

The major effort of this book has been to synthesize the theories and practices of American ethnic politics. There is no dearth of scholarly and popular writing about the political consequences of race, religion, and nationality within the country. Accordingly, it is surprising that no previous effort has been made to systematically discuss ethnic politics from a sustained theoretical position. Possibly, the chapters in this book devoted to that task may stimulate further efforts to write the "definitive" account of a rich and continuing influence in American politics.

At this writing, the nation is engaged in a critical struggle to accommodate itself to the demands of black people who are seeking a larger stake in the American dream. The dimension of democratic participation discussed in Chapter Nine and the productive abilities of the polity to provide creative responses are very much at issue. Although little in these pages provides prescriptive guidelines for experts and policymakers, this analysis ought to at least clarify the variety of issues at stake in the present struggle.

For every ethnic group operating under given political conditions, particular political mechanisms have produced responses designed to award group members various human values. *Accommodation politics* has been the most persistent type of American ethnic politics; indeed, it has become for many investigators the "natural" form of politics in general. This type of politics is a legacy from the efforts of white immigrant groups to wrest urban power from the Anglo-Saxons, channel it into the urban party "machine," and distribute specific benefits and prerogatives to ethnic group members. In its emphasis on divisible benefits and on the awarding of particular political positions to representatives of designated groups, the accommodation framework has accomplished several things. It has provided some necessary goods, services, and recognition to groups struggling for survival in American society. It has restrained the divisive proliferation of class and ideological politics that would have aroused public passions. By carefully absorbing ethnic political leaders, while providing mass recognition and services, it has promoted a genuinely liberal social policy within the framework of generally conservative religious and nationality attitudes. By heeding the practical and immediate claims for material benefits, accommodation politics has avoided the passionate tensions with which the politics of blood and believer have been plagued throughout history. By recognizing the existence and claims of discernible ethnic groups, accommodation politics has infused considerable stability into the growing American society. In retrospect, and with the fresh experience of newly developed nations to guide us, we can see that all these accomplishments in the American political melting pot were brought about with a minimum of cost and repression.

Yet, the accomplishments of the political "melting pot" are likely to be exaggerated with the passing of time. Circumstances have now altered, although there is a tendency to apply the yardsticks and assumptions of ethnic accommodation politics to contemporary problems—an historic fallacy that should be strenuously resisted. Classic accommodation politics has had some specific and limiting conditions that make it an unreliable guide to contemporary varieties of ethnic politics.

First, accommodation politics was exceedingly limited in scale. It was essentially urban politics, bound by perimeters and the dominant political institutions of the central city. Our understanding of ethnic accommodation politics rests on an analysis of urban politics as something essentially separate from the national political horizon. When one considers the range of party patronage and other rewards dispersed to accommodate competing ethnic groups, it can be seen that these benefits are meaningful only within the urban area and the sphere of operations of the local politicians.[1] Accommodation politics presented a picture of discrete urban solutions, whose impact was meaningful only in the aggregate.

Second, accommodation politics, founded as it was on the rapport between local governmental and party systems and ethnic communities, was not well suited to handle mass *collective claims* for housing, jobs, education, and other human valuables. As a variety of pluralistic politics, accommodation politics rested on the existence of organized and cohesive ethnic communities making limited claims on the government. The stock-in-trade of accommodation politics was divisive benefits, such as the judgeship and the precinct committeemanship, in which a single recipient was the beneficiary. Since mass "public welfare" programs were not at issue, the largesse of the urban machine had little impact on masses of urban dwellers. Moreover, accommodation politics had built-in barriers to the solution of collective problems, those where broad group claims or major public programs were sought. Political reform and the rational use of governmental programs were anathema to the pragmatic and mechanistic style of accommodation politics. More concerned with obtaining and holding support through representative machinery such as the political party, the architects of urban accommodation never devised an effective means of handling broad political claims engendered by major social changes within the polity itself.

Third, the essence of accommodation politics and ethnic "recognition" was an underlying consensus on the enduring stability of pluralistic politics. By channeling discontent into legitimate political forms, accommodation politics reduced the level of political tension, the importance of political ideology, and the excesses of political passion. Accommodation politics was never designed to cope with expansive changes in public policies and institutions of the polity; rather, it fostered the continuity of old ethnic communal values. The legacy of Jewish cultural liberalism and Irish Catholic conservatism reviewed in these pages testifies to the tenacity of the accommodating political style.

A slack system designed to produce selective change within a seemingly stable social order, the accommodation system is of limited value to either the ghetto Negro or the contemporary policymaker seeking solutions for new ethnic politics. The confrontations between nihilism and gradual integration and the impact of federal programs on the cities combine to expand the range and increase the tempo of contemporary politics. Thus, party and ethnic communities are no longer sufficient instruments for determining and distributing such collective social goods as were part of the accommodation model.

Those with a narrow perspective might view each of the alternate political strategies discussed in this book as a deviation from the basic accommodation model. That approach would permit us to retain an illusion of historical and political continuity in the contest of ethnic assimilation, for the political theme of accommodation nicely parallels the sociological emphasis on the assimilation of American ethnic groups to the core values of the system. That accommodation and absorption have resulted is perfectly evident. However, the tendency has been to overstate the case and to fail to note that the so-called deviant political styles are really responses to those values suppressed in classical accommodation politics. Rather than deviations from a norm, other political styles can be seen as substitutions of different kinds of politics in order to obtain new political values.

For instance, in *separatist politics*, ethnic political drives are converted into social and psychological forms as group members withdraw from the dominant political system in order to find a stronger foundation for cultural and personal identity. In the "quaint" ways of the Amish and the Mormons, in the practices of the Black Muslims and the other varieties of black nationalists, men have sought social and political identity outside of the accommodating system. Indeed, the very avoidance of questions of culture and identity within pragmatic accommodation politics encouraged the pursuit of meaningful alternatives. Accommodation politics was highly repressive of cultural and psychological values, limited as it was to the hammering out of short-term, pragmatic compromises. Separatist politics promises to provide individual and group reconstruction where accommodation politics had only a limited response.

Turning to yet another approach, consider *"old-style" radical politics*, namely, the joining of ethnicity with a broad-based political coalition guided by a forensic ideology describing a preferred set of power relations and means of distributing political values. Accommodation politics, a pragmatic system that filled certain group and individual needs, had little appeal to the ideologues who attempted to infuse Marxism and socialism within the American urban process. Such ideologues have seldom had an easy time in influencing American politics, nor have they found the going any easier when their efforts involved integrating ethnic appeals within a coherent ideological framework. Indeed, the history of American ideological politics is littered with failures of whites and blacks to unite under such banners as that of Agrarian Populism; the "Red and Black" strategy of the Communists and Trotskyites failed dismally in the industrial doldrums of the 1930's; even the present loose relationship between "white radicals" of the "New Left" and the ghetto Negro seems to suffer the same problems of internal discord. It is a rare case where an appeal reinforced by ideological symbolism has succeeded in achieving ethnic unity.

This point is made in a description of the National Conference for New Politics, which was held by black and white radical groups in the autumn of 1967:

> The issue of Vietnam, which brought most delegates to Chicago, is not of consuming interest in the black ghettos. The single wholehearted display of radical togetherness came on Sunday, in response to the appearance of a black private, a W. E. B. DuBois Club member from Philadelphia who announced that he was refusing to go to Vietnam (and he has since been arrested for his refusal). For a few minutes, as whites and blacks chorused, "Hell no, we won't go," the convention was one. The blacks could cheer the soldier for his color, the communists for his affiliation, the peace fighters for his act, but such a combination of qualities is not likely to come along every day.[2]

In addition, accommodation politics had little to offer in terms of psychic needs and emotional catharsis. The antics of a James Michael Curley or an Adam Clayton Powell, although they provide marvelous anecdotes, were never dominant in the politics conducted under the urban tent of ethnic accommodation. In many ways, traditional ethnic politics was a solemn deliberation of small and shrewd political businessmen rather than a violent or exotic interchange of ethnic culture and style. Here, too, the gains and losses of settled practices must be carefully assessed. While cooling the passions based on discriminatory experiences, accommodation politics may have been incapable of promoting an even more important element of sane and expressive politics, the ability to create and sustain ethnic communities capable of expressing intense political feelings without constituting a basic threat to the stability of the commonweal.

This reinterpretation of American ethnic politics has grown out of the context of contemporary events, particularly the swirling controversies in our core cities, that the variants on the accommodation theme we have explored were supposed to have rendered impossible. The ideology and passion, supposedly suppressed in the knowing embraces of carefully calculating political professionals, have never been more volatile than they are in mid-twentieth-century urban America. Indeed, ethnic politics itself, purportedly presiding over the disappearance of anachronistically hyphenated Americans, has shown surprising resiliency within the last two decades in the claims of racial, and to a lesser extent, religious factions.

The limitations of the accommodation system lie primarily in its inability to explain the persistence of ideology and passion as ethnic groups respond to new national policies. This failure to account for current American political trends also stems, paradoxically, from the emergence of the new political organizations, many specifically created to deal with a "problem area," such as Negro-white relations, and composed of individuals with conflicting political goals. The new emphasis on bargaining or compromise politics, i.e., the stress on negotiation about specific, tangible benefits, limited the utility of the accommodation model. In its haste to avoid the dysfunctional consequences of aroused emotions, psychological dislocations, and class and racial conflict, accommodation theory failed to explain the fact that the diffuseness of values being sought is itself evidence of a structural change in ethnic politics.[3] As long as ethnic politicians kept the securing of psychological and other intangible values on the periphery, they could effectively maintain that acts to secure such values only muddled the rationale of the ongoing system of political accommodations. As long as accommodation meant essentially the distribution of benefits within a fixed arena of power relations, the accommodation framework served as a blanket of *realpolitik* in dealing with a complex human condition. All of the key terms in accommodation—recognition, collective benefits, and preferments—referred to a persisting political environment, namely, the American city, within which power relations were fairly consistent over time. Once new governmental powers are exerted or new social problems are defined, however, the terms of who is to be accommodated under what political conditions become the heart of ethnic political controversy. The enduring characteristic of the accommodation model was its reliance on an organic and Newtonian series of concepts about the relations among ethnic groups, major political actors, and political strategies within a common political framework of the large American city.

Neither the varieties of the human condition nor the range of workable alternatives in a political arena thus defined justified a continuation of so narrow a view of ethnic politics. In the largest sense, ethnic politics always involved the attainment, in both the public sphere and the private economy, of a wide variety of human values including recognition, enlightenment, power, cultural acceptance, and material rewards. It has only been when major shifts in power relations developed among groups and between levels of government dealing with multi-ethnic claims that the varieties of ethnic politics not "accommodated" in times of social change became apparent. This is true because accommodation politics propounded the view of a nightwatchman state or balancing community sensitive to shifting claims made by established social, religious, and nationality groups. Much of this political balancing developed before ethnic politics became integral to federal government concern. However, when federal agencies became the major dispensers of political, social, economic, and cultural recognition, it became apparent that not all ethnic groups were effectively organized for dialogue with the federal government. No longer were ethnic leaders tied to clearly defined community relationships. No longer were the political institutions developed by ethnic groups, such as the party machine, able to direct the distribution of national resources on a broad scale. No longer were ethnic strategies rationally directed toward the securing of local political patronage. Providing for human needs had become the central domestic business of the *federal* political system. The development of mass media and instant communications were additional factors to consider in selecting an appropriate political strategy. Moreover, it was no longer clear that separatist tactics and other variants of radical political strategies would be ineffective in influencing the distribution of social goods within national governmental and economic institutions. As the control over the distribution of basic human values became more and more the province of federal power, it became more difficult to apply the accommodation model on a national scale. The limited scale of the old urban political order paralleled a limited set of demands that required accommodation by the polity, but the enlarged federal impact on housing, education, and the distribution of political power enhanced the potential effectiveness of several different strategies available to ethnic politists. Since formerly subordinate ethnic groups are most likely to seek maximum social, political, and psychological benefits from the national system, the clear rules and restraints of the older urban political game based on gradual accommodation no longer obtained. Thus, to understand the expansion of ethnic politics beyond the accommodation model, it is necessary to examine further the impact of federal policies upon the variety of ethnic politics.

Accommodation politics, as was previously noted, was primarily concerned only with the distribution of settled political rewards, particularly judgeships and party positions, that could be quantified and calculated in a political balance sheet of ethnic group advantages and disadvantages. The substantive shift in contemporary ethnic politics is marked by a dislocation of the older urban structure that secured ethnic political adjustments, that is, the use of such mechanisms as the city council and the party machine. The national scope of racial and ethnic politics now requires the development of normative integration, the reconciliation of ethnic group beliefs about how political rewards ought to be distributed. Once before, in the period of mass immigration, the nation had to develop means of linking ethnic identities to the citizenship of a multi-racial and multi-religious society. The accommodation model helped to facilitate this process. Today, the primacy and urgency of Negro demands require an effort to determine the scope of political action necessary to satisfy social, economic, political, and psychological needs of ethnic group members. In carrying out this effort, the governmental apparatus frequently will supplant local ethnic leaders and communities in fashioning a politics of identity that distributes status and rewards by massive governmental action. The core issues of race and poverty are involved here because the new awareness of cultural identity among American Negroes, for example, has been reached in a political setting vastly different from that which housed the politics of eastern and southern European immigrants. While accommodation politics showed that men of different ethnic backgrounds could obtain important political positions, the requirement of normative integration at present is to fashion agreement about the scope and quality of governmental efforts to improve the distribution of human valuables. Therefore, the importance of cultural and psychic values gained through politics, values sought heretofore by separate efforts of ethnic groups, is indicated by the government's role as cultural and political arbitrator of group values as well as group demands for traditional welfare values. The accommodation model functioned as well as it did because local ethnic communities were able to provide the sentiments and symbols of shared cultural and psychic attachments. Hence, pragmatic political negotiations could proceed so long as politicians granted general respect to ethnic beliefs and sentiments. However, the decline of ethnic symbols and organizations with broad political appeal means that governmental policies now determine the future of cultural and psychological identity among ethnic groups. A depressing example of the impact of this situation is found in the influence of federal policies on the beliefs and identities of American Indians. A contemporary and hopefully more positive case of governmental influence on ethnic identity is the effort, promoted as a secondary goal of poverty and community action programs, to change basic patterns of Negro social and cultural life. Since the federal government, despite its new role in fashioning ethnic polities, cannot take the articulation of group norms for granted, social policies themselves become major influences on the cultural and psychological fabric of ethnic group political life.

Furthermore, the issue of psycho-social integration assumes new political significance. Heretofore, particularly in the terms of the accommodation model, minority ethnic groups were to be socially assimilated and raised from their prior position of subordination gradually, as they achieved political power. All of this was to occur in a stable social system motored by urban political institutions. The problems of prejudice, self-hatred, and ethnocentrism were to be gradually overcome as adjustments were made in the attitudes prevailing among both the majority and minority groups. However, the basic political demands of Negro politics raise important questions about the meaning of assimilation. No longer is social and psychological adjustment to the norms of "white society," a particular ruling economic caste, or even to the actions of public officials politically meaningful. The new social and psychological integration of American Negroes and other nonwhite minorities must take place by means of relationships formed with political institutions, whose actions are reshaping the character and life opportunities of these people. Social and psychological integration will constantly be reshaped in conjunction with changing housing, educational, and political patterns, patterns in which the impact of Negro protest on governmental agencies is considerable. It is ironic that having made a major impact on the political status of their race, assertive Negro Americans now face problems of personal adjustment to the rewards and responsibilities of their new positions. More than in the case of any other ethnic group in America, the patterns of these rewards and responsibilities are shaped by the relationship between Negro protest groups and government agencies.

The political consequences of the Negro revolt in America raise the necessity for *environmental integration,* that is, the development of a satisfactory relationship between political institutions and the demands they are designed to satisfy in the emerging order of urban politics. Heretofore, the matrix of political institutions remained essentially unchanged, and accommodation politics proved remarkably resilient in the face of sporadic demands by reform groups for changes in political boundaries and the creation of new political institutions in our cities. However, by accelerating the intervention of federal agencies and the impact of specially designed federal programs, the Negro protest movement has helped to bring about major changes in the responsibilities of political institutions themselves. The failure of the neighborhood school to prepare minority group children for adult life, the total inadequacy of older local agencies to cope with the magnitude of political problems involving race, and the importance of federal agencies with power to settle disputes about housing and job discrimination all mean that basic political institutions are being called into question in the drive to secure complete racial integration. As a result, the boundaries of the family, the ward, and the political party that effectively provided the environment of earlier ethnic politics are rendered increasingly less meaningful. The problem of the American Negro becomes that of creating and maintaining a supportive political environment that leads directly to the acquisition of competence within a national political economy.

The combination of these additional demands of "integration" insures the continuation of significant ethnic politics at a time when the impact of race and religion on American life had been thought to have diminished. The search for something more adequate than the old accommodation model represents more than the need for new political institutions capable of responding to public claims made by ethnic groups at the national level. It also raises anew the cultural, environmental, and psycho-social problems that were more or less effectively submerged in low-tension urban politics.

Nevertheless, the political problems raised by the new scope and demands of national ethnic politics ought not obscure the tenacity of ethnicity in political choice and the viability of the accommodation model itself. More than evidence of a "cultural lag," the fierce persistence of ethnic politics in modern American history illustrates the tenacity of ethnic groups in their efforts to survive and shape new cultural and social structures. This proposition applies equally to those white immigrant groups who prospered in the melting pots of urban political and social accommodation and to ghetto Negroes seeking political power in Newark and Detroit. It applies to the urban style of the local political machine and to the more sophisticated federal programs that now employ social, economic, and political resources to satisfy American Negroes while retaining the political allegiances of urban whites. Here lies an important message for political leaders in both the inner cities and the affluent suburbs.

> In general terms, the new "affluence" (among white ethnic groups) may actually provide minorities with the financial and psychological wherewithal for building even more elaborate parallel subsocietal structures, including those needed for political action. In prosperous suburban locales, while the oldest and most exclusive country clubs belong to old-stock Protestant families, the newer clubs are of Jewish or varying Catholic-ethnic antecedents. . . .
>
> That many urban and suburban politicians persist in giving attentive consideration to minority social groupings in American-born constituencies, then, may be due less to the

> [limitations of politicians] than to the fact that ethnic substructures and identifications are still extant, highly visible, and, if handled carefully, highly accessible and responsive. The political practitioner who chooses to ignore the web of formal and informal ethnic substructures on the presumption that such groupings are a thing of the past does so at his own risk.[4]

The thesis that ethnic group acculturation does not mean the end of ethnic politics receives powerful support from the crisis of the contemporary accommodation system of urban politics. In short, theories of accommodation and cultural lag seem outdated primarily because European immigrants have made the successful entry into the American polity.

The brunt of this analysis has been that the passions of racial politics in America are not merely a case of the same political song being played with new, more dissonant lyrics. The point is that Negro Americans have not been able to accommodate themselves to the patchwork of political machines, elective positions, and fraternal organizations that comprised the old accommodation system. That system is no longer viable, and the scope of political demands now encompasses the whole range of human valuables men seek from government and society. Moreover, the American Negro confronts a number of other ethnic groups, each with its own cultural and political stakes in American society. The latter groups used the accommodation system successfully to stockpile economic and social resources of their own. Yet, in part, they helped destroy accommodation politics because they no longer affiliated themselves with it; instead, they worked openly to "reform" the political system or simply became uninterested in national and local politics.

However, the impact of Negro political demands has convinced us that the social base of ethnic politics remains viable within American society. Accommodation politics meant the successful political and social mobility of certain white ethnic groups. Its political viability has been revealed during the unprecedented efforts of the federal government to eradicate racism and poverty during the past decade. Based on the liberal assumption that poverty and racism can be uprooted by providing a wide variety of social benefits and collective forums for deprived groups, the federal effort has often encountered restraints from the "dead hand" of the political edifice constructed by white immigrants. The hope was that, at least in the urban North, the granting of these federally sponsored collective benefits would not encounter strenuous opposition from white ethnic groups and the working class. But white ethnics, particularly the working classes, have felt threatened by direct Negro competition for jobs, housing, and status and have often responded in conformity with their acquired belief system, which is strongly influenced by the acculturation of their immigrant forefathers. Past ethnic group experiences resulted in a strong emphasis on personal achievement and security. Accustomed to the political accommodations of the party ethnic association, many white urban dwellers saw the Negro protest movement as but one more, albeit a difficult and troublesome, case of accommodating the interests of a specific group.

Nevertheless, American ethnic politics persists long after the political structure of urban accommodation has decayed. Despite the federal impact on major social policies, the effort to "accommodate" the Negro is really part of a larger effort to meet the needs of a complex urban society. In the process, the handling of social conflict and debates about federal policies is becoming another means of redefining mutual identification among citizens and the relation between specific groups and the national society; such questions, dealt with at a local level in the historical debates about immigration and the melting pot, are now being settled at the federal level.

The answers to the problems of the new ethnic politics, problems involving salient group values and a local structure inadequate to cope with them, are beyond the purview of these pages. Suffice it to say that we must recognize the existence of these problems in order to comprehend the evolution of ethnic politics beyond the accommodation thesis. For instance, in a controversial report, Daniel Moynihan pointed out that the Negro family structure was in bad shape. Moynihan advocated family benefits to restore the well-being of the Negro family. The negative response was vastly different from responses to previous accounts of Negro family problems in the works of Franklin Frazier and a whole generation of sociologists in race relations. The meaning of the admonition to Moynihan lies only partly in a matter of political tactics, growing out of the fear that his public criticism of Negro family life would strengthen conservative forces who desired a reduction of welfare benefits to Negroes and other deprived groups. In broader perspective, the Moynihan controversy involved a dispute about what sort of political role the federal government should play in the amelioration of the family unit as a basic agent of proper values and beliefs in modern society. Since the family unit is also a prime carrier of ethnic social and political beliefs, the federal involvement in social policy can drastically change the nature of the ethnic group structure which was relatively autonomous from politics in the accommodation period.

As long as the accommodation system was viable, cultural and psychological attitudes toward race could be neatly compartmentalized into a category of "moral and personal" values. However, the present reality persuades us that ethnic politics is neither withering away nor being effectively dealt with under the liberal assumptions about racial integration and equality currently in vogue. That message has been the core contribution of black militants and nationalists in the Black Power movement and of other more disturbing forums in the streets of our major cities. Ethnic politics has become a major and broad-gauged *political* matter involving the necessity for a reassessment of the entire American value system and the psychological supports on which it is based. Whether American politicians can or will face up to this necessity cannot be answered now.

There is substantial evidence that the very broadening of passions and cultural issues in current ethnic politics makes pragmatic accommodation all but impossible to achieve. Yet, the most obvious alternative to a situation in which the granting of rewards no longer achieves its ancient purpose is the overt or covert use of political repression. A nation fed up with behavior that violates its working assumptions and political mythology may seek to punish group members who have exercised the majority power. Numerous ethnic groups, from the Mormons to the Amish and Japanese, have felt the sting of rejection at critical points in American history. The least we can contribute is a comprehension that the broad issues of personal meaning and group identity are also political matters. In a curious way, the implications of this conclusion have usually been better understood by conservatives than by liberals. For conservatives have been particularly sensitive to those situations in which myths and folkways no longer command the respect or loyalty of a visible element in the population. It is to such questions of belief and identification, rather than to the more calculating level of incremental advantage, that the present brand of ethnic politics addresses itself in the continuous search for new theories and practical remedies.

The long-term contribution of the accommodation model was to provide political stability facilitating the mobility of ethnic groups within a permissive political environment. Although muted by cultural assimilation and the passing of generations, the ethnic factor remains with us, and it requires no more than the politicization of passions about the needs of nonwhites to revitalize the saliency of race and religion in American public life. The primary political benefactors of the accommodation model currently shape public policy in the Democratic party coalition and, to a lesser degree, through the trade union and fraternal associations. Their immigrant forefathers left a political legacy that guided urban America through its growing pains and fashioned some rules about the proprieties to be observed in American political life. The ability of these descendants of Irish, Jewish, and Italian immigrants to reconstruct a political order capable of making qualitative distributions of human valuables among all ethnic and social groupings may well provide the true historical test of the melting pot dream that animated Israel Zanger and his contemporaries in their search for a political culture that combined individual opportunity and collective action to heal the mental and physical ills of a discriminatory society.

FOOTNOTES

CHAPTER ONE

1. J. Hector St. John Crèvecoeur, *Letters From an American Farmer* (New York: Boni, 1925 [original edition Longdon 1782]), pp. 10, 48.

2. Frederick Jackson Turner, *The Frontier in American History* (New York: Henry Holt, 1920), pp. 22-23; Nathan Glazer and Daniel Moynihan, *Beyond the Melting Pot* (Cambridge: M.I.T. Press and Harvard University Press, 1963), pp. 289-290. Reprinted from *Beyond the Melting Pot* by permission of the M.I.T. Press, Cambridge, Massachusetts. Copyright 1963 by the Massachusetts Institute of Technology; especially pertinent to the above discussion are Milton M. Gordon, "Assimilation in America: Theory and Reality," *Daedalus* 90 (Spring 1961): 263-285 and Oscar Handlin, *Immigration As a Factor in American History* (Englewood Cliffs, N.J.: Prentice-Hall, Inc., 1959), pp. 146-166.

3. T. J. Wertenbaker devotes a great deal of attention to the non-English elements in colonial America in his *The Founding of American Civilization.*

4. Glazer and Moynihan, *op cit.*, p. 28ff.

5. *Ibid.,* pp. 311-313.

6. For data on the development of New York's Chinese community, see *The New York Times,* January 15, 1964, p. 33.

7. Horace M. Kallen, "Democracy Versus the Melting Pot," *The Nation,* February 1915. Excerpts reprinted in Handlin, *op. cit.,* pp. 153-155.

8. See H. S. Commager, "Leadership in Eighteenth Century America and Today," *Daedalus* 90 (Fall 1961): 652-673 (664ff); Ray A. Billington, *The Protestant Crusade, 1800-1860* (Chicago: Quadrangle Books, Inc., 1964); Handlin, *op. cit.,* pp. 158-188.

9. For a more detailed discussion of this topic, see Maldwyn A. Jones, *American Immigration* (Chicago: University of Chicago Press, 1960), pp. 308-319.

10. For documentation of what follows see Oscar Handlin, *The Uprooted* (New York: Grosset & Dunlap, Inc., 1951); R.E. Park and H.A. Miller, *Old World Traits Transplanted* (New York: Harper, 1921); E. V. Stonequist, *The Marginal Man: A Study in Personality and Culture Conflict* (New York: Charles Scribner's Sons, 1937); W. L. Warner and L. Srole, *The Social Systems of American Ethnic Groups* (New Haven: Yale University Press, 1945); W. L. Warner, *American Life: Dream and Reality* (Chicago: University of Chicago Press, 1962, rev. ed.), chapter 7; W. I. Thomas and F. Zananiecki, *The Polish Peasant in Europe and America,* 5 vols. (Boston: Badger, 1918-1920).

11. Peter Munch, "Social Adjustments Among Wisconsin Norwegians," *American Sociological Review* 14 (December 1949): 780-787.

12. See Henrik Infield, *Cooperative Communities at Work* (New York: Dryden Press, 1945); Munch, *op cit.*; J. A. Hossetler, *Amish Society* (Baltimore: Johns Hopkins University Press, 1963).

13. William Foote Whyte, *Street Corner Society* (Chicago: University of Chicago Press, 1943); Herbert Gans, *The Urban Villagers* (New York: The Free Press, 1962).

14. See Erich Rosenthal, "Acculturation Without Assimilation?" *American Journal of Sociology* (November 1960): 275-288; Amitai Etzioni, "The Ghetto—A Re-evaluation," *Social Forces* (March

1959): 255-262; J. Milton Yinger, "Social Forces Involved in Group Identification or Withdrawal," *Daedalus* 90 (Spring 1961): 247-262; M. Gordon, *op. cit.*

CHAPTER TWO

1. Response of a Buffalo industrial worker quoted in Lucy S. Dawidowicz and Leon J. Goldstein, *Politics in a Pluralist Democracy: Studies of Voting in the 1960 Election* (New York: Institute of Human Relations Press, 1963), p. 18.
2. James Reichley, *The Art of Government* (New York: The Fund for the Republic, 1959), p. 104.
3. "A Conversation with James Baldwin," transcript of a documentary broadcast by WGBH-TV (Boston, June 24, 1964), p. 5.
4. Compare Bernard B. Berelson, Paul F. Lazarsfeld, and William N. McPhee, *Voting: A Study of Opinion Formation in a Presidential Campaign* (Chicago: University of Chicago Press, 1954), ch. 4; Robert A. Dahl, *Who Governs: Democracy and Power in an American City* (New Haven: Yale University Press, 1961), chs. 4, 5; Gerhard Lenski, *The Religious Factor: A Sociologist's Inquiry* (New York: Doubleday & Company, Inc., 1961), ch. 4; and Edward C. Banfield and James Q. Wilson, *City Politics* (Cambridge, Mass.: Harvard University Press and M.I.T. Press, 1963), pp. 28-44.
5. Robert R. Alford, *Party and Society* (Chicago: Rand McNally & Company, 1963), pp. 241-249. See also Robert T. Bower, *Voting Behavior of American Ethnic Groups* (New York: Bureau of Applied Social Research, 1944), pp. 16-17. But see also V. O. Key, Jr., and Frank Munger, "Social Determinism and Electoral Decisions: The Case of Indiana," in *American Voting Behavior,* ed. Eugene Burdick and Arthur Brodbeck (Glencoe, Ill.: The Free Press, 1959).
6. The political ramifications are spelled out in V. O. Key, Jr., *Politics, Parties, and Pressure Groups,* 5th ed. (New York: Thomas Y. Crowell, 1964), p. 250n. Long-term consequences of urban ethnic majorities in American politics are examined by Samuel Lubell, *The Future of American Politics* (New York: Harper & Row, Inc., 1952); Samuel J. Eldersveld, "The Influence of Metropolitan Party Pluralities in Presidential Elections Since 1920," *American Political Science Review* 43 (1949): 1189-1206; Alan P. Grimes, *Equality in America: Religion, Race, and the Urban Majority* (New York: Oxford University Press, 1964).
7. Alford, *op.cit.,* p. 325. One of the reasons for this endurance is the secularization of American religious and ethnic institutions that adjust and sustain traditional loyalties. See the discussion by Seymour M. Lipset, *The First New Nation: The United States in Historical and Comparative Perspective* (New York: Basic Books, Inc., 1963), pp. 151-159; see also Will Herberg, *Protestant, Catholic, Jew* (New York: Doubleday & Company, Inc., 1960), pp. 46-71; Lenski, *op. cit.,* ch. 1.
8. Dahl, *op. cit.*, p. 279. Supporting evidence from a different, but related, approach to the relationship among political power, participation, and community structure is provided by Robert Presthus, *Men at the Top: A Study in Community Power* (New York: Oxford University Press, 1964), especially pp. 175-238.
9. Cf. Theodore H. White, *The Making of the President, 1960* (New York: Atheneum House, Inc., 1961).

10. See, for example, the complex of factors involved in the battle over Chicago's public housing, which included an ethnic element, [namely,] the selection of sites for low-rent housing in a Jewish ward as a sanction against Jewish politicians who had supported plans for public housing, as described by Martin Meyerson and Edward C. Banfield, *Politics, Planning, and the Public Interest* (Glencoe, Ill.: The Free Press, 1955).
11. The theme is central to V. O. Key, Jr., *Public Opinion and American Democracy* (New York: Alfred A. Knopf, Inc., 1961), especially chs. 16, 21.
12. Oscar Handlin, *The Uprooted* (New York: Grosset & Dunlap Inc., 1951), p. 217.
13. William I. Thomas and Florian Zaniecki, *The Polish Peasant in Europe and America* (Boston: Richard G. Badger, 1917); M. Brewster Smith, Jerome S. Bruner, and Robert W. White, *Opinions and Personality* (New York: John Wiley & Sons, Inc., 1956).
14. Angus Campbell, Phillip E. Converse, Warren E. Miller, and Donald E. Stokes, *The American Voter* (New York: John Wiley & Sons, Inc., 1960), p. 220.
15. See Berelson and others, *op. cit.;* Campbell et al., *op. cit.*
16. On resistance to cognitive dissonance, that is, confusion to conflicting stimuli, see Leon Festinger, *A Theory of Cognitive Dissonance* (Palo Alto: Stanford University Press, 1957); Charles E. Osgood, C. J. Suci, and P. H. Tannenbaum, *The Measurement of Meaning* (Urbana, Ill.: University of Illinois Press, 1957).
17. Leon J. Damin, "Ethnic and Party Affiliations of Candidates as Determinants of Voting," *Canadian Journal of Psychology* 12 (1958): 205-212.
18. Campbell et al., *op. cit.,* pp. 207-212; Michael Parenti, "Ethnic-Political Attitudes: A Depth Study of Italian Americans," Ph.D. thesis (Yale University, 1962); on low political information and parochial sources of voting clues, see the comparative data of Gabriel A. Almond and Sidney Verba, *The Civic Culture: Political Attitudes and Democracy in Five Nations* (Princeton, N.J.: Princeton University Press, 1959), pp. 62-68.
19. See Banfield and Wilson, *op. cit.,* pp. 304-307.
20. Duane Lockard, *New England State Politics* (Princeton, N.J.: Princeton University Press, 1959), pp. 62-68.
21. V. O. Key, Jr., *American State Politics* (New York: Alfred A. Knopf, Inc., 1956), p. 157.
22. The communication of shared interests in face-to-face groups is the key here. See Herbert Gans, *The Urban Villagers* (New York: The Free Press, 1962). The relation between the concentration of distinct ethnic group populations and electoral politics is discussed in Robert E. Lane, *Political Life: Why People Get Involved in Politics* (New York: The Free Press, 1961).
23. Berelson et al., *op. cit.,* p. 315.
24. See Lenski, *op. cit.,* pp. 83-95.
25. See Daniel Moynihan's chapter on "The Irish" in Nathan Glazer and Daniel Moynihan, *Beyond the Melting Pot* (Cambridge, Mass.: Harvard University and M.I.T. Press, 1963).
26. Lenski, *op. cit.,* pp. 164-165; Scott Greer, "Catholic Votes and the Democratic Party," *Public Opinion Quarterly* 25 (Winter 1961): 611-625.
27. Consult, respectively, Benjamin J. Ringer and Charles Y. Glock, "The Political Role of the

Church as Defined by its Parishioners," *Public Opinion Quarterly* 18 (Winter 1954-1955): 337-347; and Benton Johnson, *op. cit.*

28. Campbell et al., *op. cit.*, p. 234. Association with group benefits rather than ideology or social class explains much of the "logic" of ethnic political behavior that is otherwise irrational from the point of view of group members.

29. On race and the southern economy, see E. E. Schattschneider, *The Semi-Sovereign People* (New York: Holt, Rinehart, and Winston, Inc., 1960), ch. 4. On nationality and the northern economy, see "Crime As an American Way of Life," in Daniel Bell, *The End of Ideology* (New York: The Free Press, 1960).

30. "Minority Hiring by City Praised," *The New York Times*, March 22, 1964, Sec. l, p. 57.

31. Scott Greer, *Metro-Politics: A Study of Political Culture* (New York: John Wiley & Sons, Inc., 1963), p. 94.

32. The data of socio-economic status and participation is summarized in Lane, *op. cit.*, chs. 16, 17. That Negroes participate at least as much as whites in comparable organizational and social milieu is established by Arthur Kornhauser, Albert J. Mayer, and Harold L. Sheppart, *When Labor Votes* (New York: University Books, 1956). Therefore, tangible political rewards remain very important to sustain the participation and interests of lower status ethnic groups. Note the evidence about New Haven Negroes in Dahl, *op. cit.*, pp. 293-296.

33. See, for instance, C. B. Nam, "Nationality Groups and Social Stratification in America," *Social Forces* 37 (1959): 328-333; A. B. Hollingshead and F. C. Redlich, *Social Class and Mental Illness* (New Haven: Yale University Press, 1945). On overt relations to political participation, see Gerhart Sanger, "Social Status and Political Behavior," *American Journal of Sociology* 51 (1946): 103-113; Wesley and Severly Allinsmith, "Religious Affiliation and Socio-Economic Attitudes," *Public Opinion Quarterly* 12 (1948): 377-389; Leonard W. Bloomberg, "The Relationship Among Rank Systems in American Society," in M. Freedman, ed., *A Minority in Britain* (London: Vallentine, Mitchell, 1955).

34. On achievement orientation and ethnicity, see Lenski, *op. cit.*, ch. 3; Bloomberg, *op. cit.*; Joseph S. Forman, "Occupation Selection Among Detroit Jews," *Jewish Social Studies* 14 (1952): 17-50; George Pasataz, "Ethnicity, Social Class, and Adolescent Independence from Parental Control," *American Sociological Review* 22 (1957): 415-423; Bernard C. Rosen, "Achievement: A Psychocultural Dimension of Social Stratification," *American Sociological Review* 21 (1956): 203-211; Bernard C. Rosen, "Race, Ethnicity, and Achievement," *American Sociological Review* 24 (1959): 47-58; John J. Kane, "The Social Structure of American Catholics," *The American Catholic Sociological Review* 16 (March 1955): 30; Bosco D. Cestelle, "Catholics in American Commerce and Industry, 1925-1945," *American Catholic Sociological Review* 17 (October 1956).

On religious aspects of political reform groups stressing "liberal" values, see James Q. Wilson, *The Amateur Democrats: Club Politics in Three Cities* (Chicago: University of Chicago Press, 1962), especially ch. 9, where middle-class and Jewish characteristics are found to be highly related to club participation. On religious differences pertaining to civil rights (so-called noneconomic liberalism), consult Seymour M. Lipset, *Political Man* (New York: Doubleday & Company, Inc., 1960), and a summary of studies in Edgar Litt, "The Political Perspectives of Jews in an Urban Community," Ph.D. thesis (Yale University, 1960), chs. 7, 8.

On psychological integration or nonimpairment and religion, see Charles A. Snyder, *Alcohol and the Jew* (New Haven: Yale University Press, 1957); evidence on Irish Americans summarized in Glazer and Moynihan, *op. cit.,* and the careful study by Leo Srole et al., *Mental Health in the Metropolis: The Midtown Manhattan Study* (New York: McGraw-Hill Book Company, 1962), ch. 16, which indicates a strong tendency toward mild symptom formation—but away from severe mental impairment—among Jews, Catholics, and Protestants. The first two groups were found more likely to fall in the top (well) and bottom (impairment) categories. The difference between Catholic and Jewish mental impairment was significant at the .01 confidence level with age and socio-economic status controlled. This is a very significant statistical relationship.

35. Kane, *op. cit.,* p. 30.

36. Litt, "Political Perspectives," *op. cit.,* p. 78.

37. The stability of Jewish partisanship and liberalism are both positively related to cultural security and broad party identifications, and inversely associated with ethnic defensiveness and Jewish insecurity. See Edgar Litt, "Jewish Ethno-Religious Involvement and Political Perspectives," *Midwest Journal of Political Science* (August 1961): 276-283. For a different interpretation of Jewish political behavior in America, see Fuchs, *op. cit.,* p. 191.

38. V. O. Key, Jr., *Southern Politics in State and Nation* (New York: Alfred A. Knopf, Inc., 1949), pp. 271-276.

39. See Elmer E. Cornwell, "Party Absorption of Ethnic Groups," *Social Forces* 38 (1960): 205-210.

40. Note two contributions by Jerome E. Myers: "Assimilation in the Political Community," *Sociology and Social Research* 35 (1951): 175-182; "Assimilation in the Ecological and Social Systems of Community," *American Sociological Review* (1950), 367-372.

41. Donald R. Matthews and James W. Prothro, "Political Factors and Negro Voter Registration in the South," *American Political Science Review* 57 (March, June 1963): 24-44, 355-367.

42. Taken from a 1963 draft of a paper by Raymond E. Wolfinger, which was later printed under the title "The Development and Persistence of Ethnic Voting," *American Political Science Review* 59 (December 1965). Wolfinger traces Italo-American Republicanism in New Haven. His data present the interesting picture of political mobilization leading to altered party allegiances. Irish exclusiveness and the stimulation of a fellow ethnic as mayoralty candidate motivate Italian Republicanism.

43. Compare 1956 and 1960 presidential voting performances of middle-class Catholics in major cities as analyzed by Lucy S. Dawidowicz and Leon J. Goldstein, *Politics in a Pluralist Democracy* (New York: Institute of Human Relations Press, 1963).

44. For variations on these themes, see Dahl, *op. cit.,* pp. 11-62;

Peter H. and Alice Rossi, "An Historical Perspective on Local Politics," paper delivered at the American Sociological Association annual meeting, 1956; Banfield and Wilson, *op cit.,* pp. 40-44. The variations are the relative weights of power, status, and ethos in the great patrician retreat.

45. Jewish fund raising and the Catholic Church sustain these two subcommunities thus providing high policy autonomy. On the same relationship between the Democratic party and ethnic members of the upperworld and underworld, see Bell, *op. cit.*

46. Andrew Hacker, "Liberal Democracy and Social Control," *American Political Science Review* 51 (December 1957): 1017. Reflections are seen in studies of diplomatic, military, and fiscal elites assembled in Suzanne Keller, *Beyond the Ruling Class* (New York: Random House, Inc., 1963), pp. 292-327. There is a tendency toward ethnic assimilation. Moreover, those who lack status because of ethnicity and social class have their best chance to succeed in corporate business hierarchies. Those lacking status only because of ethnicity do best through education and professionalization. Advancement of Roman Catholics and Jews tends to vary accordingly.

47. This is a matter of concern to the Jewish community, as the following citations suggest: Tom Brooks, "Negro Militants, Jewish Liberals, and the Unions," *Commentary* 32 (September 1961); Norman Podhoretz, "My Negro Problem—and Ours," *Commentary* 35 (February 1963); "Liberalism and the Negro: A Round-Table Discussion," *Commentary* 37 (March 1964).

48. Lane, *op. cit.*, p. 249.

49. E. Franklin Frazier, *Black Bourgeoisie* (Glencoe, Ill.: The Free Press, 1957), p. 149. Reprinted by permission.

50. Litt, "Political Perspectives," *op. cit.,* p. 121. See also Joseph Adelson, "A Study of Minority Group Authoritarianism," *Journal of Social and Abnormal Psychology* 48 (1953): 477-485; Irving Sarnoff, "Identification with the Aggressor," *Journal of Personality* 20 (1951): 199-218.

51. The quotation is from a verbal contribution by Wallace Markfield to "Jewishness and the Younger Intellectuals: A Symposium," printed in *Commentary* 31 (April 1961): 343.

52. Litt, "Political Perspectives," *op. cit.*, p. 81. On the political effects of ethnic marginality, consult Howard W. Brotz, "Social Stratification and the Political Order," *American Journal of Sociology* 64 (1959): 575-585; William T. Lee, "The Marginal Catholic in the South," *American Journal of Sociology* 65 (1960): 383-390; Gerhard Lenski, "Status Crystallization: A Non-Vertical Dimension of Social Status," *American Sociological Review* 19 (1954): 405-413.

53. Litt, "Political Perspectives," *op. cit.*, p. 81.

54. Judith R. Kramer and Seymour Levantman, *Children of the Gilded Ghetto* (New Haven: Yale University Press, 1961), p. 196. See also the important article by Murray Edelman, "Symbols and Political Quiescence," *American Political Science Review* 54 (September 1960): 695-704.

55. On the greater concern about status in an equalitarian nation (such as the United States) compared with a deferential, ascriptive society (such as Great Britain), see Howard Brotz, "The Position of the Jews in English Society," *Jewish Journal of Sociology* 1 (1959); Brotz, "The Outline of Jewish Society in London," in Milton Freedman, ed., *A Minority in Britain, op. cit.* Compare these studies with Marshall Sklare, *The Jews: Social Patterns of an American Group* (Glencoe, Ill.: The Free Press, 1950).

56. "Across the Land White Discontent Bubbles Angrily," *The National Observer*, March 23, 1964, pp. 1, 14. Data on the Wisconsin primary is based on United States Bureau of the Census, *City and County Data Book* (1962); United States Bureau of the Census, *The Congressional District Data Book* (1963); and *The Milwaukee Journal*, April 6, 1964, p. 2. A useful guide to an almost unmanageable literature about integrated housing is Arnold M. Rose, "Inconsistencies in Attitudes Toward Negro Housing," *Social Forces* (1961). For the genesis of deeper doubts about the scope of Negro demands by so-called equalitarian liberals, consult Michael Parenti, "White Anxiety and the Negro Revolt," *New Politics* 3 (Winter 1964): 35-39.

57. Hacker, *op. cit.*, p. 1016.

58. Keller, *op. cit.*, pp. 162-163. The same reasons seem to have hastened the political decline of the Congregational elite. See Dahl, *op. cit.*, on New Haven at pp. 25-51.

CHAPTER THREE

1. See Daniel Glaser, "The Dynamics of Ethnic Identification," *American Sociological Review* 23 (1950): 31-40; Milton M. Gordon, *Social Class in American Society* (Durham, N.C.: Duke University Press, 1958).

2. Oscar Handlin, *The Uprooted* Boston: Beacon Press, 1951); Emile Benoit-Smullyan, "Status, Status Types, and Status Interrelations," *American Sociological Review* 9 (1944): 151-161.

3. Howard Brotz, "Social Stratification and the Political Order," *American Journal of Sociology* 64 (1959): 575-585; Handlin, *op. cit.*, pp. 133-156; Everett V. Stonequist, *The Marginal Man* (New York: Charles Scribner's Sons, 1957).

4. A useful theoretical discussion of the advantages and hazards of social reward exchanges is found in Peter M. Blau, *Exchange and Power in Social Life* (New York: John Wiley & Sons, Inc., 1964), expecially pp. 115-139.

5. Edward M. Levine, *The Irish and Irish Politicians* (Notre Dame, Indiana: University of Notre Dame Press, 1966), p. 60.

6. Samuel J. Eldersveld, *Political Parties: A Behavioral Analysis* (Chicago: Rand McNally & Company, 1966), pp. 85, 87, 95.

7. Robert A. Dahl, *Who Governs: Democracy and Power in an American City* (New Haven: Yale University Press, 1961), p. 42.

8. *Ibid.;* see also Matthew Holden, Jr., "Party Politics and Ethnic Politics," in *Political Science: Some New Perspectives*, ed. Clyde Wingfield (El Paso, Texas: Texas Western Press, 1966), pp. 124-145.

9. Note Oliver P. Williams and Charles Press, *Democracy in Urban America* (Chicago: Rand McNally & Company, 1961), pp. 22-28; Elmer E. Cornwell, "Party Absorption of Ethnic Groups," *Social Forces* 38 (March 1960): 205-216.

10. Allan H. Spear, *Black Chicago* (Chicago: University of Chicago Press, 1967), pp. 52-123; Matthew Holden, Jr., "Ethnic Accommodation in a Historical Case," *Comparative Studies in Society and History* 28 (January 1966): 165-174.

11. Gerhard Lenski, *The Religious Factor* (New York: Doubleday & Company, Inc., 1961), pp. 120-167.
12. Note Benjamin Ringer and Charles Y. Glock, "The Political Role of the Church as Defined by its Parishioners," *Public Opinion Quarterly* 18 (1954-1955): 337-343.
13. Marshall Sklare, *Conservative Judaism: An American Religious Movement* (Glencoe, Ill.: The Free Press, 1955).
14. Edgar Litt, *The Political Culture of Massachusetts* (Cambridge, Mass.: The M.I.T. Press, 1965), p. 123.
15. Suzanne Keller, *Beyond the Ruling Class* (New York: Random House, Inc., 1963), p. 137.
16. David R. Manwaring, *Render unto Caesar: The Flag-Salute Controversy* (Chicago: University of Chicago Press, 1961), pp. 117-118.
17. Organizational restraints on church groups in politics are assessed in Louis C. Kesselman, *The Social Politics of F. E. P. C.* (Chapel Hill, N.C.: University of North Carolina Press, 1948). Note also Murray Stedman, *Religion and Politics in America* (New York: Harcourt, Brace & World, Inc., 1964), pp. 20-47.
18. William Lee Miller, "American Religion and American Political Attitudes," in *The Shaping of American Religion,* Vol. 2, ed. James W. Smith and A. Leland Jamison (Princeton, N.J.: Princeton University Press, 1961), pp. 81-118.
19. *Ibid.*
20. H. Richard Niebuhr, "The Movement and Democracy in the United States," in Smith and Jamison, *op. cit.,* Vol. 1, p. 56.
21. Stedman, *op. cit.,* pp. 109-110.
22. Tracey Ellis, *American Catholicism* (New York: Alfred A. Knopf, Inc., 1958).
23. See High D. Price, "Federal Aid to Education Bill," in Allan P. Westin, ed. *The Uses of Power: Seven Cases in American Politics* (New York: Harcourt, Brace, & World, Inc., 1962), pp. 1-73.
24. A fuller account is found in Litt, *op. cit.*, ch. 3.
25. See *Zorach* v. *Clausen*, 369 U.S. 420 (1961).
26. The Regents' Prayer case was *Engel* v. *Vitale,* 370 U.S. 421 (1962). Note also the case analysis in Westin, *op. cit.*, pp. 118-132.
27. Will Herberg, *Protestant, Catholic, Jew* (New York: Doubleday & Company, Inc., 1956), p. 225.
28. Litt, *op. cit.*, p. 133.
29. *Ibid.*, p. 134.
30. Robert E. Lane, *Political Ideology: Why the American Common Man Believes What He Does* (New York: The Free Press, 1962), pp. 199-200. Reprinted by permission.
31. The evidence is found in a pioneering study of religion and politics, George L. Lundberg, "The Social Position of the Protestant Clergy," *Journal of Social Issues* 8 (1944): 16-33.
32. This section draws heavily on Henry Pratt, "Adaptation to Change: The Case of the New York Protestants," unpublished manuscript, 1965.
33. *Ibid.,* p. 25. Reprinted by permission of the author.

CHAPTER FOUR

1. Robert A. Dahl, *Who Governs: Democracy and Power in an American City* (New Haven: Yale University Press, 1961), p. 34.
2. Consult James Q. Wilson, *The Amateur Democrat* (Chicago: University of Chicago Press, 1962).
3. Raymond E. Wolfinger, "Some Consequences of Ethnic Politics," in *The Electoral Process*, ed. M. K. Jennings and L. H. Zeigler (Engle-

wood Cliffs, N. J.: Prentice-Hall, Inc., 1966), p. 52.

4. See Edgar Litt, "Jewish Ethno-Religious Involvement and Political Perspectives," *Midwest Journal of Political Science* (August 1961): 276-283.

5. Edward C. Banfield and James Q. Wilson, *City Politics* (Cambridge, Mass.: Harvard University Press, 1963), p. 43.

6. On the subject of the balanced ticket, note Gerald M. Pomper, "Ethnic and Group Voting in Nonpartisanship Municipal Elections," *Public Opinion Quarterly* 30 (Spring 1966): 79-97; on the value of patronage records as "proof" of ethnic justice, note the mechanisms for handling ethnic claims developed by the Harriman administration in Daniel P. Moynihan and James Q. Wilson, "Patronage in New York State, 1955-1959," *American Political Science Review* 58 (June 1964): 296-300.

7. Matthew Holden, Jr., "Party and the Persistence of Ethnic Politics," unpublished manuscript, 1966, p. 7. I have relied heavily on Holden's description of the organizational uses of ethnicity in political bargaining.

8. Samuel J. Eldersveld, *Political Parties: A Behavioral Analysis* (Chicago: Rand McNally & Company, 1964), pp. 73-97.

9. Holden, *op. cit.*

10. Murray R. Levin, *Kennedy Campaigning* (Boston: Beacon Press, 1966), p. 25.

11. The classic study is Samuel Lubell, *The Revolt of the Moderates* (New York: Harper & Row, Inc., 1956).

12. The combination of ethnic and status politics in McCarthyism is explored by Seymour M. Lipset, "The Sources of the Radical Right," in Daniel Bell, ed., *The New American Right* (New York: Doubleday & Company, Inc., 1962 ed.), pp. 308-356.

13. See the sources cited in chapter two and Grace M. Anderson, "Voting Behavior and the Ethnic-Religious Variable," *Canadian Journal of Economics and Political Science* 32 (February 1966): 27-37; Raymond E. Wolfinger, "The Development and Persistence of Ethnic Voting," *American Political Science Review* 59 (December 1965): 896ff.

14. See Edgar Litt, *The Political Cultures of Massachusetts* (Cambridge, Mass.: The M.I.T. Press, 1965), ch. 3; Theodore Lowi, *At the Pleasure of the Mayor* (New York: The Free Press, 1964), ch. 2.

15. Compare Dahl, *op. cit.*, p. 52.

Certain benefits are divisible in such a way that they can be allocated to specific individuals. . . . Other benefits are more nearly indivisible; parks, playgrounds, schools, national defense, and foreign policies, for example, either cannot or ordinarily are not allocated by dividing the benefits piecemeal and allocating various pieces to specific individuals.

16. Note the concern of the "mayoralty-centered coalition" of New Haven with urban renewal in *Ibid.*, pp. 117-140; or its visibility in Chicago politics as described by Martin Meyerson and Edward C. Banfield, *Politics, Planning, and the Public Interest* (Glencoe: The Free Press, 1953); Peter Rossi and Robert Dentler, *The Politics of Urban Renewal* (Chicago: University of Chicago Press, 1965).

17. Note James Q. Wilson, "The Strategy of Protest: Problems of Negro Civic Action," *Journal of Conflict Resolution* 4 (September 1961): 291-303.

18. Matthew Holden, Jr., "Ethnic Accommodation in a Historical

Case," *Comparative Studies in Society and History* 8 (January 1966): 168-180.

19. See Bernard Weissbourd, *Segregation, Subsidies, and Megalopolis* (Santa Barbara, Calif.: Center for the Study of Democratic Institutions, 1964).

20. St. Clair Drake and Horace R. Clayton, *Black Metropolis: A Study of Negro Life in a Northern City* (New York: Harper & Row, Inc., 1961 ed.), p. vii in Appendix.

21. Catherine Bauer, "Social Questions in Housing and Community Planning," *Journal of Social Issues* 7 (1963): 21-22.

22. J. David Greenstone and Paul Peterson, "Reformers, Machines, and the War on Poverty," paper presented at the Annual Meetings of the American Political Science Association, New York City, 1966.

23. Holden, "Party and Ethnic Politics," *op. cit.*, p. 24.

24. Banfield and Wilson, *op. cit.*, p. 43.

25. Holden, "Ethnic Accommodation," *op. cit.*, p. 176. Yankee Protestant withdrawal from Massachusetts politics is described by Peter H. and Alice S. Rossi, "An Historical Perspective on Local Politics," paper delivered at the 1956 meeting of the American Sociological Association (mimeo.); for similar data on New Haven, see Dahl, *op. cit.*, pp. 12-86.

26. Note James Reichley, *The Art of Government* (New York: The Fund for the Republic, 1959).

27. See Wolfinger, "Persistence of Ethnic Politics," *op. cit.;* Edgar Litt, *The Political Cultures of Massachusetts* (Cambridge, Mass.: The M. I. T. Press, 1965), ch. 3.

CHAPTER FIVE

1. Accommodation politics involves an ethnic group in making overt demands on existing political institutions; in separatist politics alternative institutions are created to solve the problems at hand.

2. The analysis in this chapter is enriched by two contributions of Michael John Parenti: "The Black Muslims: From Revolution to Institution," *Social Research* 31 (Summer 1964): 175-194; "Black Nationalism and the Reconstruction of Identity," in *Personality and Social Life*, ed. Robert Endelman (New York: Random House, Inc., 1965), pp. 1-16.

3. The best full-length study of the Muslims to date is E. U. Essien-Udom, *Black Nationalism, A Search for an Identity in America* (New York: Dell, 1964). Other titles worth mentioning are C. Eric Lincoln, *The Black Muslims in America* (Boston: Beacon Press, 1961); Louis Lomax, *When the Word Is Given* (New York: The World Publishing Company, 1963).

4. See for instance A. B. Southwick, "Malcolm X: Charismatic Demagogue," *Christian Century* 80 (June 5, 1963): 741; C. Eric Lincoln, "Extremist Attitudes in the Black Muslim Movement," *Journal of Social Issues* 19 (April 1963): 82-83; *The New York Times*, editorial, March 14, 1964; Max Lerner, "White Devils?" *New York Post*, March 9, 1964. For an analysis suggesting that the Muslims are moving toward a more moderate position in American society despite the occasional vehemence of their rhetoric, see William Worthy, "The Nation of Islam: Impact and Prospects," *Midstream* 8 (Spring 1962): 26-44.

5. Cf. Hans Kohn, *Prophets and Peoples* (New York: The Macmillan Company, 1964), for a study of rising nationalisms that documents this observation.

6. E. Franklin Frazier, *Black Bourgeoisie* (New York: Free Press, 1962 edition), p. 114.
7. *Ibid.*; see also A. Kardiner and L. Ovesey, *The Mark of Oppression* (New York: W. W. Norton & Co., Inc., 1951).
8. Muhammad writes: ". . . It has been written that God would choose the rejected and the despised. We can find no other persons fitting this description in these last days more than the so-called Negroes in America." *Muhammad Speaks,* September 27, 1963.
9. For accounts of the Muslim eschatology see Essien-Udom, *op. cit.,* pp. 140-159; Lincoln, "Extremist Attitudes . . . ," *op. cit.;* Elijah Muhammad, "What the Muslims Believe," reprinted in every issue of *Muhammad Speaks.*
10. Essien-Udom, *op. cit.,* p. 141.
11. This rehabilitation phenomenon is well-documented in *Ibid.*, ch. 4, and in the testimonies offered by Muslims in "What Islam Has Done for Me," a feature now appearing in every issue of *Muhammad Speaks*; see also Claude Brown, "Ally Bush," *Dissent* 10 (Summer 1963): 265; and Worthy, *op. cit.*, pp. 31-32.
12. Essien-Udom, *op. cit.,* p. 121ff; Lincoln, *The Black Muslims in America, op. cit.*, pp. 17-18, 24, 60-64.
13. Lincoln, *Black Muslims . . . , op. cit.*, pp. 199-203. While the Fruit of Islam has been described as a "paramilitary" group, it should be remembered that its own members, like all Muslims, are unarmed.
14. See *Muhammad Speaks*, July 5, 1963, and other issues over the past few years; also Lincoln, *op. cit.*, *passim,* and Essien-Udom, *op. cit., passim.*
15. See Lincoln, *op. cit., passim.*
16. This can explain the rigidity and ostensible triviality of many ideologues on the question of symbols. For example, congregations have suffered schisms over disputes about stained glass windows. A seemingly minor decorative question is really a fight over symbols, which in turn is a struggle having fundamental religious implications. Thus, such windows may "symbolize" the church's position toward "idolatry" and a host of related theological questions. One might also think of the secular religion of nationalism and the recent Canadian dispute over the design of the national flag.
17. One such notable is the former heavyweight boxing champion Cassius Clay, who now is known as Muhammad Ali. The issues of military service and religious belief involved in Ali's loss of his boxing title are a cogent example of society's response to separatism. Elijah Muhammad himself is another who has his "real" surname. Muslims of lesser renown usually use a numbered X, thus James X, James 2X, James 3X, etc. At some future day Allah will bestow upon them their lost names.
18. Quoted in Essien-Udom, *op. cit.*, p. 225.
19. In a study of another sect, J. A. Hostetler (*Amish Society* [Baltimore: Johns Hopkins University Press, 1963], pp. 132-133.) writes: "The horse and buggy, the beard of the married man, and the styles of dress . . . all take on symbolic meaning. All Amish know that this is the accepted way of doing things, and symbolism becomes an effective means of social control as the nonconformist can quickly be detected from the conformist."
20. *Muhammad Speaks*, August 28, 1964.

21. The absence of Black Muslims from anomic urban riots has been noted on several occasions. For instance, see Gertrude Samuels, "Feud Within the Black Muslims," *The New York Times Magazine*, March 22, 1964, pp. 17, 104-107; Worthy, *op. cit.*, p. 39.
22. See Parenti, *op. cit.*
23. *Muhammad Speaks*, November 22, 1963.
24. Those upset by separatist politics and institutions with seemingly bizarre symbols might reflect on the potentiality of long-term ghetto violence on the part of those lacking such relationships. On the psychological components of anomie, consult Herbert McClosky and John H. Schaar, "Psychological Dimensions of Anomie," *American Sociological Review* 30 (February 1965): 14-40.
25. Max Weber, "The Sociology of Charismatic Authority," in *From Max Weber: Essays in Sociology*, eds. H. Gerth and C. W. Mills (New York: Oxford University Press, 1958), pp. 248, 253; also Weber, "The Protestant Sects and the Spirit of Capitalism," *loc. cit.*, pp. 302-322; Max Weber, *The Protestant Ethic and the Spirit of Capitalism* (New York: Charles Scribner's Sons, 1958); Robert Merton, "Puritanism, Pietism, and Science," in Merton, *Social Theory and Social Structure,* rev. ed. (Glencoe, Ill.: The Free Press, 1957), pp. 574-606.
26. Cf. Essien-Udom, *op. cit.,* pp. 81-82. Lomas (*op. cit.*) is persuaded of the morality of Muslim leaders: "I am convinced that they would no more fight publicly over the question [of Muhammad's successor] than would the cardinals of the Roman Church." Essien-Udom notes that Muhammad is training his son, Minister Wallace Muhammad, to be his successor.
27. Eric Hoffer, *The True Believer* (New York: Harper & Row, Inc., 1963), p. 134.
28. Essien-Udom, *op. cit.,* p. 170n.
29. Cf. Merton's "Social Structure and Anomie," in Merton, *op. cit.,* pp. 131-160, for a pertinent theoretical statement.
30. See *Muhammad Speaks,* winter issues of 1961; Lincoln, "Extremist Attitudes in the Black Muslim Movement," *loc. cit.*, p. 82; "Black Supremacy Cult," *U.S. News and World Report,* 47 (November 9, 1959), 112-114.
31. *Muhammad Speaks,* October 11, 1963; also "New Move by the Black Muslims," *U.S. News and World Report,* 47 (November 9, 1959): 112-114.
32. See issues of *Muhammad Speaks* from August 1963 to the present.
33. Lincoln, *Black Muslims, op. cit.,* pp. 18-19.
34. "Call to All Black Leaders," *Muhammad Speaks,* October 11, 1963.
35. *Ibid.,* August 16, 1963.
36. Nat Hentoff, "Elijah in the Wilderness," *Reporter* 23 (August 4, 1960): 40.
37. Hentoff quoted in Lincoln, *op. cit.,* p. 38.
38. Karl Mannheim, *Ideology and Utopia* (New York: Harcourt, Brace & Co., Harvest Paperback, no date), p. 213.

CHAPTER SIX

1. Nat Hentoff, *The New Equality* (New York: The Viking Press, Inc., 1964), p. 231.
2. See David A. Shannon, *The Socialist Party of America* (New York: The Macmillan Company, 1955); Murray S. and Susan W. Stedman, *Discontent at the Polls* (New York: Columbia University Press, 1950).
3. Cogent accounts of Commu-

nist party relations with Negroes are found in Irving Howe and Lewis Coser, *The American Communist Party* (New York: Praeger, 1962), pp. 175-273.

4. Henry Lee Moon, *Balance of Power: The Negro Vote* (New York: Doubleday & Company, Inc., 1948), pp. 120-121; see also the major study by Wilson Record, *The Negro and the Communist Party* (Chapel Hill, N.C.: The University of North Carolina Press, 1951).

5. Harry Rogoff, *An East Side Epic: The Life and Work of Meyer London* (New York: Vanguard Press, Inc., 1930), p. 15. See also *The Immigrant Jew in America,* ed. Edmund J. James (New York: Buch and Co., 1907), pp. 261-277.

6. Much of the evidence is reviewed in Edgar Litt, "The Political Perspectives of Jews in an Urban Community," Ph.D. thesis, Yale University, 1960. See also Nathan Glazer, *The Social Basis of American Communism* (New York: Harcourt, Brace, & World, Inc., 1961), pp. 130-168; Seymour M. Lipset, "Three Decades of the Radical Right," in *The Radical Right,* ed. Daniel Bell (New York: Doubleday & Company, Inc., 1964 ed.), pp. 413-421. Lipset's data support the conclusion that anti-Semitism was not a significant contributant to McCarthyism.

7. See William Brink and Louis Harris, *The Negro Revolution in America* (New York: Simon & Schuster, Inc., 1963), p. 201, on the multiple problem of being "black and red" in America; note Record, *op. cit.*, pp. 131-197.

8. Robert E. Lane, *Political Ideology: Why the American Common Man Believes What He Does* (New York: The Free Press, 1962), p. 426. Reprinted by permission.

9. Lane, *Ibid.*, pp. 425-435.

10. Herbert McClosky and John H. Schaar, "Psychological Dimensions of Anomie," in *Political Behavior in America,* ed. Heinz Eulau (New York: Random House, Inc., 1966), p. 475.

11. Brink and Harris, *op. cit.*, pp. 206-209.

12. Edward Banfield and James Q. Wilson, *City Politics* (Cambridge, Mass.: Harvard University Press, 1963), p. 297. On the relation between weak social structure and mass political action by civil rights groups, see James Q. Wilson, "The Strategy of Protest: Problems of Negro Civic Action," *Journal of Conflict Resolution* (September 1961): 291-303.

13. The "vicious circle" thesis is propounded by Daniel P. Moynihan, in his "Employment, Income, and the Ordeal of the Negro Family," *Daedalus* (Winter 1967). See also Thomas Pettigrew, *A Profile of the American Negro* (New York: Van Nostrand, 1964). Theories about benefits to be derived from the consequences of urbanization and education to Negroes stem from Robert E. Park, *Race and Culture* (Glencoe, Ill.: The Free Press, 1950), and the equally positive view stressing white initiation of ameliorative change is traced to Gunnar Myrdal's influential *An American Dilemma* (New York: Harper & Row, Inc., 1962), pp. 927-1004.

14. Concludes John Dizard: "Reports from various people involved in training programs on the West Coast indicate that many trainees refer to their internship as "the poverty hustle," indicating that their interest is hardly one of getting into the occupational structure and beginning the long trek to the American Dream. They are not making it in the system; . . . they are, in their eyes, beating the system." From a working manuscript on Negro unemployment which Professor Dizard kindly made available to me (Spring 1967, p. 7).

15. Sol Stern, "The Call of the Black Panthers," *The New York Times Magazine*, August 6, 1967, p. 62, © 1967 by the New York Times Company. Reprinted by permission.

16. James S. Coleman, *Equality of Educational Opportunity* (Washington, D.C.: Government Printing Office, 1966), p. 289.

PART THREE

INTRODUCTION

1. See Edward C. Banfield and James Q. Wilson, *City Politics* (Cambridge, Mass.: Harvard University Press, 1963), pp. 33-44, and their "Public-Regardingness As a Value Premise in Voting Behavior," *American Political Science Review* 58 (December 1964): 876-887.

2. For instance, Raymond E. Wolfinger and John O. Field, "Political Ethos and the Structure of City Government," *American Political Science Review* 60 (June 1966): 306-326.

CHAPTER SEVEN

1. Nathan Glazer and Daniel P. Moynihan, *Beyond the Melting Pot* (Cambridge, Mass.: The M.I.T. Press, 1963), pp. 179-180. Reprinted from *Beyond the Melting Pot* by permission of the M.I.T. Press, Cambridge, Massachusetts. Copyright 1963 by the Massachusetts Institute of Technology.

2. Lawrence Fuchs, *The Political Behavior of American Jews* (Glencoe, Ill.: The Free Press, 1956), p. 187. Reprinted by permission.

3. The evidence is reviewed in Edgar Litt, "The Political Perspectives of Jews in an Urban Community," Ph.D. thesis, Yale University, 1960, pp. 89-100; Litt, "Ethnic Status and Political Perspectives," *Midwest Journal of Political Science* (August 1961): 328-332; Glazer and Moynihan, *op. cit.*, pp. 166-180; Seymour M. Lipset, *Political Man: The Social Bases of Politics* (New York: Doubleday & Company, Inc., 1963 ed.), pp. 251-263; Fuchs, *op. cit.*, pp. 171-204.

4. Sources cited in footnote 3 and Gerhard Lenski, *The Religious Factor* (New York: Doubleday & Company, Inc., 1961), pp. 120-191.

5. Glazer and Moynihan, *op. cit.*, p. 171. For documentation of Jewish participation in reform politics in New York, note James Q. Wilson, *The Amateur Democrats* (Chicago: The University of Chicago Press, 1962); on Massachusetts, see Edgar Litt, *The Political Cultures of Massachusetts* (Cambridge, Mass.: The M.I.T. Press, 1965), ch. 6 and Litt, "The Politics of a Cultural Minority," in *The Electoral Process*, ed. M. K. Jennings and L. H. Zeigler (Englewood Cliffs, N.J.: Prentice-Hall, Inc., 1966), pp. 105-121.

6. Lenski, *op. cit.*, pp. 91-102.

7. *Ibid.;* George Psatz, "Ethnicity, Social Class, and Adolescent Independence from Parental Control," *American Sociological Review* 22 (1957): 415-423; and the work of Bernard C. Rosen in his "Achievement: A Psychocultural Dimension of Social Stratification," *American Sociological Review* 21 (1956): 203-211; and his "Race, Ethnicity, and Achievement," *American Sociological Review* 24 (1959): 47-58.

8. Erich Rosenthal, "Five Million American Jews," *Commentary* 18 (1958): 499-507.

9. Nathan Glazer, "The Immigrant Group and American Culture," *Yale Review* 48 (1959): 387-392; Daniel Glaser, "The Dynamics of Ethnic Identification," *American*

Sociological Review 23 (1958): 31-40; Joseph S. Forman, "Occupation Selection Among Detroit Jews," Jewish Social Studies 14 (1952): 17-50; Leonard W. Blumberg, "The Relationship Among Rank Systems in American Society," in Maurice Freedman, *A Minority in Britain* (London: Vallentine, Mitchell, 1955), pp. 404-444; Nathan Glazer, "The American Jew and the Attainment of Middle Class Rank," in Marshall Sklare, ed. *The Jews: Social Patterns of an American Group* (Glencoe, Ill.: The Free Press, 1958), pp. 138-146.

10. August B. Hollingshead and Fredrick G. Redlich, *Social Class and Mental Illness* (New York: John Wiley & Sons, Inc., 1958), pp. 61-122; see also their "Social Structure and Psychiatric Disorders," *American Sociological Review* 18 (1953): 163-169.

11. Lenski, *op. cit.*, p. 92.

12. See Sklare, *op. cit., passim*; Aileen D. Ross, "The Social Control of Philanthropy," *Americal Journal of Sociology* 63 (March 1953): 451-469; Solomon Sutker, "The Jewish Organizational Elite of Atlanta," *Social Forces* 31 (December 1952): 136-143.

13. Fuchs, *op. cit.*, pp. 177-178.

14. Lipset, *op. cit.*, p. 308.

15. Litt, "Ethnic Status and Political Perspectives," *op. cit.*, Jerome Himmelhoch, "Tolerance and Personality Needs Among Minority Group Students," *American Sociological Review* 15 (1950): 79-88; Edgar Litt, "Jewish Ethno-Religious Involvement and Political Liberalism," *Social Forces* (May 1961): 328-332.

16. Litt, "The Political Perspectives of Jews," *op. cit.*, p. 81.

17. The composite picture of modern welfare politics is drawn from such works as David M. Potter, *People of Plenty: Economic Abundance and the American Character* (Chicago: The University of Chicago Press, 1954); Seymour M. Lipset, *The First New Nation* (New York: Basic Books, Inc., 1964); Daniel Bell, *The End of Ideology* (New York: The Free Press, 1960).

18. See Fuchs, *op. cit.*, pp. 187-191 and the evidence cited in Glazer and Moynihan, *op. cit.*, pp. 155-159.

19. The value sources are reviewed by Fuchs, *loc. cit.*, pp. 182-189; the ameliorative stance with regard to such matters as mental illness is documented by Hollingshead and Redlich, *op. cit.*

20. That, for example, college education is more important than ethnicity in supporting civil libertarianism has been shown in such studies as Samuel Stouffer, *Communism, Conformity, and Civil Liberties* (New York: Doubleday & Company, Inc., 1955).

21. See John R. Seeley et al., *Crestwood Heights* (New York: Basic Books, Inc., 1956); Herbert J. Gans, "Park Forest: Birth of a Jewish Community," *Commentary* 7 (1951): 330-339; Albert I. Gordon, *Jews in Suburbia* (Boston: Beacon Press, 1960).

22. Glazer and Moynihan, *op. cit.*, pp. 176-178.

23. Nat Hentoff, *The New Equality* (New York: The Viking Press, Inc., 1964), p. 241.

24. Note Michael Parenti, "White Anxiety and the Negro Revolution," *New Politics* (May 1964): 35-39. See also the symposium on "Liberalism and the Negro," *Commentary* 35 (February 1963).

CHAPTER EIGHT

1. See Angus Campbell et al., *The American Voter* (New York: John Wiley & Sons, Inc., 1960), ch. 7; Dennis G. Sullivan, "Psychological Balance and Reactions to the Presidential Nominations in 1960," in *The Electoral Process,* ed. M. K. Jennings and L. H. Zeigler (Englewood Cliffs, N.J.: Prentice-Hall, Inc., 1966), pp. 238-264.

2. See Scott Greet, "The Catholic Voter and the Democratic Party," *Public Opinion Quarterly* 26 (Winter 1962): 735-776.

3. Nathan Glazer and Daniel P. Moynihan, *Beyond the Melting Pot* (Cambridge, Mass.: The M.I.T. Press, 1963), pp. 265-266. Reprinted from *Beyond the Melting Pot* by permission of the M.I.T. Press, Cambridge, Massachusetts. Copyright 1963 by the Massachusetts Institute of Technology.

4. Campbell, *op. cit.*, pp. 323-327.

5. See the classic account of the "politics of revenge" in Samuel Lubell, *The Future of American Politics* (New York: Harper & Row, Inc., 1952).

6. James Q. Wilson and Edward C. Banfield, "Public-Regardingness As a Value Premise in Voting Behavior," *American Political Science Review* 58 (December 1964): 876-887.

7. Compare James Q. Wilson, *The Amateur Democrat* (New York: The Free Press, 1962); Seymour M. Lipset, "Religion and Politics in American History," in *Religious Conflict in America*, ed. Earl Raab (New York: Doubleday & Company, Inc., 1964), pp. 6-89; Murray S. Stedman, Jr., *Religion and Politics in America* (New York: Harcourt, Brace, & World, Inc., 1964), pp. 83-110.

8. On Catholic fundamentalism and political heterodoxy, note Gerhard Lenski, *The Religious Factor* (New York: Doubleday & Company, Inc., 1961), pp. 144-171; H. C. Selvin and W. O. Hagstrom, "Determinants of Support for Civil Liberties," *British Journal of Sociology* 11 (March 1960): 51-64; Milton Rokeach, *The Open and the Closed Mind* (New York: Basic Books, Inc., 1962), pp. 348-355.

9. See Suzanne Keller, *Beyond the Ruling Class* (New York: Alfred A. Knopf, Inc., 1963), pp. 315-325.

10. Lenski, *op. cit.*, p. 86.

11. John J. Kane, "The Social Structure of American Catholics," *The American Catholic Sociological Review* 16 (March 1955): 30; compare Bosco D. Costello, "Catholics in American Commerce and Industry, 1925-1945," *American Catholic Sociological Review* 17 (October 1956); Bernard C. Rosen, "Race, Ethnicity, and Achievement," *American Sociological Review* 24 (1959): 47-58; Keller, *op. cit., passim*; Lenski, *op. cit.*, ch. 3.

12. See Robert Presthus, *The Organizational Society* (New York: Alfred A. Knopf, Inc., 1963), and Guy Swanson, et al., *Bureaucracy and the American Family* (Ann Arbor: University of Michigan Press, 1964).

13. See V. O. Key, Jr., *Public Opinion and American Democracy* (New York: Alfred A. Knopf, Inc., 1961), pp. 221-223; Seymour M. Lipset, "The Sources of the Radical Right," in *The Radical Right*, ed. Daniel Bell (New York: Doubleday & Company, Inc., 1964 ed.), pp. 307-376.

14. Robert E. Lane, *Political Ideology: Why the American Common Man Believes What He Does* (New York: The Free Press, 1962). Reprinted by permission.

15. Thomas F. O'Dea, *American Catholic Dilemma* (New York: Sheed and Ward, 1958), pp. 112-113.

16. Joseph P. Fitzpatrick, "Catholics and Scientific Knowledge of Society," *The American Catholic Sociological Review* 15 (March 1954): 6.

17. See, for instance, Robert L.

Crain and Morton Inger, "Urban Society," *The American Catholic Sociological Review* 15 (March 1954: 6. 18, 1967): 76-77, 97-98.

18. The influence of "status politics" on Catholics may be traced to this development. See Seymour M. Lipset, "Three Decades of the Radical Right," in Bell, *op. cit.*, pp. 373-446; Lenski, *op. cit.*, pp. 165-176.

19. A cogent analysis of this problem is found in John Courtney Murray, "America's Four Conspiracies," in Raab, *op. cit.*, pp. 209-228.

20. William H. Honan, "A Would-Be Candidate For This Season," *The New York Times Magazine*, December 10, 1967, p. 36, © 1967 by the New York Times Company. Reprinted by permission.

CHAPTER NINE

1. The synopsis of participation's characteristics and the qualities of Negro civic readiness is drawn from Robert E. Lane, *Political Life: Why People Get Involved in Politics* (New York: The Free Press, 1959); Lester Milbrath, *Political Participation* (Chicago: Rand McNally & Company, 1965), Phillip E. Converse, "The Nature of Belief Systems in Mass Politics," in *Ideology and Discontent,* ed. David E. Apter (New York: The Free Press, 1964), pp. 206-261.

2. Dwaine Marvick, "The Political Socialization of the American Negro," *The Annals of the American Academy of Political and Social Science* 361 (September 1965): 117 (112-127); see also Joseph S. Roucek, "Majority-Minority Relations in Their Power Aspects." *Phylon* 17 (1956): 24-30; Alfred B. Clubock et al., "The Manipulated Negro Vote: Some Pre-Conditions and Consequences," *Journal of Politics* 26 (February 1964): 112-129, and Allan P. Sindler, "Protest Against the Political Status of the American Negro," *The Annals of the American Academy of Political and Social Science* 357 (January 1965): 48-54.

3. The personal and political values of participation are stressed in James C. Davies, *Human Nature in Politics* (New York: John Wiley & Sons, Inc., 1963); Paul Heist, "Intellecy and Commitment: The Faces of Discontent," in *Order and Freedom on the Campus* (Western Interstate Commission for Higher Education and the Center for the Study of Higher Education, 1965); Christian Bay, "The Cheerful Science of Dismal Politics," in *The Dissenting Academy*, ed. Theodore Roszak (New York: Pantheon, 1967).

4. This dominant motif runs through such modern social science classics as William Kornhauser, *The Politics of Mass Society* (New York: The Free Press, 1959), Seymour M. Lipset, *The First New Nation: The United States in Historical and Comparative Perspective* (New York: Basic Books, Inc., 1963); Daniel Bell, *The End of Ideology* (New York: Critendon, 1954); Edward Shills, *The Torments of Secrecy* (Glencoe, Ill.: The Free Press, 1956); Richard Hofstadter, *Anti-Intellectualism in American Life* (New York: Alfred A. Knopf, Inc., 1963).

5. An example of this most conservative approach to widespread political apathy is Bernard Berelson, P. F. Lazarsfeld, and W. N. McPhee, *Voting* (Chicago: The University of Chicago Press, 1954); E. E. Schattschneider makes a spirited case for the "responsible elite" thesis in his *The Semi-Sovereign People: A Realist's View of Democracy in America* (New York: Holt, Rinehart, and Winston, Inc., 1960); the "group leader recognition" approach to the participation issue dominates in such respected works as Robert Dahl and Charles Lindblom, *Politics, Economics, and Welfare* (New York: Harper & Row, Inc., 1953), Robert A. Dahl, *Who Governs: Democracy and Power in an American City* (New Haven: Yale University Press, 1961), and V. O. Key, Jr., *Public Opinion and American Democracy* (New York: Alfred A. Knopf, Inc., 1961).

6. See Arthur I. Waskow, *From Race Riots to Sit-In* (New York: Doubleday & Company, Inc., 1966), especially pp. 225-303; evidence of personal behavior other than violent reactions to politics growing from creative disorder politics is examined in Robert Coles, "Serpents and Doves: Non-Violent Youth in the South," in *The Challenge of Youth*, ed. Erik H. Erikson (New York: Doubleday & Company, Inc., 1965 ed.), pp. 223-259; John Moore, "Social Deprivation and Advantage As Sources of Political Values," *Western Political Quarterly* 15 (1962): 217-226; Richard Flacks, "The Liberated Generation: An Exploration of the Roots of Student Protest," *Journal of Social Issues* (1967); Kenneth Kenniston, *The Uncommitted: Alienated Youth in American Society* (1965).

7. Bayard Rustin, "The Lessons of the Long Hot Summer," *Commentary* 44 (October 1967): 40-41.

CHAPTER TEN

1. See Allan P. Grimes, *Equality in America: Religion, Race, and the Urban Majority* (New York: Oxford University Press, 1964), and Harry A. Bailey, ed., *Negro Politics in America* (Columbus, Ohio: Merrill, 1967).

2. Walter Goodman, "When Black Power Runs the New Left," *The New York Times Magazine*, September 24, 1967, sec. 6, p. 127., © 1967 by the New York Times Company. Reprinted by permission.

3. The proliferation of political conflicts in ethnic change has received some theoretical attention. See Gino Germani, "Social Change and Intergroup Conflict," in *The New Society*, ed. Irving Horowitz (New York: Oxford University Press, 1965), pp. 341-408.

4. Michael Parenti, "Ethnic Politics and the Persistence of Ethnic Identification," *American Political Science Review* 61 (September 1967): 721, 725.

BIBLIOGRAPHICAL ESSAY

CHAPTER ONE

The conflicting theories of ethnic accommodation, assimilation, and the melting-pot concept are of long standing in American scholarship. Historical views are provided by Oscar Handlin, *Immigration as a Factor in American History* (Englewood Cliffs, N.J.: Prentice-Hall, Inc., 1959); W. I. Thomas and F. Znaniecki, *The Polish Peasant in Europe and America*. 5 vols. (Boston: Badger, 1918–1920); and Ray A. Billington, *The Protestant Crusade, 1800–1860* (Chicago: Quadrangle Books, Inc., 1964).

Pertinent social and political adaptations among ethnic groups are highlighted by Milton M. Gordon, "Assimilation in America: Theory and Reality." *Daedalus* 90 (Spring 1961): 263–285; Horace M. Kallen's classic "Democracy Versus the Melting Pot." *The Nation*, February 1915; Amitai Etzioni, "The Ghetto—A Reevaluation." *Social Forces* (March 1959), pp. 255–262, and J. Milton Yinger, "Social Forces Involved in Group Identification or Withdrawal." *Daedalus* 90 (Spring 1961): 247–262.

The politics of ethnic acculturation are richly detailed in William Foote Whyte, *Street Corner Society* (Chicago: University of Chicago Press, 1943); Herbert Gans, *The Urban Villagers* (New York: The Free Press, 1962); and in Nathan Glazer and Daniel P. Moynihan, *Beyond the Melting Pot* (Cambridge: M.I.T. Press, 1963).

CHAPTER TWO

Excellent overviews of ethnic political patterns are Robert A. Dahl, *Who Governs: Democracy and Power in an American City* (New Haven: Yale University Press, 1961); Robert R. Alford, *Party and Society* (Chicago: Rand McNally & Company, 1963); Edward C. Banfield and James Q. Wilson, *City Politics* (Cambridge: Harvard University Press, 1963); and V. O. Key, Jr., *Politics, Parties, and Pressure Groups*. 5th ed. (New York: Thomas Y. Crowell, 1964).

The persistence and stability of ethnic politics are dominant themes in Gerhard Lenski, *The Religious Factor: A Sociologist's Inquiry* (New York: Doubleday & Company, Inc., 1961); V. O. Key, Jr., and Frank Munger, "Social Determinism and Electoral Decisions," in *American Voting Behavior*. Edited by Eugene Burdick and Arthur Brodbeck. (Glencoe, Ill.: The Free Press, 1959); and the pioneering work of Samuel Lubell, *The Future of American Politics* (New York: Harper & Row, Inc., 1952). The application of ethnic political stability to urban America is developed by Samuel J. Eldersveld, "The Influence of Metropolitan Party Pluralities in Presidential Elections Since 1920." *American Political Science Review* 43 (1949): 1189–1206. The secularization of American religious and ethnic institutions in sustaining traditional political loyalties is a major point in Seymour M. Lipset, *The First New Nation: The United States in Historical and Comparative Perspective* (New York: Basic Books, Inc., 1963).

Major explanations of ethnic party and political behavior are found in Angus Campbell, Phillip E. Converse, Warren E. Miller, and Donald E. Stokes, *The American Voter* (New York: John Wiley & Sons, Inc., 1960); Michael Parenti, "Ethnic-Political Attitudes: A Depth Study of Italian Americans." Ph.D. thesis, Yale University, 1962; Raymond E. Wolfinger. "The Development and Persistence of Ethnic Voting." *American Political Science Review* 59 (December 1965); and Michael Parenti, "Ethnic Politics and the Persistence of Ethnic Identification." *American Political Science Review* 61 (September 1967).

CHAPTER THREE

The psychological and group dynamics of ethnic politics are cogently dealt with in Nathan Glazer, "The Dynamics of Ethnic Identification." *American Sociological Review* 23 (1950): 31–40; Howard Brotz, "Social Stratification and the Political Order." *American Journal of Sociology* 64 (1959): 575–85; Samuel J. Eldersveld, *Political Parties: A Behavioral Analysis* (Chicago: Rand McNally & Company, 1966); and Edgar Litt, *The Political Culture of Massachusetts* (Cambridge: M.I.T. Press, 1965).

Those desiring to learn more about politics and religious groups should consult Marshall Sklare, *Conservative Judaism: An American Religious Movement* (Glencoe, Ill.: The Free Press, 1955); Tracey Ellis, *American Catholicism* (New York: Alfred A. Knopf, Inc., 1958); Murray Stedman, *Religion and Politics in America* (New York: Harcourt, Brace & World, Inc.); and David R. Manwaring, *Render Unto Caesar: The Flag-Salute Controversy* (Chicago: University of Chicago Press, 1961).

CHAPTER FOUR

The varieties of ethnic benefits exchanged in politics are treated in James Q. Wilson, *The Amateur Democrat* (Chicago: University of Chicago Press, 1962); Raymond E. Wolfinger, "The Development and Persistence of Ethnic Voting." *American Political Science Review* 59 (December 1965): 896–908; and also by Wolfinger, "Some Consequences of Ethnic Politics," in *The Electoral Process*. Edited by M. K. Jennings and L. H. Zeigler. (Englewood Cliffs, N.J.: Prentice-Hall, Inc., 1966), pp. 49–61; and Edgar Litt, "Jewish Ethno-Religious Involvement and Political Perspectives." *Midwest Journal of Political Science* (August 1961): 276–283.

The dynamics of divisible and collective ethnic benefits are often best seen in the analysis of state and local politics. See Matthew Holden, Jr., "Ethnic Accommodation in a Historical Case." *Comparative Studies in Society and History* 8 (January 1966): 168–180 (Cleveland); Martin Meyerson and Edward C. Banfield, *Politics, Planning and the Public Interest* (Glencoe, Ill.: The Free Press, 1953), (Chicago); Theodore Lowi, *At the Pleasure of the Mayor* (New York: The Free Press, 1964); and Daniel P. Moynihan and James Q. Wilson, "Patronage in New York State, 1955–1959." *American Political Science Review* 58 (June 1964): 296-300 (New York).

CHAPTER FIVE

Two studies important to a general understanding of the history and psychology of separatist politics are Hans Kohn, *Prophets and People* (New York: The Macmillan Company, 1964), and Herbert McClosky and John H. Schaar, "Psychological Dimensions of Anomie." *American Sociological Review* 30 (February 1965): 14–40. Of particular relevance to Black America are C. Eric Lincoln, *The Black Muslims in America* (Boston: Beacon Press, 1961); Abraham Kardiner and Lionel Ovesey, *The Mark of Oppression* (New York, W. W. Norton, 1951); and Michael John Parenti, "Black Nationalism and the Reconstruction of Identity," in *Personality and Social Life*. Edited by Robert

Endelman. (New York: Random House, Inc., 1965), pp. 1–16.

CHAPTER SIX

Robert E. Lane, *Political Ideology: Why the American Common Man Believes What He Does* (New York: The Free Press, 1962) is the best account of ideological dimensions pertaining to American radicalism. Specific radical appeals to ethnic groups are dealt with in David A. Shannon, *The Socialist Party of America* (New York: The Macmillan Company, 1955); Nathan Glazer, *The Social Basis of American Communism* (New York: Harcourt, Brace, & World, Inc., 1961); Seymour M. Lipset, "Three Decades of the Radical Right," in *The Radical Right*. Edited by Daniel Bell. (New York: Doubleday & Company, Inc., 1964 ed.), pp. 413–431; and Nat Hentoff, *The New Equality* (New York: The Viking Press, 1964).

CHAPTER SEVEN

Jewish political culture is reflected in publications of *Commentary,* the socially and politically important outlet of the American Jewish Committee. Scholarly interest and diversity of Jews in public life are expressed in Lawrence Fuchs, *The Political Behavior of American Jews* (Glencoe, Ill.: The Free Press, 1956); Nathan Glazer and Daniel P. Moynihan, *Beyond the Melting Pot* (Cambridge: M.I.T. Press, 1963); and Edgar Litt, "Jewish Ethno-Religious Involvement and Political Liberalism." *Social Forces* (May 1961), pp. 328–332.

CHAPTER EIGHT

The most brilliant single piece on American Irish-Catholic politics is found in Glazer and Moynihan's *Beyond the Melting Pot*, cited above. The classic account of the politics of revenge among ethnic groups is Samuel Lubell, *The Future of American Politics* (New York: Harper & Row, Inc., 1952). On Catholic fundamentalism and political heterodoxy, see Gerhard Lenski, *The Religious Factor* (New York: Doubleday & Company, Inc., 1961). The periodical *Commonweal* is an excellent guide to public and religious issues as seen within the liberal American Catholic community. The application of a political ethos, influenced by religion and ethnicity, may be appraised in James Q. Wilson and Edward C. Banfield, "Public-Regardingness as a Value Premise in Voting Behavior." *American Political Science Review* 58 (December 1964): 876–887. The most sensitive account of modern-fundamental social and political strains in American Catholicism is by Thomas F. O'Dea, *American Catholic Dilemma* (New York: Sheed and Ward, 1958).

CHAPTER NINE

Theories of political participation congenial to ethnic accommodation are William Kornhauser's *The Politics of Mass Society* (New York: The Free Press, 1959); and Daniel Bell's *The End of Ideology* (New York: Critendon, 1954). Useful divergent views are in E. E. Schattschneider, *The Semi-Sovereign People* (New York: Holt, Rinehart and Winston, Inc., 1960); and James C. Davies, *Human Nature in Politics* (New York: John Wiley & Sons, Inc., 1963). The reader ought to also carefully consider Robert Dahl and Charles Lindblom, *Politics, Economics, and Welfare* (New York: Harper & Row, Inc., 1953).

Political implications of collective benefits and mass politics outside the conventional mode are the concerns of Dwaine Marvick, "The Political Socialization of the American Negro." *The Annals of the American Academy of Political and Social Science* 357 (January 1965): 112–127; Allan P. Sindler, "Protest Against the Political Status of the American Negro." *Annals of the American Academy of Political and Social Science* 357 (January 1965): 48–54; Arthur I. Waskow, *From Race Riots to Sit-In* (New York: Doubleday & Company, Inc., 1966); and Michael John Parenti, "White Anxiety and the Negro Revolution." *New Politics*, May 1964.